UNBUILT TORONTO

For Patricia –
All the best,
Mark Osbaldeston.

UNBUILT TORONTO

A HISTORY OF THE CITY THAT MIGHT HAVE BEEN

Mark Osbaldeston

DUNDURN PRESS
TORONTO

Editor: Barry Jowett
Copy-editor: Ruth Chernia
Design: Erin Mallory
Printer: Transcontinental

Library and Archives Canada Cataloguing in Publication

Osbaldeston, Mark, 1966-
    Unbuilt Toronto : a history of the city that might have been / by
Mark Osbaldeston.

ISBN 978-1-55002-835-5

    1. Toronto (Ont.)--History. 2. Toronto (Ont.)--Buildings, structures,
etc.--History. 3. City planning--Ontario--Toronto--History. I. Title.

FC3097.3.O72 2008   971.3'541   C2008-904905-5

3 4 5   12 11 10 09

We acknowledge the support of the **Canada Council for the Arts** and the **Ontario Arts Council** for our publishing program. We also acknowledge the financial support of the **Government of Canada** through the **Book Publishing Industry Development Program** and **The Association for the Export of Canadian Books**, and the **Government of Ontario** through the **Ontario Book Publishers Tax Credit program**, and the **Ontario Media Development Corporation**.

Care has been taken to trace the ownership of copyright material used in this book. The author and the publisher welcome any information enabling them to rectify any references or credits in subsequent editions.

J. Kirk Howard, President

Printed and bound in Canada.
www.dundurn.com

Dundurn Press
3 Church Street, Suite 500
Toronto, Ontario, Canada
M5E 1M2

Gazelle Book Services Limited
White Cross Mills
High Town, Lancaster, England
LA1 4XS

Dundurn Press
2250 Military Road
Tonawanda, NY
U.S.A. 14150

For Steve

ACKNOWLEDGEMENTS

I AM GRATEFUL TO A NUMBER OF PEOPLE for their help during the researching and writing of this book:

To Bert Archer, Paul Challen, Rollo Myers, and Stephen Otto for their comments on content and their advice and assistance on research.

To the architects who provided illustrations of their firms' projects and background about them and to the archives and institutions that were a source of written and visual documents.

To the many other people and entities who helped in any number of ways, including: Howard Chapman, Ken Coit, Pauline Kay, Loren Kolar, Fr. James McConica, Michael Moir, Elizabeth Osbaldeston Troyer, Greg Osbaldeston, Douglas Richardson, Peter Richardson, Peter Skrepichuk, and Mark Sterling.

To James Dawson for taking an afternoon off to photograph a concrete hole in the ground, and to the understanding people at the TTC for letting him do it.

And finally, to my spouse Steven Vieira for his help throughout the writing of this book, in everything from marshalling electronic images to gamely spending a winter's day chasing down a ghost canal.

CONTENTS

TRANSPORTATION

TOWERS

ARTS, LETTERS AND LEISURE

EPILOGUE

INTRODUCTION

GHOST TOWN

IF YOU WERE TO THINK OF A GHOST town, Toronto probably wouldn't spring to mind. After all, a ghost town is a town filled with abandoned buildings that continue to haunt the place, long after the inhabitants and their dreams have vanished. But ghosts come in many forms. The most ephemeral are the ghosts of things that never were, the buildings that were themselves the dreams.

It is those buildings and plans, in Toronto and the surrounding area, that are the subject of this book: elegant opera houses; scenic lakeside parks; soaring towers; and the latest in bridges, highways, and transit systems.

The projects covered span more than two centuries. Each has something to say, for better or for worse, about the era in which it was proposed and the people who proposed it. One or two of the projects, such as the Spadina Expressway, have taken on a kind of legendary status in their spectral incarnation. Most have simply faded from public memory, along with the excitement or controversy that surrounded them.

Whether the loss of these projects was in any instance a good or bad thing will be for you to decide. As you consider the city-building dreams of the past, you may be led to reflect on those of the present and future. What foregone projects of the past would we do well to resurrect today? What big ideas of today will end up lining the streets of Unbuilt Toronto?

Mark Osbaldeston
Toronto, 2008

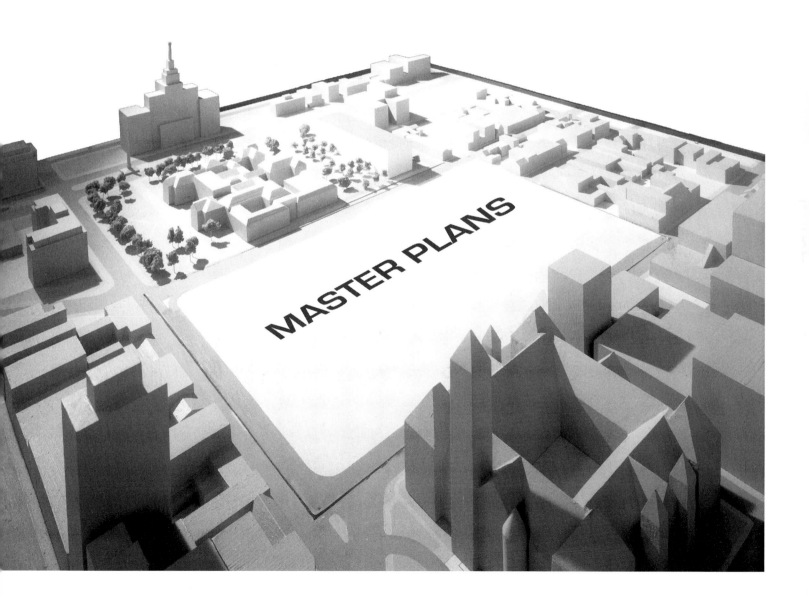

MASTER PLANS

Chapter 1

1788 PLAN FOR TORONTO

1788 / Unbuilt

JOHN GRAVES SIMCOE, UPPER CANADA'S first Lieutenant Governor, is credited with directing surveyor Alexander Aitkin to lay out ten square blocks (in what is now the St. Lawrence Market area) that would form the nucleus of modern-day Toronto. But this 1793 plan for Toronto wasn't the first. In December of 1788, Captain Gother Mann of the Royal Engineers prepared a plan for a proposed town on "Torento Harbour," a year after the Crown purchased, from the Mississauga First Nation, more than a quarter million acres of land surrounding Toronto Bay (Fig. 1-1).

Mann's proposal was typical of those being drawn up by the imperial authorities for what was then the western frontier. Its symmetry and simplicity are hallmarks of the Georgian influence that was dominant in England at the time. The town site is one mile square, situated roughly in the area now bounded by King, Harbord, Bathurst and Bay streets. Encircling the town is a public commons, which is itself surrounded by "town parks," probably lots for larger homes. Farm lots,

not demarcated here, would occupy the area surrounding these larger town lots.

A public square is at the centre of the town, and four secondary public squares are arranged symmetrically around it. A sixth square is shown to the south. This break from the otherwise absolute symmetry of the scheme is probably a nod to the settlement's location on Lake Ontario. If so, it is a rare concession to natural topography: for the most part, ravines, streams and even the mighty Don, whose outlet is shown to the right, disappear under the imperial grid.

Although not reflected on this particular plan, blocks for government, church, court and military buildings would be designated around the central square, forming the heart of the community and emphasizing the social order. Cemeteries, hospitals, workhouses and the like would be given blocks on the periphery of the town. The remainder of the blocks are divided into six one-acre town lots, the whole being served by a perfect grid of streets.

None of these high Georgian schemes proposed for Upper Canada saw the full light of day. In Toronto's case, Mann's scheme was replaced by Aitkin's more practical and less ambitious gridiron. But this 1788 plan provides the perfect graphic representation of the British government's attempt to impose eighteenth-century rational order on the Canadian wilderness. It is a view of Toronto as a tabula rasa, a canvas on which to project grand plans and hoped-for futures. The perfect starting point for the history that follows.

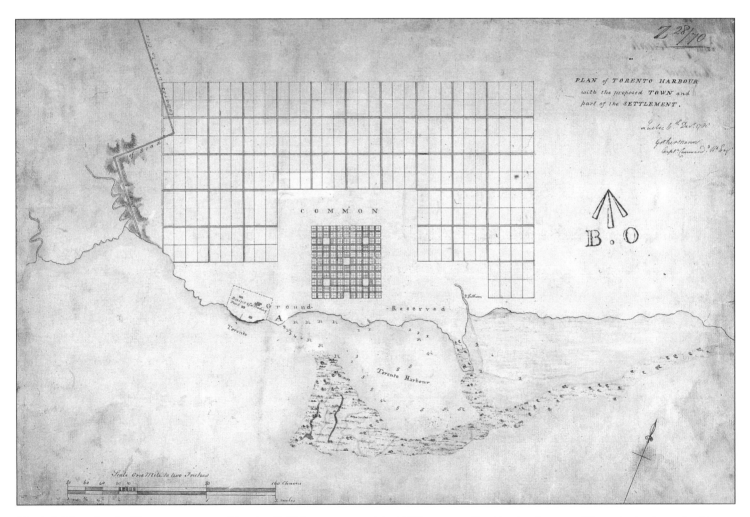

Fig. 1-1. The plan for Toronto prepared by the British government in 1788, a year after the land around Toronto harbour had been purchased from the Mississauga First Nation. [Library and Archives Canada, n0004434k]

Chapter 2

WATERFRONT WALKS AND GARDENS

1852 / Partially built

I N 1852, PROMINENT LOCAL ARCHITECT John Howard prepared plans for a park stretching between York and Bathurst Streets. The park would follow the Lake Ontario shoreline, occupying all the land south of Front Street. Howard's plan was titled "Sketch of a Design for laying out the north shore of the Toronto Harbour in pleasure drives, walks and shrubbery for the recreation of the citizens" (Fig. 2-1). The title said it all. Walkways winding through landscaped shrubbery would afford the opportunity for lakefront promenades. A scenic drive would wend its way through the western half of the park, allowing carriage passengers to take in lake vistas. The following year the city, which had commissioned Howard's plan, actually acquired all the land necessary to carry it out. How is it then, that instead of beautiful public parks and open space bordering the waterfront, Toronto ended up with railways, factories, highways and condos?

The origin of Howard's scheme goes to the very beginnings of Toronto. During the clearing of the site for the new town in 1793, Lieutenant Governor Simcoe was so taken by the beauty of the waterfront that he decided to preserve it in perpetuity. His motives and intentions were reflected in a letter from Peter Russell, his fellow executive councillor. In September of 1793, Russell wrote to his sister Elizabeth that Simcoe "has fallen so much in love with the land that he intends to reserve from population the whole front from the Town to the Fort — a space of nearly three miles." As an integral part of the plan, Simcoe immediately set aside public reserves on either end of his proposed waterfront commons. To the west was the 1200-acre Garrison Reserve surrounding Fort York; to the east was the King's Park (also known as Government Park) in the area south of what is now Queen, between Berkeley and the Don River (Figs. 2-2, 2-3).

Apart from its scenic benefits, Simcoe's lakeshore corridor would serve as a link between the eastern and western reserves, allowing soldiers to march between the fort and the parliament buildings to be located in the King's Park. It

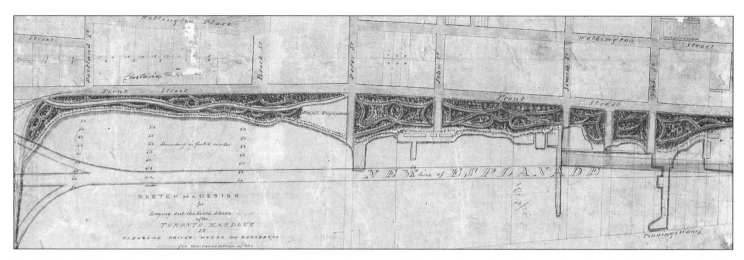

Fig. 2-1. In 1852, at the city's request, architect John Howard prepared this plan for a shoreline park on lands held in trust for the purpose. Within a few years, as additions to the map foreshadowed, decisions would be made that would see Toronto's waterfront end up crowded with railways and factories instead. [Library and Archives Canada, n0011447k_a1 (detail)]

would be another twenty-five years, however, before these two reserves would be officially connected. In 1818, the government granted thirty acres of lakefront property between the Garrison Reserve and the King's Park to a committee of five public trustees and their heirs. The purpose of the trust was to ensure that the strip of land between Front Street and the top of the bank of the Lake Ontario shore would be held for the benefit of the citizens of York, to be used for a "public walk or mall."

But even before the creation of the waterfront trust, the integrity of Simcoe's original vision had been compromised. Just before the start of the War of 1812, almost 350 acres of the Garrison Reserve were granted by Isaac Brock, acting as administrator of Upper Canada, to his secretary (and cousin) James. The reduction of the reserves continued in the 1820s as lands were severed from the King's Reserve to pay for what would later become the Toronto General Hospital. In the same decade, more lands were sold from the Garrison

Reserve to pay for the New Fort (or Stanley Barracks). In 1848, 287 acres of the Garrison Reserve (shown on Fig. 2-2) were leased to the city by the British Board of Ordnance. The city intended to build a park on the land, and John Howard drew up plans for that too. But the city was forced to surrender what was supposed to have been a lease of 999 years in fewer than four. Shortly afterwards, the Ontario, Simcoe and Huron Railway was pushed through the city's planned Western Park. Toronto's two other railway companies, the Great Western and Grand Trunk, took additional land from the reserve. And under the railway legislation in place at the time, the city was powerless to stop it.

As for the waterfront corridor, known as the "Walks and Gardens," it was threatened from the start by the land-use tension inherent in the waterfront location itself. The waterfront was a source not only of beauty ideal for recreational use, it also was the hub of marine transportation, perfect for commercial and industrial uses. In 1840, the government granted

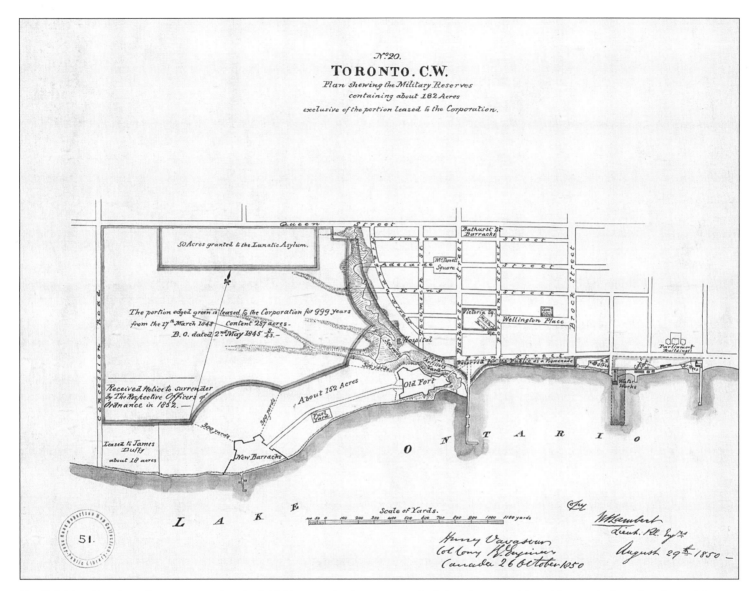

Fig. 2-2. The Garrison Reserve consisted of 1200 acres in the west end of the city set aside at Toronto's founding for public use. By the time of Howard's Walks and Gardens plan, much of it had been conveyed away. This map from 1850 shows the Reserve land leased to the city for 999 years for the never-built "Western Park." As a notation on the map indicates, the city was forced to surrender the lease four years later. [Toronto Public Library]

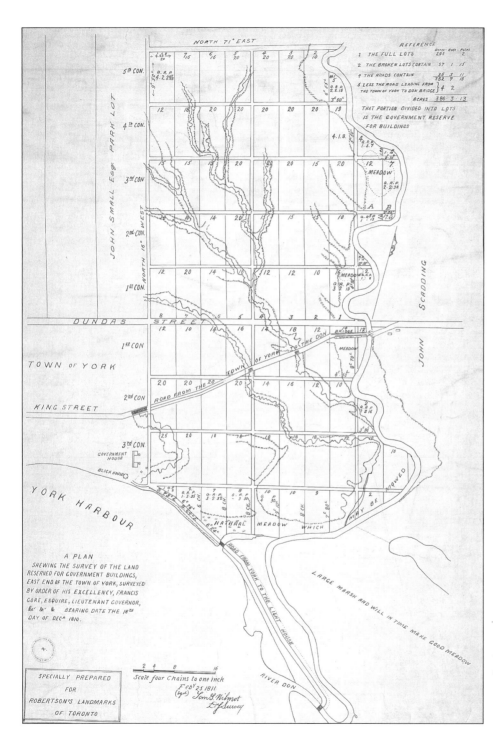

Fig. 2-3. The King's Park (shown divided into lots), the eastern counterpart of the Garrison Reserve. This reproduction of an 1811 map by Samuel Street was prepared for *Robertson's Landmarks of Toronto*. [Toronto Public Library]

the municipality land south of the Walks and Gardens in the form of the shoreline between Berkeley and Simcoe streets, as well as water lots in Lake Ontario. The city was permitted to lease this land out for periods of up to fifty years, with the provision that within three years of the city or a lessee taking up occupation, a one-hundred-foot "esplanade" would be constructed along the water's edge. As the city used this new power and granted waterfront leases, wharves developed to the south of the esplanade land, on the waterfront, while industrial uses developed to its north. The Walks and Gardens lands were left as little more than a service road between them.

Even as commercial and industrial uses were beginning to erode the Walks and Gardens concept, however, some steps were being taken to realize it. In 1841, an area of land between Berkeley and Princess Streets was fenced off and a public garden was planted, called the Fair Green. And in 1845, the city instructed John Howard to survey the waterfront as a first step in the comprehensive waterfront plan he would release in 1852.

The problem was, by then the railways posed a new threat to the dream of a waterfront esplanade. And, undoubtedly, it was this very threat that spurred the city into a final effort to realize Simcoe's dream. In 1853, the Province of Canada passed the Toronto Esplanade Act, allowing the Walks and Gardens trustees to convey the Walks and Gardens lands to the city. The city was bound to ensure that the land was used as a public walk or mall, but the act also stipulated that it could be used for a railway, provided the provincial government consented.

Not surprisingly, a year after Howard released his Walks and Gardens design, plans were already prepared showing the land used for railway purposes instead. Indeed, the copy of Howard's plan illustrated here was used by someone as a handy base to sketch the "New Esplanade," which would be produced by harbour filling, and the railway tracks that would run along it. The protection offered by the Toronto Esplanade Act lasted only three years. In 1857, the province amended it to allow the city to sell the Walks and Gardens land outright. If there was any bright side to this turn of events, it was the legislation's requirement that the sales money was to be used for the "purchase, planting, ornamenting and care of some other piece or parcel of land." Because of this provision, improvements were made to several parks (including Riverdale Park and High Park). As for the Walks and Gardens themselves, the dream had died. The same year the railway-friendly legislation was passed, trains were already chugging through the waterfront park that had been Toronto's birthright.

Chapter 3

PLAN OF THE CIVIC IMPROVEMENT COMMITTEE

1911 / Partially built

PLAN OF THE ADVISORY CITY PLANNING COMMISSION

1929 / Partially built

THE 1893 WORLD'S COLUMBIAN Exposition held in Chicago is credited with starting the City Beautiful movement in civic planning. It may seem strange that the design of a fairground could inspire an entire school of town planning. But, to many architects and city builders of the period, the White City (as the site of the exposition was known), with its monumental beaux arts architecture and formal symmetry, was more than a temporary fairground; it was a fleeting vision of how cities, including Toronto, could look.

City Beautiful planning in Toronto had its genesis in 1897, with the formation of the Guild of Civic Art. The guild was a group of artists and architects who had banded together to promote the beautification of Toronto. By 1901 it had begun to consider the issue of a comprehensive plan for the city. With council showing little interest in pursuing the idea, the guild took on the work itself. By 1905 it had developed a plan focusing on playgrounds, parks and road

improvements and hired English architect Sir Aston Webb to review it. That the guild would bring in Webb, who had designed the mall and Victoria Monument in front of Buckingham Palace, gave an indication both of the seriousness with which it took its task, and the effect it was aiming for.

The guild released its final plan in 1908 (Fig. 3-1). The following year, council succumbed to the guild's lobbying, and appointed a Civic Improvement Committee to take up the guild's planning efforts in an official capacity. Both the chair of the committee, architect Edmund Burke, and its consulting architect, John Lyle (Fig. 15-2), had worked on the guild's plan, and the committee met with guild members throughout the course of its work. It is not surprising, then, that the committee's report, released in December 1911, reflected the guild's plan to a great degree. In the area of parks, for instance, the committee's plan simply adopted the recommendations found in the earlier guild plan.

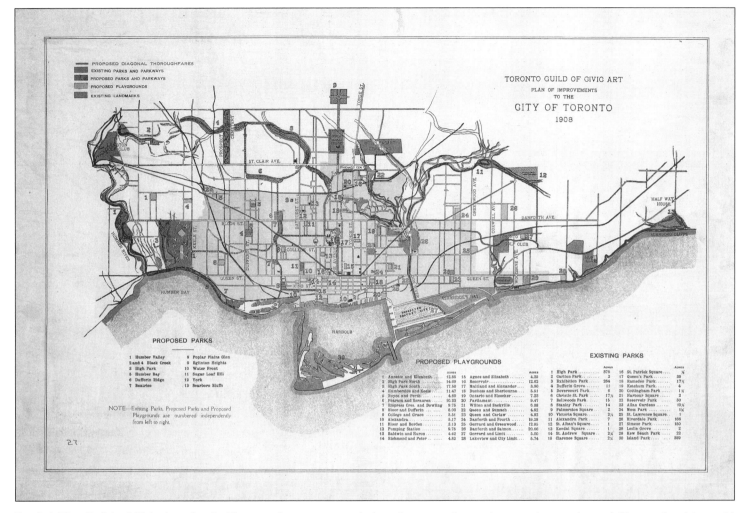

Fig. 3-1. The Guild of Civic Art plan for Toronto. Its recommendation, that new diagonal streets be cut through Toronto's grid, would influence city plans for the next two decades. [Toronto Public Library]

The chief focus of the committee's report was road improvements, with Toronto's lack of continuous thoroughfares seen as the most pressing issue. Two of its proposals to remedy this problem involved connecting existing smaller streets to produce an eastward extension of Dundas (from its terminus at Ossington) and a northern extension of Bay (it stopped at Queen). Dundas and Bay have become so integral to the city's road network that it's hard to believe they are largely twentieth-century accretions.

The committee's most dramatic recommendations, however, were those that drew their inspiration not from the existing streets of Toronto, but from the more rarified tenets of the City Beautiful. Radial thoroughfares — that is, roads that cut through the street grid on the diagonal — were a favourite City Beautiful device. As the committee noted, radial roads were found in the great cities of Europe and, more recently, had figured heavily into the plan that Daniel Burnham, the principal architect of the White City, had prepared for Chicago in 1909. In the Toronto plan, the committee recommended two major radial routes heading into the core. The idea for both these routes, like the proposal for a lakeshore drive, had been kicking around for some years, finding their way into the committee's plan via that of the guild. The first radial thoroughfare would head northwest from Queen and University; the second would head northeast from Queen and Church, to connect with Parliament Street (and ultimately the viaduct, then being planned, see chapter 15) at Carlton. In addition to these two major roads, a number of other radial routes were envisaged extending to the edges of the city and beyond.

Another feature of the plan in keeping with the times was its parkways. The concept of the parkway — a landscaped carriageway connecting parks in different parts of the city — had been used by Frederick Law Olmsted and Calvert Vaux in their parks plan for Buffalo, developed between 1868 and 1898. Adapted for the era of the motor car, it continued to find favour among City Beautiful planners. The committee proposed two for Toronto. The first, connecting the Humber with the area between the Stanley Barracks and Fort York, would be partially carried out as Lake Shore Boulevard (in the committee's plan, it would have continued across the western gap to the islands). The second parkway, which never developed beyond a line on a map, would have connected High Park and Queen's Park, via a westward extension of Hoskin.

A "civic centre," a collection of majestic public buildings grouped around a grand square, was another hallmark of City Beautiful plans. Daniel Burnham's 1903 plan for Cleveland had one, as did his plan for Chicago. In Toronto, a public square had been proposed for the area between Osgoode Hall and Terauley Street (now Bay) since before E.J. Lennox's City Hall had opened (see chapter 10). The committee took this idea and fit it firmly into the City Beautiful stylebook by surrounding the square with three formal public buildings (Fig. 10-2). To the rear of these buildings, extending to Agnes Street (now Dundas), a garden and parade ground would complete the public precinct. Burnham's civic centres for Cleveland and Chicago were joined by grand axial boulevards to train stations near the water. Toronto had purchased land for a new train station on Front Street after the great fire of 1904 (see Figs. 33-2a, 33-2b). It was perfectly situated to allow for a connection with Toronto's new civic centre via a grand boulevard: Federal Avenue.

The choice of the name "Federal Avenue" was significant. In 1911, what we now call Old City Hall had been around for little more than ten years. Even if its Romanesque styling was already dated (certainly it was not in keeping with the beaux arts aesthetic favoured by the City Beautiful), calling for a new city hall in 1911 simply to be able to join the civic centre club would have seemed profligate, something Toronto could never be accused of. In naming the principal approach to the civic centre Federal Avenue, the committee was signalling its intention that the federal government would be a major occupant of the precinct's grand buildings. Indeed, both the *Globe* and the *World* (a daily newspaper published between 1880 and 1921) had earlier that year called for the Dominion government to expropriate land for just that purpose, and the Board of Trade held meetings with the government on its involvement.

In the end, the federal government didn't build in the civic square area, but the city began work on the complex the following year when it held a competition for a new Registry Building, which would be the easternmost structure in the

Fig. 3-2. Looking south down Cambrai Avenue. Union Station terminates the vista. The new Royal York Hotel is visible on the right. [City of Toronto Archives, Series 59, Item 7]

complex. A neoclassical design by Charles S. Cobb was chosen the winner. As well, a number of buildings constructed over the next two decades anticipated the arrival of Federal Avenue. Most significantly, Union Station, on which building began in 1915 (with John Lyle as a collaborating architect), was centred at the base of the street's proposed route. The Graphic Arts Building (1913) at the southeast corner of Richmond and Sheppard was designed with the thought that its Sheppard frontage would eventually become Federal Avenue frontage. The western façade of the Toronto Daily Star Building on King Street, west of Bay (1928, Fig. 24-4) was designed to flank the street, as was the eastern façade of the Royal York Hotel (1929). The city permitted the construction of two buildings in the block between Richmond and Adelaide, however, in what would have been the route of Federal Avenue, thwarting the scheme as conceived (the first, built in 1922, was ironically called the Federal Building). Even so, the notion of a roadway centred on Union Station was too attractive to disappear completely.

By the late 1920s, with the increase in car ownership, downtown traffic congestion had become even worse and the need for more thoroughfares through the core even more pressing. One obvious improvement would be to extend University Avenue — which then stopped at Queen Street — southward. In April of 1928, the provincial government enacted special legislation giving the city broadened powers to expropriate the land necessary for the extension. The next month, the city appointed the Advisory City Planning Commission to recommend the best route for the extension. The commission consisted of four outside experts, with Mayor Samuel McBride as chair (Fig. 17-2). Its report of March 1929 recommended an extension south to Richmond. From there, the extension would angle across York Street to Adelaide before heading due south on the line of the proposed Federal Avenue. It would emerge, as that street would have, dead centre at Union Station.

Or, at least, that was the recommendation if no other work was done. But the commission said that the traffic situation could not be solved by one extension; it proposed a comprehensive scheme. In its plans, Federal Avenue was resurrected in the form of Cambrai Avenue, which would run from Front to Queen (Fig. 3-2). Like all the new roadways proposed by the commission, the street bore the name of a First World War battle site. Because of the new construction that blocked the route between Richmond and Adelaide, the commission had, in its words, made a "virtue of a necessity" by splitting Cambrai around a new monumental building and plaza just south of Adelaide (using Sheppard as one branch). The branches of the street would join up again north of Richmond. The idea of a civic centre was retained from the 1911 plan, now formed by Osgoode Hall, Cobb's Registry Building and a new civic building to the east. These buildings would define a public garden. In keeping with the battle theme, the new square would be called St. Julien Place (Figs. 10-3, 10-4).

In the comprehensive scheme (Fig. 3-3), University would terminate at a vast new traffic circle, to be known as Vimy Circle, centred at Richmond. South of Vimy Circle, University would continue in a southeastern direction to Front, just west of York. The break provided by Vimy Circle would serve to mask this shift in alignment, and indeed, south of Vimy Circle, University Avenue would have an entirely different name, Queen's Park Avenue. The commission proposed that a public plaza, to be known as York Plaza, be built at the northeastern corner of the intersection of

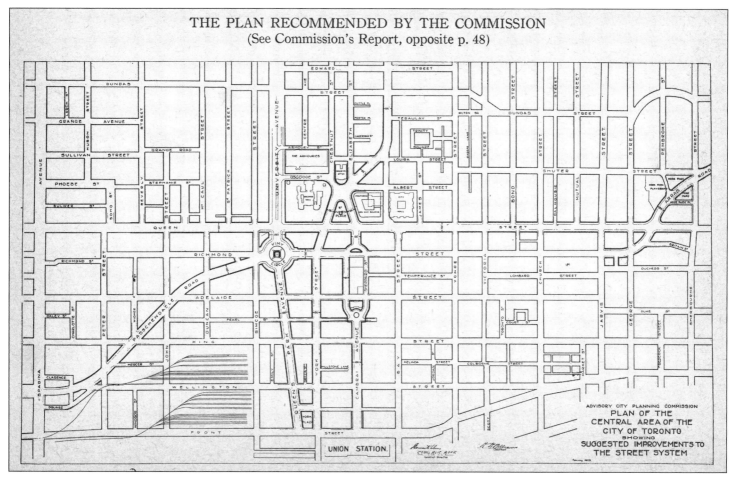

THE PLAN RECOMMENDED BY THE COMMISSION
(See Commission's Report, opposite p. 48)

Fig. 3-3. The road improvements proposed by 1929's Advisory City Planning Commission. Its hallmarks were Cambrai Avenue, a grand boulevard linking Union Station with St. Julien Place (at the current site of Nathan Phillips Square), and Queen's Park Avenue, an extension of University south from Queen. [City of Toronto Archives, Series 97, Sub-series 2, Item 139]

Fig. 3-4. Looking northward up University Avenue from Vimy Circle. The new Canada Life Assurance Building is visible in the distance, to the left. [City of Toronto Archives, Series 59, Item 7]

Queen's Park Avenue and Front Street (city staff would later recommend that a plaza be built at the northwestern corner as well). In addition to serving the University Avenue extension, Vimy Circle would also be the starting point of Passchendaele Road, a southwestern radial road that would merge with Wellington at Spadina (a northeastern radial, Arras Road, would connect with Parliament at Dundas). In the centre of Vimy Circle, the commission proposed a memorial to Canada's war dead. Vimy Circle, even more so than Cambrai Avenue, would have become Toronto's most monumental public space. Beautiful illustrations in the report by Earle C. Sheppard convey the grandeur of the scheme proposed (Fig. 3-4).

In a question put on the municipal ballot in January 1930, Torontonians were asked to authorize the issuance of debentures to finance the improvements recommended by the Advisory City Planning Commission. By a vote of 28,489 to 26,789, they refused. The stock market crash three months earlier had certainly altered the appetite for expensive public works, despite efforts by the plan's supporters to draw attention to the jobs its construction would bring. It didn't help matters that the works were limited to a small downtown area at a time when infrastructure improvement was needed throughout the city.

Ultimately, the University Avenue extension went ahead, but financed now as a "local improvement," with a special levy on property owners in the vicinity. The route chosen was the Queen's Park Avenue alignment, which had been cherry-picked from the larger scheme. Against the recommendations of city staff, Vimy Circle was lopped off as a frill. Gone too was York Plaza. Cambrai Avenue disappeared from the public discourse entirely, despite some initial talk of its being financed as a local improvement as well. Like Federal Avenue, it had always been more about giving the core a grandeur and spatial cohesion than it was about improving traffic flow. And in the end, despite the efforts of the Civic Improvement Committee and the Advisory City Planning Commission, the city's comfort zone didn't extend beyond improving traffic flow.

Chapter 4

EATON CENTRE

1965 / Built to different plans

TWO OF TORONTO'S PLACE-MAKING structures, Old City Hall and the Eaton Centre, are next-door neighbours on Queen Street West. The 1890s municipal complex and the 1970s shopping mall are about as different functionally and aesthetically as two buildings can be. And yet there is something about each that has made it integral to Toronto's urban sense of itself; the city would be a poorer place if either one of them disappeared. But, in the 1960s, when Eaton's first unveiled its plans for a massive new commercial and residential complex, the view was that Queen Street wasn't big enough for both.

The perception that the time had come for the Eaton Centre — and also that time had run out for Old City Hall — sprang from the construction of New City Hall. In June 1958, while the finalists in the international competition for that commission were busy refining their submissions (see chapter 12), city planners approached Eaton's about the possibility of the retailer's redeveloping its sprawling holdings between Yonge and Bay into something that would be a more fitting neighbour for the new City Hall and square. The way the bureaucrats saw it, Eaton's could acquire and redevelop the whole Yonge/Bay/Queen/Dundas superblock, turning it into a retail and office complex that the planners had named "Project Viking," after Eaton's in-store line of consumer goods.

As it happened, at the time, Eaton's was already actively considering reconstructing its downtown store; with the seed of the Project Viking idea sown, it put these plans on hold. Over the next three years, Eaton's worked with American-based developer Webb and Knapp, which had built Montreal's Place Ville Marie, on a redevelopment scheme for the superblock. Boston-based architect I.M. Pei, who had also worked on Place Ville Marie (and had been a finalist in the city hall competition, see Fig. 12-6) was brought on to lead the design team. With the withdrawal of the financially troubled American developer in 1962, Eaton's partnered with Canadian financier E.P. Taylor, developer of Don Mills. In

Fig. 4-1. Metro Chairman William Allen studies Eaton's plans for the redevelopment of its downtown holdings, October 1965. Eaton's proposed to buy Old City Hall in order to get its valuable frontage at Queen and Bay. Just the clock tower would remain. [Clara Thomas Archives and Special Collections, York University, Toronto Telegram Photograph Collection, ASC04399]

the summer of 1964, that joint venture dissolved as well. But Eaton's was undeterred. With the additional lands that Taylor's company had acquired in the superblock and with the name that was now being applied to the development, "Eaton Centre," Eaton's decided to go it alone.

Torontonians got their first look at Eaton's proposed $260-million scheme in October 1965, when a delegation from Eaton's arrived at the Executive Committee of Metro council with a formal proposal to buy Old City Hall for $8 million. The 1899 neo-Romanesque building by E.J. Lennox (Fig. 33-1) had been purchased by Metro in 1961. The cenotaph and a 100- by 140-foot parcel of land surrounding it, however, had been retained by the City of Toronto. In Eaton's plans, the cenotaph would be left where it was, as would the City Hall clock tower (Fig. 4-1). Holy Trinity Church, which Eaton's hadn't been able to buy, would also be retained, but now in a setting of "dignity and symbolism." Eaton's was aware that the proposal to demolish Old City Hall could prove contentious, and it left the job of explaining the necessity for demolition to its planners and architects. They assured council that the recommendation to demolish had been reached only after "exhaustive studies" of potential ways to work around the building had proven fruitless. If left in place, Old City Hall would be "an insuperable barrier" that would "prejudice beyond any possible realization" Eaton's grand scheme, cutting it off visually and physically from the established commercial area surrounding Bay Street to the south. Even more significant than the above-ground barrier, in their view, was the barrier that Old City Hall would present below ground, thwarting the ability to connect to a continuous below-grade pedestrian network to the south and to the New City Hall parking garage to the west.

The committee deferred making a recommendation on the matter, asking Eaton's to return with conceptual plans for the whole project. Eaton's formally unveiled its plans on March 1, 1966 (Fig 4-2). In addition to a shopping mall, the twenty-two-and-a-half-acre site would contain five towers, including the three tallest in the Commonwealth. The seven-storey Eaton's store would be in the southeast corner of the site, at Yonge and Queen. The store would back onto a seven-storey atrium, rising from the second level below ground up to the fifth floor. Two hundred other smaller stores would front onto the atrium on all levels, resulting in almost two million square feet of retail space, the largest retail complex in the world. To the north of this retail complex, the project would be dominated by a sixty-nine-storey office and apartment tower, roughly in the centre of the superblock, fronting Yonge Street. Twin fifty-seven-storey office towers would face Bay Street, one at the Bay/Dundas corner, and one just north of the Old City Hall tower. A twenty-storey, 550-room circular hotel, with a circular interior court, also faced Bay, between the twin towers. A thirty-two-storey office building would be located on Dundas, near Yonge (Eaton's had not managed to secure the actual southwest corner of Yonge and Dundas) (Figs. 4-3, 4-4, 4-5). All the streets within the superblock would be closed, resulting in "splendid buildings set in open space, plazas and landscaped areas in which people can walk undisturbed on a great traffic-free plaza."

The architects for the scheme were Mathers and Haldenby of Toronto, with the American firm of Skidmore, Owings and Merrill as consultants. The overall rectilinear geometry of the scheme they devised was meant to complement Viljo Revell's sculptural New City Hall and square, which had opened officially a few months earlier. The three large office buildings were to be built around a courtyard aligned with Revell's curved towers. The circular hotel, which was lower than the City Hall, was on an axis with a circular opening to the underground pedestrian mall below, in the centre of the plaza. Both were meant to echo the bold curvilinear lines of Revell's twin towers, the whole site reading as a piece with

Fig. 4-2. Toronto city councillor Herbert Orliffe and councillor (later mayor) William Dennison (second and third from left) talk to reporters at the official unveiling of plans for the Eaton Centre, March 1966. Dennison fought to save Old City Hall, but the majority of councillors were willing to see it go. [Clara Thomas Archives and Special Collections, York University, Toronto Telegram Photograph Collection, ASC04288]

Fig. 4-3. A photomontage of the Eaton Centre. The proposed complex included the three tallest towers in the Commonwealth. [Archives of Ontario, F 229-501-135; used with permission of Sears Canada Inc.]

Fig. 4-4. The Eaton Centre seen from the south. The new department store and mall are on the southeast corner of the site, the largest retail complex in the world. In response to complaints from council, the fifty-seven-storey office building in the southwest corner of the site would later be reduced to forty-four storeys, but at the price of the City Hall clock tower. [Archives of Ontario, F 229-501-135; used with permission of Sears Canada Inc.]

Fig. 4-5. The Eaton Centre seen from the northeast. The complex was meant to be read as a piece with Viljo Revell's New City Hall, which had opened the year before. The twenty-storey circular hotel was meant to evoke Revell's curved city hall towers. A plaza, with circular opening to a pedestrian concourse below, was placed on an axis with the towers. [Archives of Ontario, F 229-501-135; used with permission of Sears Canada Inc.]

the New City Hall complex. In the words of an Eaton's executive at the time, the Eaton Centre would "become an important part of the physical image of Toronto … the mind's eye picture of the city itself." There was some concern among the politicians about the loss of Old City Hall, but not much. The overwhelming view seemed best summed up by Swansea reeve Lucien Kurata, who felt the plan was "so gorgeous it's almost sexy."

In June, after a nine-hour debate, Metro Council approved, in principle, the conveyance of Old City Hall to Eaton's. Despite the dogged lobbying efforts of the Friends of Old City Hall, an ad hoc preservation group, the vote was a decisive sixteen to five. In fact, ground had actually been lost in the preservation battle. By this time, even preserving the clock tower was no longer on offer. In response to concerns that the proposal loomed over Nathan Phillips Square, Eaton's offered to lop fourteen storeys off the tower on Bay near Queen. In return, however, it wanted to widen the building's floor plate, requiring removal of the Old City Hall clock tower.

Although council was willing to see its old headquarters demolished (as, for that matter, were all three daily newspapers and the city's commissioner of planning), the near-awe with which most councillors had greeted the unveiling of the proposal a few months earlier had been replaced with more clear-sighted appraisals. Now there was some criticism of the centre's architectural design (which was described as conceptual only), with one councillor calling it "a collection of cereal boxes." And there was concern over whether those cereal boxes would ever be built. Aware that the 1920s Eaton's plans for a grand development at Yonge and College had fizzled (see chapter 22), council resolved to ensure that a bond or other guarantee of performance would be in place before handing over Old City Hall. Council also voted to lease the land rather than sell it. Although a lease arrangement was agreeable

to Eaton's, the parties were still close to two million dollars apart on the issue of Old City Hall's value, which would factor into the rent charged. Eaton's was insistent that it was not interested in purchasing the cenotaph site (as it would be left as open space in any event), and had discounted the purchase price accordingly. For its part, council felt that the cenotaph lands should be part of the deal. Council wanted the flexibility to move the memorial, since veterans' groups were, rather reasonably, not wild about its being stranded in the front yard of a department store.

Negotiations continued among Eaton's, Metro and the city over the next year, with compensation for the sale of the five streets that would be closed also part of the discussions. Then, in May of 1967, Eaton's made a bombshell announcement: it was cancelling the project. In a letter delivered to Mayor William Dennison and Metro Chairman William Allen, Eaton's said that the municipalities' planning and financial demands had made the Eaton Centre uneconomical. The municipal politicians were puzzled; they had believed that a deal on the financial matters was close at hand. Metro quickly responded by creating a special committee to try to get the project back on track, but Eaton's declined to meet with them, not wanting "to suggest we wanted a reduced price for the civic property." This was a strange response given the official reason for the cancellation. Clearly there was more afoot than just unreasonable municipal demands. Eaton's admitted that the Old City Hall controversy played a role, but said it was just not interested in being in the development business. It would look at proposals that private developers or the city might devise, but it was done with going it alone. There was speculation that Eaton's had come to the conclusion that the whole scheme was simply more than the market would bear. Indeed, when the Eaton Centre was first announced, the Town Planning Institute of Canada doubted that Eaton's could fill its projected eleven million square feet of space. And, with the erection of the Toronto-Dominion Centre and a proposed Bank of Commerce development, a critical mass of office space was developing at King and Bay. It was an open question whether high-end office tenants would want to move north of Queen. Now that question was moot.

By 1968, Eaton's was already back at the drawing board, beginning work on scaled-down plans. But now, it had decided that Old City Hall could be dropped from the scheme after all. In the end, the "insuperable barrier" would outlast Eaton's itself.

Chapter 5

PROJECT TORONTO

1968 / Unbuilt

PROJECT SPADINA

1971 / Unbuilt

CHANGE WAS IN THE AIR IN 1968. *Hair* opened on Broadway, Rochdale College opened on Bloor Street, Trudeau was going to create a just society and Buckminster Fuller had a plan to turn Toronto the Good into Toronto the Groovy, the "livingest" city on earth.

A true Renaissance man, Fuller had made his mark in the 1920s and 1930s with his futuristic designs for an innovative mass-produced house, a three-wheeled car and an undistorted map of the world. With his optimistic message and emphasis on ecology, the seventy-two-year-old, pre-war futurist had found a new following among the hippy generation. In 1968 "Bucky" was known the world over for the American Pavilion at Expo '67, the most famous application of his most famous invention, the geodesic dome. Expo had transformed the image of Montreal — of Canada even — and Fuller's dome had stolen the show at Expo.

Like many people who visited the fair's artificial islands in the summer of 1967, Toronto sculptor Gerald Gladstone, who had been commissioned to produce three major pieces for the grounds, including the sculpture in front of the Canadian Pavilion, found the Expo experience inspiring. He was convinced that staid Toronto could benefit from the imagination and insight that Fuller could bring to its city planning. He got Fuller, then in high demand, interested in the job. What was needed now was a sympathetic sponsor capable of paying the freight. Gladstone, who had earlier done a sculpture for the new Telegram Building, found it in *Telegram* publisher and CFTO-TV president John Bassett. In February, the *Telegram* and CFTO jointly commissioned Fuller's architectural and planning firm, Fuller-Sadao/Geometrics, to prepare a report outlining the Toronto of the twenty-first century. They would have three months to do it.

Intellectually, Fuller was given free reign: there were no terms of reference. Consequently, no one knew what to expect. This was a man who had, after all, proposed that a giant plastic dome be placed over a large chunk of Manhattan. If

Fig. 5-1. In 1968, philosopher, inventor and architect Buckminster Fuller explained Project Toronto, his visionary plan for the future of the city, at a press conference in the newly opened Toronto-Dominion Centre. [Clara Thomas Archives and Special Collections, York University, Toronto Telegram Photograph Collection, ASC04389]

Metro councillors had any concerns about what he might propose, they were probably not comforted when, in a speech to council on the upcoming report, he said he saw his job as assisting in "the ballistics and navigation of humanity on spaceship earth." For politicians used to dealing with bureaucrats and ratepayers' groups, it was heady stuff.

On June 1 Fuller presented his seventy-eight-page report (plus illustrations) at a press conference held on the top floor of the Toronto-Dominion Bank Tower, which had opened only two weeks earlier (Figs. 5-1, 5-2). The report emphasized that it was considering Toronto in a larger temporal and geographic horizon than normally taken in

Fig. 5-2. "Bucky" in front of display panels for Project Toronto. [Clara Thomas Archives and Special Collections, York University, Toronto Telegram Photograph Collection, ASC04390]

traditional city-planning documents. In the North American context, it saw Toronto as a "second order metropolitan area" similar in size and function to cities such as St. Louis, Indianapolis, Cincinnati/Dayton and Boston. As with all second-order cities, Toronto was susceptible to brain drain. To attract and keep the best and the brightest it would have to develop a unique identity: "It must maintain a unique role, some pre-eminent capability which will generate a meaningful influence beyond the boundaries of English-speaking Canada, relating in a distinct and individual way to the world at large."

The report concluded that Boston provided a good precedent in this regard; that city had carved out a special niche for itself in the areas of education and health. The Project Toronto report recommended that Toronto could similarly distinguish itself as an education centre. It had a good start with the University of Toronto and York University, but the report recommended that a third institution be founded, which could be "an entirely new kind of teaching/research university." A downtown site was recommended, Exhibition Place being ideal. As for the Ex, it could move up to Downsview, which could also be developed as a site for the 1976 Olympics.

The establishment of a waterfront university would work to mend a problem identified in the report that remains to be solved: the city's lack of connection with Lake Ontario, its most scenic and significant geographic feature (at the time of this writing, forty years after Fuller proposed a post-secondary institution on the waterfront, George Brown College announced its plans for an East Bayfront campus). The Fuller group was clearly taken aback by the fact that "when moving around in the downtown, one is totally unaware that Toronto is a waterfront and not a prairie city." To create a link between the waterfront and the city, Fuller recommended straightening University Avenue and extending it over the railway corridor and then under the Gardiner. Looking south

from Queen's Park, University Avenue would touch the horizon and then disappear as it dipped down again. An enclosed galleria stretching three thousand feet would parallel University from King Street to the waterfront. It would be a twenty-four-hour, climate-controlled civic and commercial space, a twenty-first-century urban amalgam of the Victorian crystal palace and the modern shopping mall.

At the point where University reached its pinnacle, a "Gateway Tower" would mark the transition from downtown to waterfront. To the west of the Gateway Tower, a four-hundred-foot Crystal Pyramid would enclose two twenty-storey commercial buildings. Together, like Expo's geodesic dome had done for Montreal, these structures would help to create a global identity for Toronto, giving it needed differentiation from the likes of Indianapolis and Cincinnati (Fig. 5-3).

In Fuller's mind, University Avenue would not merely extend to Lake Ontario, but into it, connecting with three floating "Pro-To-Cities" (the name was taken from Project Toronto, and "prototype"). These neighbourhoods of 3,500 to 6,500 people would consist of pre-fabricated residential units inserted into floating three-sided steel structures with inward sloping walls. They would be self-contained, with elementary schools, supermarkets, parks and other amenities, and could be towed to different locations if desired. Residential development would also be constructed in the harbour on traditional fill. In this way, the report, which noted Toronto's rapid suburban growth, treated the lake as another frontier for expansion. Land-based Pro-To-Cities could be built in Metro's traditional suburban fringe, in various shapes and configurations, capitalizing on what Fuller identified as Toronto's rather unusual attribute of having suburban high-rise apartment buildings. Clustered in groups of three to six neighbourhood units, they would form new towns.

Fuller had made it clear that his plan, which had been costed at roughly a billion dollars, was merely conceptual and

Fig. 5-3. A glassed-in arcade parallelling an extended University Avenue, a twenty-storey pyramid and floating and suburban "Pro-To-Cities" characterized the Fuller proposals for Toronto. [Clara Thomas Archives and Special Collections, York University, Toronto Telegram Photograph Collection, ASC04387]

that detailed work would need to be done on its various components. Having done their part by paying for the initial report and delivering it to all levels of government, the *Telegram* and CFTO made it clear that the ball was now in the governments' court. Despite Gerald Gladstone's efforts to keep the project alive, no level of government knew quite what to do with it. Certainly none was keen on single-handedly ponying up the $200,000 that Fuller required for more detailed study and models. Mayor William Dennison wrote to the Metro chairman, William Allen, telling him he thought that Metro should take the lead, as Project Toronto was really more a Metro issue than a city issue. Allen wrote to the provincial minister of municipal affairs and housing, Darcy McKeough, stating that he felt it was really a provincial issue. The province considered having Fuller look at surplus government lands at Bay and Wellesley (two decades later they would be offered for the opera house, see chapter 31), but the idea wasn't pursued. The feds thought that some of the theories in Project Toronto might be worth exploring, but they weren't committing to anything. One provincial bureaucrat privately noted at the time that the idea of further study on the report seemed to be kept alive simply because no government wanted to be the one to say that it thought Fuller's ideas didn't really merit further study.

Fuller met with senior politicians from all levels of government in October of 1968, but nothing came of it. The railway companies were about to formally announce their redevelopment plans for 187 acres of railway lands in the downtown core (see chapter 6). It gave the governments the excuse they seemed to be looking for to take a pass on Project Toronto: events had superseded it. Fuller's theoretical proposals were interesting but there was a real waterfront megadeal on the table that needed attention.

Provincial politicians may not have known what to do with Fuller in 1968, but three years later they were beating a path to his door. The cancellation of the Spadina Expressway in June 1971 left a six thousand-foot-long right-of-way between Lawrence and Eglinton — a right-of-way that now had no purpose (Fig. 20-4). A week before the general provincial elections that were held in October of that year, Premier William Davis unveiled a possible solution: Buckminster Fuller's "Project Spadina." In Project Toronto, Fuller had not discussed particular areas where his land-based Pro-To-Cities might go. Now he had a very specific idea: they would go in the empty expressway corridor, providing housing for ten to twelve thousand people in four thousand residential units.

But times had changed, and pyramid-shaped high-rises, climate-controlled streets and moving sidewalks didn't seem as exciting as they might have on the tail of Expo. A headline in the *Toronto Daily Star* said it all: "The big plan with a small future." The *Star* was right. Toronto never got Bucky's pyramids; just six thousand more feet of expressway.

Chapter 6

METRO CENTRE

1968 / Partially built

FOR OVER THIRTY YEARS THE CN Tower held the record as the world's largest freestanding structure, a slightly arcane distinction familiar to every Torontonian. What is decidedly less known is that the CN Tower was originally supposed to have been part of a vast new development built on surplus railway lands south of Front Street. Metro Centre, as it was to be called, was 187 acres of office towers, apartment buildings, shops and schools — the largest downtown redevelopment scheme in North American history. But the planning and land negotiations for the massive development dragged on years after Metro Centre's initial fanfare had turned into the organized opposition that ultimately killed it.

It's not every day that nearly two hundred acres of a downtown core become available for development. In the case of Metro Centre, it was the removal of the railway freight yards from the city core in the early 1960s that produced an enormous tract of surplus land, bounded by Bathurst, Yonge, the Gardiner Expressway and Front Street, as well as a contiguous block up to King Street between John and Simcoe. The developer of Metro Centre was Metro Centre Developments Ltd., a company jointly controlled by Canadian National and Canadian Pacific. The railways had been considering their development options in the area for years and, in 1967, announced that they were undertaking intensive planning studies. John Andrews, chair of the University of Toronto's school of architecture, was lead designer on the project, in conjunction with Webb, Zerafa and Menkes. On December 19, 1968, in a ballroom at the Royal York Hotel, two hundred invited guests got the first glimpse of the proposal that resulted from the development team's year and a half of studies. Motioning to the twenty-foot-long model of the dazzling new world that was set shortly to rise from the railway lands, Metro Centre's president, Stewart Andrews, captured the team's excitement and pride: "Here you are," he said. "Merry Christmas." (Fig. 6-1.)

Fig. 6-1. Metro Centre, a plan for 187 acres of land owned by Canadian National and Canadian Pacific south of Front Street was unveiled to the public at a press conference in December 1968. [Clara Thomas Archives and Special Collections, York University, Toronto Telegram Photograph Collection, ASC04394]

It was truly massive in its scope: a "city-within-a-city," consisting of 4.5 million square feet of office space, 600,000 square feet of commercial space and 9,300 residential units. Key to the complex was the consolidation of the remaining railway tracks to the south of the site, alongside the Gardiner Expressway. A new transportation complex would sit diagonally over the tracks, serving as a terminal for rail, subway and bus services. The Yonge-University subway loop would be extended south from Union Station to Queen's Quay, allowing direct subway access to the new transportation hub from one of the three new subway stations. The Metro Centre people noted that pushing the tracks to the south would create a single

Fig. 6-2. Looking west over Metro Centre, down Esplanade Street. Octagonal office buildings replace Union Station to the north. A convention centre is to the south, between new office towers for each of the railway companies. The telecommunications tower (what would later become the CN Tower) terminates the view. [City of Toronto Archives, Fonds 1652, File 804, id 08]

Fig. 6-3. A view from the south, showing the extension of University Avenue looping around the new transportation terminal, and the residential area to the west of the telecommunications tower. [City of Toronto Archives, Fonds 1652, File 804, id 09]

Gardiner/rail corridor. But moving the city's train station southward had another advantage: it freed up land adjacent to the existing downtown core for redevelopment. In the Metro Centre plans, Union Station was to be demolished, replaced by six octagonal office buildings, three at eighteen storeys, and three at thirty-six storeys. The buildings would be joined by pedestrian bridges extending from the tops of the eighteen-storey buildings to the middles of the thirty-six storey buildings. The western end of the site contained apartment buildings. Between this residential area and the office area was the communications area, site of the new CBC English-language headquarters, and the 1,575-foot high broadcasting tower (Figs. 6-2, 6-3).

As in Buckminster Fuller's Project Toronto (see chapter 5), University Avenue would be straightened and extended south. But in Metro Centre, it would be split into two levels. The inside lanes would tunnel underground, surfacing south of the rail lines to connect with Lake Shore Boulevard. The outside lanes would loop over the tracks and circle around the new transportation complex, as well as a new CN hotel that would sit adjacent to it. The Esplanade would be extended (or more precisely, reintroduced) east of Bay as Esplanade Street, a broad boulevard that would form the development's major east-west artery. The Metro Centre report drew a link between this new boulevard and the original Esplanade conceived at Toronto's founding (discussed in chapter 2). In Metro Centre's updated version, instead of enjoying views of the lake in a Walks and Gardens setting, pedestrians would be underground in a pedestrian mall. Natural light would filter in from skylights in the boulevard. It was in keeping with a blurring of the traditional distinction between private buildings and public streets that typified Metro Centre generally. On the south side of Esplanade Street would be a new convention centre and, at opposite ends, two twenty-six-storey slab office buildings, one each for Canadian National and Canadian Pacific.

A multi-government technical review committee studied the Metro Centre plans. A year after the big announcement, however, there was no word of any progress. The CBC's tower and headquarters were an integral part of the first phase, but a federal spending freeze had put the broadcaster's participation in limbo (Fig. 6-4). The project encountered another major snag when Metro Toronto and the Toronto Transit Commission refused to extend the Yonge-University subway loop southward. Apart from the cost of the subway construction (which Metro Centre was not willing to pay), the TTC felt that extending the lines southward would make the University line less attractive to those who rode it southward with the intention of rounding the loop at Union to avoid changing trains at Bloor. Also, with the collapse of the Eaton Centre still fresh in people's minds (see chapter 4), there was a hesitancy to make major infrastructure changes on the basis of a single developer's plans. Even without the subway extension, Metro planners estimated that Metro Centre would give rise to a minimum of $90 million in transit and other public infrastructure costs, and there was no agreement about how these would be paid for.

Despite these problems, Metro Toronto approved the proposal in principle in December 1970. It would take another year for the City of Toronto to give its assent. For the city, there was an additional wrinkle: Union Station. Not its loss (although that would become an issue later) but its ownership. The nine acres of land on which Union Station sat — and on which Metro Centre Developments proposed four towers — belonged to the city. It had been leased to the railways since 1905, but only for railway purposes. No one was making the argument that commercial office towers were covered under those terms. If Metro Centre wanted the land, it would have to pay; the question was how much. Ultimately, a land swap was agreed to, whereby the city would get the old beltline railway lands in the northern part of the city (for use

Fig. 6-4. Members of the CBC's board of directors inspect the proposed communications area that would house the CBC's English-language headquarters as well as its new broadcasting tower, March 28, 1969. [City of Toronto Archives, Fonds 1652, File 804, id 06]

as a park) as well as land in the Metro Centre development for "new Massey Hall" (ultimately Roy Thomson Hall) and a convention centre. Alderman John Sewell called the deal a swindle, but council voted against his request for an independent evaluation.

Once the city approved the land deal, it was expected that its planners would green-light the Metro Centre plan and prepare the necessary official plan amendments. The bureaucrats' report was not a rubber stamp, however. They wanted changes to the scheme, including increased parkland, low-income housing and a guarantee of public meetings before the implementation of the various stages of the development. The city's planning board adopted the report only after amending it to exclude all these recommendations. In the end, almost three years to the week after the big Christmastime press conference, Toronto city council approved the Metro Centre planning guidelines. Although a number of councillors had voiced concerns, ultimately only John Sewell, who had tirelessly tried to call attention to what he felt was a sellout of the public interest in favour of the railway companies, voted in opposition. Perhaps attrition played a part: the vote ended five days of debate, the longest council debate in Toronto's history.

Metro Centre's troubles were far from over, however. Community organizations took up the fight. The Confederation of Resident and Ratepayer Associations, an umbrella organization of over thirty-five ratepayer groups, lobbied the legislature to refer the Metro Centre official plan amendments to the Ontario Municipal Board. Despite its public support of the project, the government obliged. An ad hoc Committee to Save Union Station was organized, with over five hundred members. The Architectural Conservancy of Ontario, which had been drawn into the debate in order to save Union Station, broadened its advocacy to a fight against the plan generally, on the basis that the "functional monstrosity" that was

Metro Centre would actually cut the city off from the lake. The opposition to Metro Centre had gone from non-existent to organized and vocal. Metro Centre officials blamed the government's decision to cancel the Spadina Expressway in 1971 (see chapter 20) for fuelling the outcry. Despite that view's minimization of Metro Centre's own problems, there was undeniably a link, and it went even further, all the way back to the fight to save Old City Hall from the Eaton Centre proposal in the mid-sixties. People who saw mega-projects like the Spadina Expressway, the Eaton Centre and Metro Centre as the antithesis of a livable, walkable, human-scaled city were organizing, and organizing successfully. Despite the years of study devoted to Metro Centre, there was the feeling that there had been little opportunity for input from the public, and that the development agreements under which Metro Centre would proceed (thanks to special legislation) would remove even more opportunity for public participation in the future.

When the OMB issued its decision in June 1972, it directed the city to restore many of the conditions that had been in the city planners' report, including a doubling of parkland from seventeen to thirty-six acres and a requirement that a minimum of 15 percent of the apartment units have at least three to four bedrooms, to accommodate families. The board also put a ceiling on commercial space. When Metro Centre was announced in 1968, it had been predicted that the communications tower, the transportation complex, a trade centre and some residential and office buildings would be completed by 1973. However, 1973 marked only the start of construction. And even then, the construction was just on the tower (initially at least, without a permit).

By that time, the pro-development council that had approved Metro Centre had been replaced in the elections of December 1972 with a so-called "reform council." It was no longer business as usual for developers. In an effort to find some middle

THE TORONTO UNION TERMINAL AND COMMERCIAL BUILDING

WATCH TORONTO GROW TO THE MILLION MARK

Fig. 6-5. Metro Centre was arguably not the most audacious plan to suggest the redevelopment possibilities of consolidating rail services. That honour must go to the Toronto Union Terminal and Commercial Building. Proposed in 1911 by an investment syndicate, it would have entailed the construction of a forty-million-square-foot, mixed-use building taking up the entire area bounded by Queen, King, Simcoe and Yonge. Trains would have entered the building via tunnels. A slight glitch was the land, none of which was owned by the promoters. [City of Toronto Archives, Series 783 , File 112]

ground in the new political reality, Mayor David Crombie asked council in November 1974 to affirm Metro Centre's existing planning approvals, subject to a series of additional conditions. Despite these new conditions, council voted against Crombie's proposal, eleven to nine. Although this vote didn't remove any official plan approvals that had already been granted, it wasn't a good sign for Metro Centre, all of whose remaining development agreements still needed council approval.

The response was swift: Stewart Andrews, who was still at the helm of Metro Centre, said that until there was a new council (elections were slated for the following month), "Metro Centre is strictly on the shelf." The die had been cast. In his own efforts to get Metro Centre back on track, Premier William Davis had struck an intergovernmental committee. Its most significant recommendation was the railways' worst-case scenario. In May of 1975, Davis held a press conference to report the committee's conclusion that Union Station should be retained as the transportation terminal for downtown Toronto. Keeping Union Station as a transportation hub altered in the most fundamental way the plan the railways had been working on for almost a decade. The railways officially announced that they were abandoning what was now clearly a doomed plan. Metro Centre had reached the end of the line.

Chapter 7

HARBOUR CITY

1970 / Unbuilt

"**H**ARBOUR CITY IS PROBABLY the most important advance in planning for cities that has been made this century." That was Jane Jacobs in May 1970 at the unveiling of the province's plans for an entire new city of sixty thousand people in Lake Ontario. The plans, which had been a closely guarded secret, would see the new city built on man-made islands between Ontario Place and the Toronto islands, its neighbourhoods connected by canals and lagoons.

It was, strangely enough, the island airport that gave rise to Harbour City. Or rather, the need for a new island airport. By the late sixties, the Toronto Harbour Commission, the federally created body that ran it, had determined that the existing Toronto Island Airport was outdated. It was suited only to small aircraft. Yet, because of its location, a stone's throw from downtown, it couldn't be expanded. The commission proposed that a new facility capable of handling inter-city jet traffic be built on fill around the southeastern part of the islands,

just off the Leslie Street spit. The bonus was that the old airport lands would become available for urban redevelopment.

The commission formally published its waterfront proposals (known as the "Bold Concept") in January 1968. It included the "Harbour City" scheme for a new city on the old airport lands and adjacent fill. In the meantime, Metro planners had picked up the commission's Harbour City idea and incorporated it into the Metro waterfront plan, which had been released the month before. The timing was right for bold waterfront concepts generally. It was known that Canadian National and Canadian Pacific had plans for their railway lands (see chapter 6), and the Marvo Construction Co. had proposed its $80-million Harbour Square project on waterfront lands along Queen's Quay (Campeau Corporation would later take over the project).

For its part, the Ontario government had its own Toronto waterfront plans underway. The Special Projects and Planning Division of the provincial Department of Trade

Fig. 7-1. From left to right: architect Eb Zeidler, Toronto mayor William Dennison and Ontario Minister of Trade Stanley Randall inspect a model at the unveiling of the province's Harbour City plans, May 20, 1970. [Clara Thomas Archives and Special Collections, York University, Toronto Telegram Photograph Collection, ASC04292]

and Development was building the Ontario Showcase (later named Ontario Place) to replace the Ontario Government Building at the CNE. This same department had been responsible for Ontario's successful pavilion at Expo '67. In preparing for the construction of the Ontario Place islands, provincial lawyers advised the government that, constitutionally, the province owned all the water lots that were not part of the federally controlled harbour. In other words, the province owned most of the land where the federal Harbour Commission intended to build Harbour City. Based on this revelation, in 1969, the provincial government took on Harbour City as its own project, assembling a team

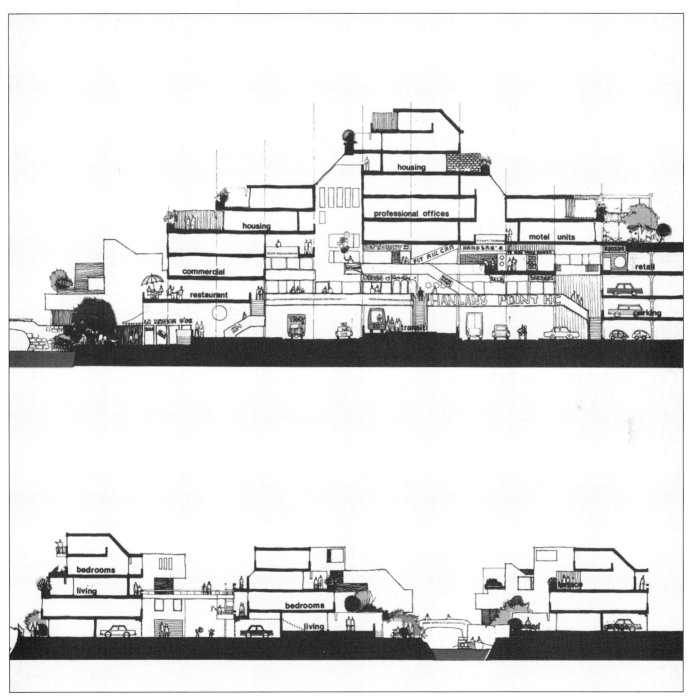

Fig. 7-2. This cross-section shows the mixing of residential and commercial uses that was a hallmark of the Harbour City plan.
[Zeidler Partnership Architects]

of outside consultants, including urban theorist Jane Jacobs and Ontario Place architect Eberhard Zeidler. The Harbour Commission was less than pleased.

If its claim on the water lots gave the province the authority to get involved, there were policy considerations that, in the opinion of Ontario Trade Minister Stanley Randall, made it incumbent on the government to do so. For one thing, Randall felt that it was important for the province to ensure that development in Harbour City would accommodate families with children (a failure that had led to criticism of the Metro Centre scheme); as well, the province wanted to provide for a mix of housing types and tenures, so that occupants of all economic means could move in. The government was skeptical of the commission's intentions on those fronts, fearing that it saw Harbour City only as a cash cow that could fund its other endeavours. Beyond that, Randall saw the province as taking a leadership role in environmental and quality-of-life issues in the seventies, just as it had been involved in education in the sixties, highways in the fifties and housing in the forties. The government saw Harbour City as a harbinger of things to come.

The province's consultants worked away in secrecy for about a year. At a press conference on May 20, 1970, the plans were finally unveiled (Fig. 7-1). The basic concept that had been proposed by the Harbour Commission, that is, a new town characterized by integral lagoons and canals and built on reclaimed land, was still there. But there were key differences. Most significantly, and in keeping with Jane Jacobs's theories on successful urban neighbourhoods, there would be no strict zoning of residential and commercial uses. Both were free to expand and contract within the development as circumstances dictated (Fig. 7-2). The potential for this flexibility would be assisted through Zeidler's design of the buildings themselves, a theme he continued from his work on the innovative McMaster Medical Centre in Hamilton.

For Harbour City, Zeidler proposed pre-engineered modules that could be arranged and stacked in any number of ways to create single-family homes, duplexes, apartments, shops, restaurants — whatever was needed. Buildings would face walkways on one side and canals on the other. Most buildings would not be over three or four storeys, and none would exceed eight (Fig. 7-3). Construction of the $500-million project would take twelve years.

Harbour City's sixty thousand residents would be spread over 220 acres of existing airport land and 510 acres of artificial islands. The goal was urban density in a low- to mid-rise built form that would allow for a sense of neighbourhood. Access from the mainland would be via Bathurst, Strachan or Spadina, onto an arterial ring road that would loop through the development (Figs. 7-4, 7-5). Traffic would not be allowed to infiltrate the community, however. Cars would be parked in courtyards off the arterial road (later versions of the scheme were car-free, with parking proposed in garages on the mainland). Internal movement would be on foot, sometimes through second-level pedestrian connections across canals, or on "travellators" (moving sidewalks).

Perhaps sensitive to criticism that the project had already been attracting in some quarters (five hundred people concerned about the pollution it would cause had held a meeting earlier in the month), Randall was tentative in his remarks at the Harbour City press conference, stressing that the project was conceptual at this stage, and reassuring his listeners that "it is not a concept that we would propose to carry out unilaterally or against the wishes of the council and people of Toronto and of Metro. Rather, it is going to require the whole-hearted co-operation of the city and of Metro if it is to proceed." Wholehearted co-operation was in short supply. Already, newly elected reform councillors John Sewell, William Kilbourn and David Crombie (who was also the chair of the city's waterfront committee) had raised concerns about

Fig. 7-3. Another view of the Harbour City model, showing the pedestrian emphasis, as well as the water frontage all units would enjoy. [Zeidler Partnership Architects]

Fig. 7-4. A view over Harbour City showing the ring road connecting at Strachan and Bathurst. Note that that the Metro Centre development is shown in this model, between Front Street and the Gardiner. Harbour Square is also shown, including square towers at the water's edge that would never be built. [Toronto Public Library]

Fig. 7-5. Harbour City, with downtown in the background. [Toronto Public Library]

the proposal publicly. The issue wasn't the architecture, which everyone seemed to like well enough, but the advisability of the concept itself.

Even though low-rise, pedestrian-friendly Harbour City was a reaction against the towers and segregated uses typified by Metro Centre, both were introduced to the public as detailed models at a grand unveiling. It was an approach that Metro Centre's chief architect would later blame for a lot of that proposal's subsequent problems. The approach was undoubtedly a miscalculation with Harbour City as well, despite the promises to consult and the strengths of the plan itself. Certainly it did nothing to allay the many specific concerns that were raised. If you were opposed to the Spadina Expressway (see chapter 20), you would be concerned that Harbour City would necessitate its completion down to the Gardiner (even with anti-expressway leader Jane Jacobs's assurances to the contrary). If you were worried about the environment, you would be concerned about the impact of introducing a city-full of people (and their motor boats and waste) into the harbour. Not to mention the basic issue of whether it made sense to give up five hundred acres of the harbour to still more landfill. If you wanted to keep the islands car-free, you would be concerned that the introduction of automobiles into Harbour City would create pressure to extend access onto the island parklands. If you lived in the Beaches, you would be concerned that Harbour City would result in a new airport a mile away from the foot of Coxwell Avenue. At a time when it was still Metro policy to bulldoze the existing island residential communities in order to create public parkland, there were those who raised the more fundamental question of who the waterfront should be developed for: all the citizens of Toronto, through the creation of parks and green space, or those lucky enough to get a unit in Harbour City.

Opponents organized a "Sink Harbour City" campaign. For a provincial government already under intense pressure from the anti–Spadina Expressway lobby, the last thing needed was another controversial project in the City of Toronto — especially one that it was proposing. In March 1971, Bill Davis became premier. By that point, a municipal–provincial committee that had been set up to consider Harbour City technical matters had not met in four months. With Stanley Randall out of the cabinet, Harbour City lost its biggest booster. Although Davis had denied that the project was dead, the next week provincial representatives failed to attend a special public meeting on the plan organized by the city.

The official pronouncement of Harbour City's demise wouldn't come until the next year, however. In March 1972, the federal and provincial governments announced that a new international airport would be built in Pickering Township (more than thirty-five years later, it has yet to be built). Under these plans, the existing Toronto Island airport was to be retained as an inter-city short take-off and -landing facility. The province now had a different new town to build, south of the new Pickering airport. The machinery to expropriate twenty-five-thousand acres for that venture was already in motion.

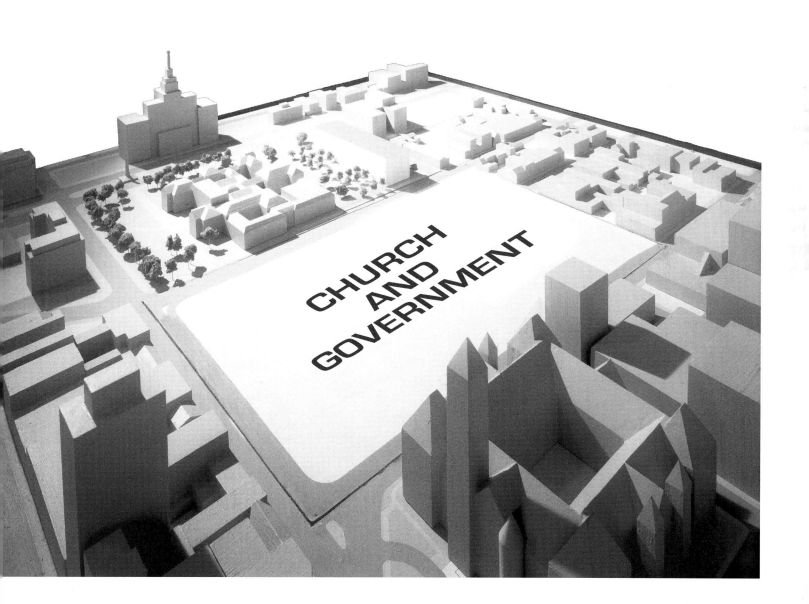

Chapter 8

ONTARIO LEGISLATIVE BUILDINGS

1880 / Built to different plans

THE LEGISLATIVE BUILDINGS AT Queen's Park are such a stoic presence at the top of University Avenue, such a symbol of staid, sensible Ontario, that it's tough to believe that they have a scandalous past. But the decision to hire an American to design them, the result of an architectural competition gone seriously off the rails, caused a firestorm in the 1880s.

By 1880, it was pretty clear that Ontario's parliament buildings, on Front Street, were in desperate need of replacement. It was more than a matter of space. Kivas Tully (Fig. 8-1), the provincial architect, warned the commissioner of public works that a fire could spread from any of the fifty stoves or forty-five open grates that heated the building, resulting in an irreplaceable loss of government records, including all the Crown lands records. Tully himself drew up plans for a new complex, offering both a Gothic and Second Empire treatment (Figs. 8-2a, 8-2b). Tully's proposal consisted of a centre block, 290 by 160 feet, joined to 80-foot-wide east

and west wings that stretched back 280 feet. The centre block would house primarily the legislative functions, with departmental buildings in the wings. Despite having prepared alternate plans, Tully had come to prefer the Gothic. Although he pointed out that this style coincided with the establishment of parliament in England, it wasn't the symbolic significance of Gothic that led him to recommend it. Rather, it was the conclusions of an 1857 British parliamentary select committee that the Gothic he advocated had been, in Tully's words, "fully proved ... to afford greater area for light, equal facilities for ventilation, and to present a more chaste and elegant external and informal effect at the same cost than that of any other style...." The purpose of the select committee that Tully quoted so favourably had been to investigate an international architectural competition for new Foreign and War offices at Whitehall. That competition had been an infamous fiasco: after the government changed, the third place winner, George Gilbert Scott, was given the commission; when the

Fig. 8-1. Kivas Tully, the provincial architect, told the government that it desperately needed new legislative buildings. [Archives of Ontario, C 158-1-0-0-2]

Figs. 8-2a (right), 8-2b (below). Tully drew up his own plans for a new complex to house the provincial parliament and government offices. Although he prepared alternate Gothic and Second Empire treatments, he preferred the Gothic (right). [Archives of Ontario, RG 15-13-2-80]

government changed again, Scott was retained, but forced to produce his building in a classical, rather than Gothic style. If Ontario's government was aware of this background, it obviously wasn't troubled by it. Taking a pass on Tully's plans, it decided to hold an international competition for the province's new parliament buildings.

The competition conditions were published in April 1880. The site would be at Queen's Park, which the government had expropriated for new parliament buildings back in 1853 (when there was the thought that Toronto might be chosen as the capital of Canada). In addition to program requirements for the new building, the conditions stressed that there was a strict budget of $500,000. The three-member jury consisted of the federal commissioner of public works, Alexander Mackenzie; an English-born architect practising in Buffalo, Richard A. Waite; and prominent Toronto architect W.G. Storm (Storm's firm, Cumberland and Storm, had actually won an earlier competition for new parliament buildings, in 1852, but the government had not pursued the matter). The first, second and third-place awards were $2,000, $1,000 and $500 respectively.

By the entry deadline of October 15, 1880, sixteen submissions had been received, eleven from Canada and five from the United States. The jury released its report a month later. It judged the entries according to a number of criteria. The entries were ranked from one to sixteen as to cost, and then they were appraised in each of five separate categories covering architectural merit; general arrangement; interior lighting; heating and ventilation; and drainage and sanitary arrangements, with the first six submissions in each of those categories being ranked. Years of difficulties followed from the result. The jury deemed the design of the Toronto firm of Darling and Curry (Fig. 8-3) highest as to architectural merit, but dead last in the cost category, which had been so important to the government. Applying all the criteria, and placing

an emphasis on budget, as it had been directed to do, the jury chose three winners. Ranked first was the entry of the Toronto firm Gordon and Helliwell.

Copies of Gordon and Helliwell's design do not appear to have survived. Based on Tully's description of its having a dome over the legislative chamber (Tully found the dome acoustically problematic), one assumes that their buildings were not in the Gothic style that the provincial architect favoured. In addition to Darling and Curry's proposal, another Gothic design survives, submitted by Augustus Laver under the pseudonym "Communi Consensu" (by common consent) (Fig. 8-4). Along with Thomas Stent, Laver had designed the East and West Blocks of the Parliament Buildings in Ottawa in 1859.

Despite being the jury's favourite, the judging criteria kept Darling and Curry's design from making the final cut. This led to an interesting jury report: the jury advised that it couldn't recommend that the government proceed with any of the winning entries, which it found unworthy of the site and lacking "evidence of design." It concluded its report by praising Darling and Curry's proposal and criticizing the government for setting an unrealistically low construction budget. The government was now in a quandary. It decided to invite six of the firms to prepare revised plans. Five responded. In 1882, the government put the revised plans of Darling and Curry and Gordon and Helliwell out to tender. That didn't solve anything. Both tenders came back well over budget. Although the province was committed to proceeding with one of the designs, a general election in 1883 resulted in the whole idea being temporarily set aside.

When the government was re-elected, it passed a bill in 1885 to increase the appropriation for the parliament buildings to $750,000. It could now move forward with one of the plans that had been tendered. But which one? Five years had passed since the competition had been announced. It was

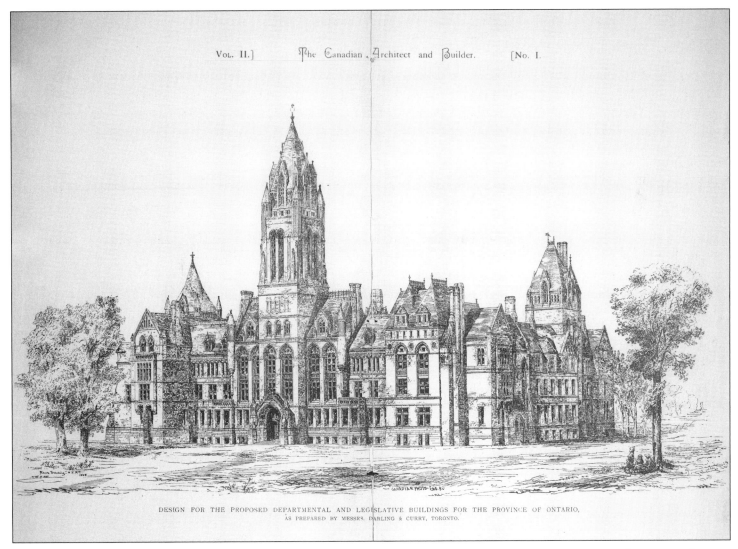

VOL. II.]   The Canadian Architect and Builder.   [No. I.

DESIGN FOR THE PROPOSED DEPARTMENTAL AND LEGISLATIVE BUILDINGS FOR THE PROVINCE OF ONTARIO,
AS PREPARED BY MESSRS. DARLING & CURRY, TORONTO.

Fig. 8-3. This design by the Toronto firm of Darling and Curry was the favourite in an international competition for new parliament buildings for Ontario. [Thomas Fisher Rare Book Library, University of Toronto]

Fig. 8-4. An entry by Augustus Laver, submitted under the pseudonym "Communi Consensu." Along with Thomas Stent, Laver had designed the east and west blocks of the Parliament Buildings in Ottawa. [Archives of Ontario, RG 15-13-2-164]

time for some outside advice again, and the government decided that both designs should be put to a full professional review. Of the original jury, this left out Mackenzie, who was not an architect. And now that the identities of the finalists were known, there was a concern that Storm might not be seen as an impartial judge of his fellow Toronto architects. That left only Richard Waite, the American.

Waite expected to take about a week to report back to the government. He ended up taking eight or nine months, submitting his report in November of 1885. Waite was now of the view that both proposals were "unsuitable and defective." In what must have proved particularly galling to the firms involved, he concluded that both designs suffered from the fact that they were devised with a $500,000 budget in mind, whereas now there was $250,000 more available. The government was in a dilemma. The competition saga had been dragging on for six years and there was no appetite for organizing another one. Its solution was simply to hire Waite himself to come up with plans. Within five weeks of submitting his report, he had a signed contract to do just that.

Waite's hiring was formally confirmed in the legislature in March 1886. Ontario architects were outraged for two reasons: first, the government had set aside the results of a competition that members of the profession had entered in good faith and, second, having done so, it unilaterally handed over to an American architect the most prestigious commission in the province. To make matters worse, not only did the government refuse to produce Waite's report, there were no published designs of what he intended to build. The *Canadian Architect and Builder* (the premier architectural journal of the day, published between 1888 and 1908) gloated when it learned two years later, that the "great American genius" was revising the design of his centre block (originally, its four domed turrets were to be taller, topped with conical roofs rising higher than the main roof).

But it noted the irony that the competition finalists had not been given the same opportunity to improve their plans. Still more frustrating — given the government's fixation on building costs during the competition — costs on Waite's building skyrocketed, reaching $1.4 million, or almost double the expanded budget, by 1890.

Even so, from the government's perspective, at least the business of the architectural competition was over and done with. And, contrary to the official view, it had produced a clear winner: Richard Waite, jury member.

Chapter 9

ST. ALBAN'S CATHEDRAL

1883 / Partially built

FOR MUCH OF TORONTO'S HISTORY — until they built the Royal York Hotel in 1929 — the spire of St. James's Cathedral at the corner of King and Church Streets was the tallest structure in Toronto. But the supremacy of St. James's as the principal church in the Anglican Diocese of Toronto was for many years eclipsed — at least officially — by plans to build a grand new cathedral in the Annex, the Cathedral of St. Alban the Martyr.

Today you can see the beginnings (and endings) of the St. Alban's project between Howland Avenue and Albany Street, north of Bloor and east of Bathurst: the completed easternmost section of the cathedral (containing the choir), as well as the massive stone foundations for the rest of the structure that was never built.

The birth of St. Alban's Cathedral was as drawn-out as its demise. Although St. James's had served as the de facto Anglican cathedral of Toronto since the diocese was founded in 1839, it remained, technically, a parish church.

Its lowish-Anglican parishioners were happy enough to allow their building to be used as the cathedral, but felt that surrendering ultimate control for this purpose to Toronto's first Anglican bishop, the decidedly high-Anglican John Strachan (Fig. 9-1), was another matter. This tension led Strachan to identify the need for a dedicated cathedral, a plan he backed up by personally funding a "cathedral establishment fund" in 1843.

It would take another forty years for things to really get moving, under Toronto's third Anglican bishop, Arthur Sweatman. In 1883, the provincial legislature passed a special act to incorporate a governing body for the new "Cathedral of St. Alban the Martyr." The next year, a four-and-a-half-acre site was made available by a syndicate that was then developing a chic new housing subdivision (later called St. Alban's Park) in Seaton Village, outside the city limits, in the part of town now known as the Annex. In an effort to attract the prestige of the cathedral to its development, it donated half the

Fig. 9-1. John Strachan, bishop of Toronto. Tensions with the parishioners at what is now the Cathedral Church of St. James led him to set up a "cathedral establishment fund" in 1843. It was the genesis of St. Alban's Cathedral. [Toronto Public Library]

purchase price (of $10,488) and promised another $2,000 if construction of the choir and chancel was completed by the end of 1886.

Local architect Richard Windeyer, Sr. was commissioned to design the new church. His Victorian Gothic plans were characterized by an unusual pairing of towers on the western facade, a massive southern tower, featuring a large clock and a smaller tower to the north, with a spire (Fig. 9-2). The design attracted criticism early on, the *Canadian Architect and Builder* dismissing it as "a design which, to say the least, is very weak," and "not by any means the best, or even the second best, which could have been obtained."

Sod was turned on August 20, 1885, but progress was slow. It took three years before the foundation stone was laid. Funding was a constant issue. To cover construction costs, the cathedral had been mortgaged from the outset. Things got worse when Canada entered a depression in the 1890s, and the need for new parish churches throughout the growing city was a constantly competing draw on the funds of the faithful. It didn't help that most of the city's Anglican elite still worshipped at St. James's, which was allowed to continue to call itself a cathedral as long as St. Alban's remained unfinished.

A bishop's residence (at 112 Howland Avenue) had been constructed in 1887. A further diocesan building immediately to the north, the chapter house, was finished in the 1890s (it housed St. Alban's Cathedral School until that institution's demise in 1910). During this time however, work on the cathedral itself had pretty much stopped. Most of what exists of the cathedral today had been completed by 1891.

Windeyer died in 1900. In 1905, architect Vaux Chadwick, who had worked on the cathedral project in Windeyer's office, prepared revised plans on which to complete the project. Significantly, they involved scrapping the western towers, which had come under particular criticism. Chadwick proposed instead a single tower on the southern

facade, nestled in the corner created by the intersection of the cathedral's aisle and transept. This change was a recognition that the southern facade, fronting on St. Alban's Square, would effectively be the cathedral's main face. But construction didn't resume. On the contrary, things got so bad financially that in 1908 some of the cathedral lands actually had to be sold in order to service the project's debt. The cathedral's great champion, Bishop Sweatman, died the following year.

Despite these hardships, in 1910 the synod of the diocese reaffirmed its commitment to completing St. Alban's. But it would not be according to Windeyer's or Chadwick's plans. That year the Great Anglican Congress was held in Halifax. Halifax's new cathedral, designed by the Boston firm of Cram, Goodhue and Ferguson, was officially opened at the congress. The firm, and particularly its principal Ralph Adams Cram, were acknowledged as masters of the Gothic style; at the time they were working on the Cathedral of St. John the Divine in New York City. Toronto's new bishop, James Sweeny, was in attendance at the Anglican congress. Clearly he liked what he saw in Halifax, because that same year the Toronto diocese hired Cram's firm to take over the St. Alban's project. The decision to hire "the distinguished architect from the United States" rankled the profession in Ontario, which was still smarting from the Richard Waite affair at Queen's Park (see chapter 8). Sweeny was unmoved by their protests. His goal was to have the cathedral substantially completed in time for the seventy-fifth anniversary of the diocese in 1914.

Sweeny sent the new architects the Windeyer plans. After reviewing them, it was their opinion that although the work done to date could be incorporated into the completed building, "there is nothing that would justify the carrying out of the original scheme for the completion of the Cathedral, nor any attempts to modify the plans as they now

WEST ELEVATION

ST. ALBAN'S CATHEDRAL

Fig. 9-2. Construction began on this design by Richard Windeyer in 1885. [Anglican Diocese of Toronto Archives]

stand. For every reason the work must be begun *de novo*." After visiting Toronto in February 1911, Cram recommended against proceeding with two towers on the western front, as their effect would be lost on narrow Albany Street; moreover, such a composition was "not British in any respect." In his view a central tower, set back on the axis of the nave and transept, would be most in keeping with the great cathedrals of Great Britain and Ireland. Cram's design did not disappoint. *Construction* magazine felt that, when completed, it "would stand with many of the great monuments of Anglican Christianity as a fitting exponent of the religion of the race." In keeping with the ever-present need for economy, however, the tower itself was planned for completion at a later date (Figs. 9-3, 9-4, 9-5).

Fig. 9-3. Construction blueprints for the plans drawn up by the American firm of Cram, Goodhue and Ferguson in 1911. A great central tower, which was intended to be built later, is not shown here. [Anglican Diocese of Toronto Archives]

On August 27, 1912, the first stone of the reconceived project was laid by the governor general, the Duke of Connaught (the Arthur of nearby Prince Arthur Street), using the same trowel that Bishop Sweatman had used almost twenty-five years earlier. Although the foundation for the rest of the structure was completed during this period (a foundation you can still see today), timing and economics were again a problem. The proposed 1911 budget of $250,000 had proven inadequate and tenders came back $200,000 higher. With the start of the Great War, construction again wound down. After the war, the estimated cost to complete the ambitious scheme was even higher and support waned. Bishop Sweeny remained committed to the project, but the synod of the diocese voted against continuing construction.

Other events conspired against the grand new church. Down at St. James's, the authorities had become concerned about the future of their church, as well-to-do parishioners

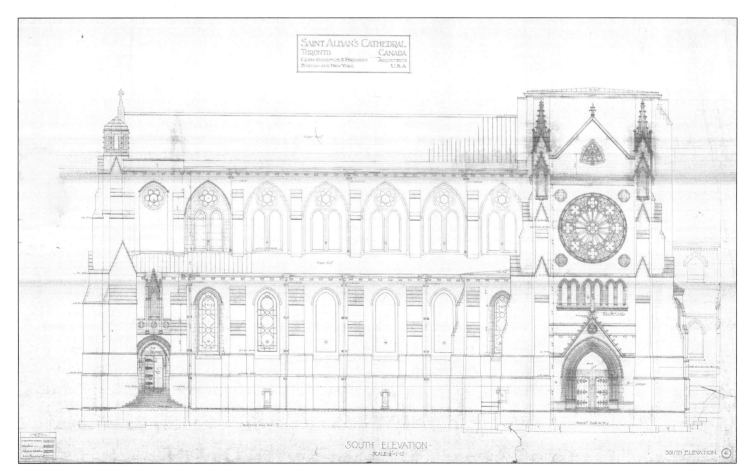

Fig. 9-4. The 1911 plans as seen from the south. [Anglican Diocese of Toronto Archives]

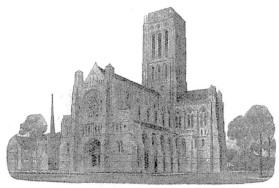

Cathedral of St. Alban the Martyr

Finance Committee:

COL. SIR HENRY MILL PELLATT, C.V.O
CHAIRMAN

REV. CANON MORLEY
SECRETARY

TELEPHONE COLLEGE 6758

87 HOWLAND AVENUE

TORONTO, *November 18, 1913*

Dear Mr Chadwick.

Sir Henry Pellatt orders that Two hundred dollars be paid to Messrs Symons & Rae on the enclosed Certificate no 4155

Please procure a fresh certificate and forward it to me.

Sincerely yours,

Geo B Morley

Fig. 9-5. In this letter dated 1913, Canon G.B. Morley, on the order of Sir Henry Pellatt, directs payment to the supervising architects, the Toronto firm of Symons and Rae. Pellatt, whose grand new home Casa Loma looked down on the cathedral site, was chair of the cathedral's Finance Committee. Note the perspective drawing of the proposed cathedral used on the letterhead. [Anglican Diocese of Toronto Archives]

were moving out of the downtown core. Taking back the cathedral role from St. Alban's seemed like a good survival strategy, and they offered their church for this purpose in 1918. Although nothing came of the offer at that time, St. Alban's continued to have its own problems. The start of the Great Depression in 1929 ensured cathedral building would remain a low priority. A fire damaged much of the completed church in the same year. St. James's took the opportunity to renew its commitment to serve as cathedral. When the new bishop, Derwyn Owen, declined to take his oath of office at St. Alban's in 1932, St. Alban's days as a cathedral were numbered.

After studying the matter for two years, a diocesan committee recommended in 1935 that St. James's should again become the Anglican cathedral. All further construction on St. Alban's was cancelled. The following year, St. Alban's status as a cathedral was revoked. St. James's was once again Toronto's only Anglican cathedral.

St. Alban's continued quietly as a parish church, serving the people of the Annex (it is now the chapel of Royal St. George's College, a private boys' school). Work done in 1956, in a contemporary style, to close in the west end of the church and provide for a little spire was a visible admission that the dream of a new cathedral on the site would never be pursued.

Chapter 10

VICTORIA SQUARE

1897/Unbuilt

OLD CITY HALL IS ONE OF Toronto's truly great buildings. It also has one of Toronto's great locations, presiding over the city's financial district from the top of Bay Street. But from its inception, it lacked a feature common to traditional town halls: there was no town square.

That the city hall site simply wasn't big enough to accommodate a square isn't surprising. The land had originally been acquired for a county court house. It was only after an architectural competition in 1884 that the city fathers decided to expand the program and build a combined court house and city hall. As a result of this decision, a second competition was held two years later, won by E.J. Lennox (Fig. 33-1). In 1897, as his building neared completion, city council was presented with two separate petitions asking that a portion of the block across Queen Street from the new municipal buildings be developed as a civic square. The idea was to extend James Street (which abuts Old City Hall to the east) south

across Queen, to Richmond. The resulting block between Bay and the James Street extension would form the square.

With the completion of Lennox's masterpiece, Toronto had a public building of which it could be proud. A square across the street would provide needed downtown parkland, as well as space so the edifice could be properly appreciated. The opportunity to remove some of the shabby low-rise buildings that continued to surround City Hall was not lost on the square's backers. Already, the southwest corner of Queen and Bay was being redeveloped, with the construction of what has been called Toronto's first skyscraper, the ten-storey Temple Building, to house the offices of the Independent Order of Foresters. Indeed, it was the Foresters who were spearheading one of the petitions, gathering two thousand signatures in support of the cause. The square's name was a natural. In 1897, Toronto was celebrating an unprecedented event along with the rest of the empire: the diamond jubilee of Queen Victoria's reign. It couldn't have been more perfect: Toronto would get its town square and at the same time provide a magnificent monument to the Queen-Empress.

Against this backdrop, and faced with the petitions in favour of the square, city council instructed the assessment commissioner to investigate the terms on which the necessary land could be obtained. After studying the situation, he was not impressed, reporting that the property would be too expensive to acquire. Although cost would always have been an issue for any such acquisition, it is understandable that there would have been particular sensitivity about expenditures related to the new city hall; originally budgeted at $1,050,000, the building ended up costing over $2.5 million by the time it was completed. Money aside, the assessment commissioner was of the view that "the small size of the square precludes it of being of much advantage as a public square."

At roughly 250 by 200 feet, Victoria Square would have been decidedly compact. But whether this would have made it inappropriate as a public square depends on one's viewpoint. Certainly it would have enhanced the architectural effect of the new City Hall. And it would have been a true urban square, in the sense that people would naturally have crossed on the diagonal as they went about their business in the city's core. Although it would not have been large, there would have been enough space to provide a pleasant haven for those who wanted to stop and enjoy a break from the bustle of the city. An illustration widely published at the time shows the park itself as essentially a green space with benches (Fig. 10-1). Diagonal walkways lead to a colossal statue of Queen Victoria. Enthroned, with orb and sceptre, the square's namesake looks less regal than placid; vapid even. Yet oddly enough, the overall effect is somewhat menacing. Despite the off-putting effect of the statue, the illustration does convey how the square would have provided a dignified setting for both the City Hall and the Temple Building.

The assessment commissioner's report had the effect of putting the project on the back burner for 1899. The *Star* even pronounced it "killed" by civic delay. But when City Hall officially opened the following year, the issue regained currency. A special subcommittee of council held hearings in May, and recommended that the land be acquired and an assessment of neighbouring landowners (who would benefit from their new frontage on the square) could be imposed to help pay for it. In August, the *Star*, which had been a strong proponent of the concept all along, reported that another constituency could likely be tapped for funds as well. The "Scotchmen" of the city, who were looking for a place to erect a statue of Robbie Burns, were now interested in the Victoria Square site (in the end, the Burns statue was placed in Allan Gardens).

In April of 1900 some of the more expensive buildings on the land proposed for the square burned to the ground. It was a lucky break (at least for proponents of the square) because the land would be cheaper to acquire. The *Star* took the opportunity to push the idea heavily, running a five-day series of endorsements of the concept from prominent citizens, including E.J. Lennox himself. Still another committee of council was struck to investigate the idea. But nothing came of it.

From the beginning, there had been those opposed to any square, primarily because of the cost. The *Telegram*, which took the position that the City Hall itself had been an unnecessary extravagance, viewed the acquisition of land for a square as an outright boondoggle. For its part, the *Globe* favoured an altogether different location for a new square. When the idea of Victoria Square was first brought before council in 1897, the *Globe* proposed that the area to the *west* of the new municipal building was the preferable site for a square. It suggested that a new art gallery could be placed at the northern end of the new space. The art gallery, along with

VOL. XI.]   CANADIAN ARCHITECT AND BUILDER.   [NO. 1.

PERSPECTIVE VIEW SHOWING EFFECT OF PROPOSED VICTORIA SQUARE, OPPOSITE THE NEW MUNICIPAL BUILDINGS, TORONTO.

Fig. 10-1. An 1897 illustration of the proposed Victoria Square, as seen from the southeast. The Temple Building is in the background. The rendering of City Hall shows E.J. Lennox's earlier design for the tower, with a smaller clock and no gargoyles. [Thomas Fisher Rare Book Library, University of Toronto]

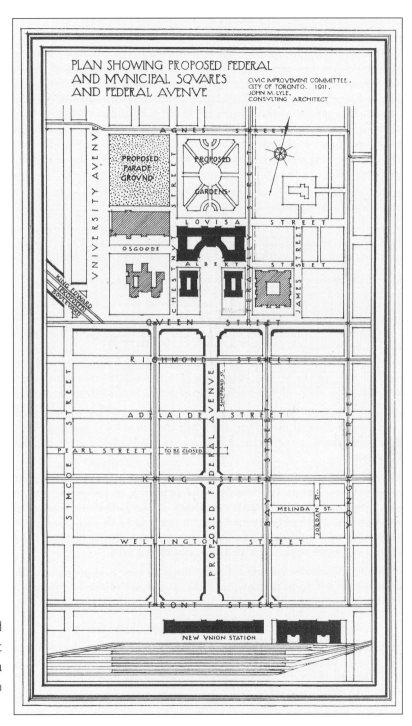

Fig. 10-2. A public square between Old City Hall and Osgoode Hall was proposed in 1911 by the Civic Improvement Committee. By now, the idea of a square on the south side of Queen Street had been abandoned. [City of Toronto Archives, Series 59, Item 7]

Lennox's structure and Osgoode Hall, would define three sides of the new plaza. The western square had two advantages over the southern site: first, it could be much larger (with the closure of streets); second, it could serve as the focus of a fine new precinct of public buildings stretching all the way over to the city's ceremonial route, University Avenue.

It was this idea that ultimately lodged in the civic imagination, appearing in various configurations over the next half-century. A western square was recommended by the Civic Improvement Committee when it submitted its report on municipal improvements in 1911 (Fig 10-2). A 1927 proposal by architect Alfred Chapman elaborated on the scheme (Fig 11-2), and it resurfaced two years later as a public garden called St. Julien Place (this time with the new public building to the east) in the *Report of the Advisory City Planning Commission* (Figs. 10-3, 10-4). Ultimately, when the site of the new City Hall was acquired after the Second World War, it was for the purpose of a civic square; New City Hall was actually an add-on. The result, Nathan Phillips Square, has become the heart of Toronto.

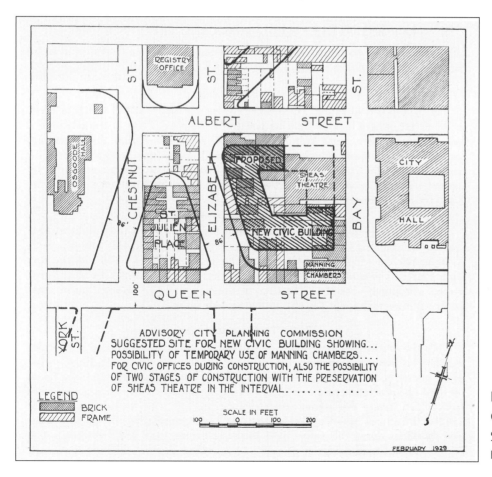

Fig. 10-3. In 1929, the Advisory City Planning Commission recommended the creation of St. Julien Place. [City of Toronto Archives, Series 59, Item 7]

In 1901 Victoria died. The provincial government announced that it was commissioning a statue of the late queen. It planned to move Sir John A. Macdonald from his spot at the top of University Avenue and place Victoria's statue there instead (she was ultimately put in front of the east wing of the legislative buildings). The *Star* and *Canadian Architect and Builder* took the opportunity to suggest Victoria Square as the site for the monarch's statue. But, by now, the advocacy was incidental and half-hearted. It was clear that the idea of Victoria Square was as dead as its namesake.

ST·JULIEN PLACE

Fig. 10-4. An illustration of St. Julien Place by Earl C. Sheppard, from the *Report of the Advisory City Planning Commission*. Osgoode Hall is on the left, the 1917 Registry Building (now demolished) is in the centre and a new public building is on the right. [City of Toronto Archives, Series 59, Item 7]

Chapter 11

TORONTO CITY HALL

1925–1955 / Built to different plans

I N SOME WAYS, THE WRITING WAS ON the wall for Toronto's magnificent third City Hall — what we now call "Old" City Hall — from the beginning. Meant to proclaim Toronto's emergence as a modern, important metropolis, its Richardsonian Romanesque styling was already seen as out of date by the time it officially opened in 1899 (after more than a decade of construction). Moreover, it wasn't long before the building was too small to accommodate the busy municipal courts and expanding bureaucracy of the growing city.

In 1925, the building's architect, E.J. Lennox (Fig. 33-1) drew up plans for an eleven-storey tower to be built in the City Hall courtyard (Fig. 11-1). Two years later, Alfred Chapman prepared plans to incorporate the 1917 Registry Building by Charles S. Cobb into a city hall and courthouse complex (Fig. 11-2). The Registry Building and a duplicate (serving as a court house) would form the eastern and western portion of the podium for a domed city hall tower. Chapman's design incorporated Cobb's more traditional neoclassicism seamlessly, but produced an overall effect that was in keeping with modern high-rise city halls such as that of Los Angeles, then under construction. Despite the handsomeness of the design, the Depression precluded any further movement on construction of new administrative space for the municipality. Instead, the city made do by putting employees off-site in seven locations, and by improvising offices in the corridors of City Hall itself.

A 1943 report to city council recommended a new city hall and square in the Bay/Queen/Chestnut block. Plans drawn up around this time by the city's buildings department show an odd reworking of the basic scheme that had been floating around for more than thirty years. Instead of putting the new city hall at the back of the square (as New City Hall is), thereby incorporating Lennox's building into an expanded civic precinct, the buildings department proposed locating it at the southeast corner of the site, facing west. The new city

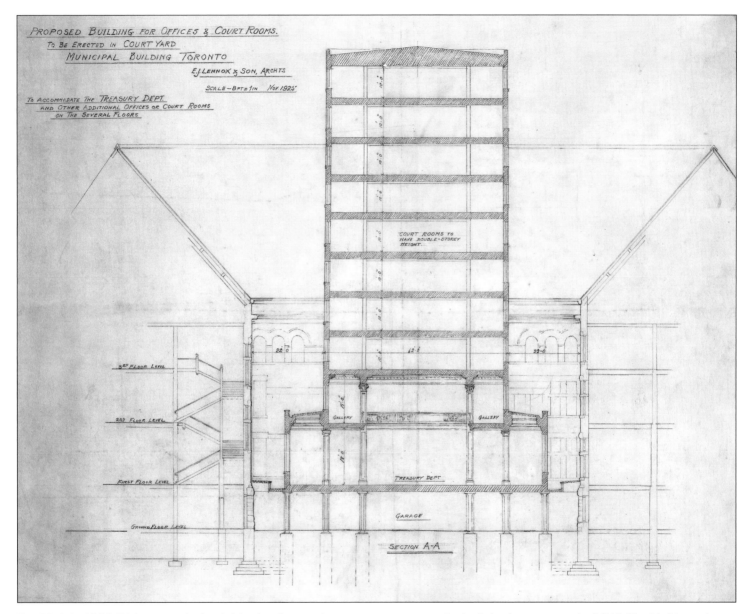

Fig. 11-1. In 1925, E.J. Lennox devised this plan for an eleven-storey tower to be built in the courtyard of Old City Hall in order to accommodate the growing municipal bureaucracy. [Archives of Ontario, C43-101, K 343]

Fig. 11-2. This 1927 design by Alfred Chapman managed to incorporate Charles S. Cobb's neoclassical Registry Building into a scheme that still reflected contemporary trends in public building. [City of Toronto Archives, Series 1188, File 3 PT 353-C-1]

hall would turn its back on the old one (Fig. 11-3). In the end, council decided to move forward with a different program entirely. It would move the courts, not the municipal workers, out of City Hall, building a new courthouse at the northern end of the proposed civic square. A ten-storey police headquarters would also occupy the site (Fig. 11-4). With this plan as the backdrop, a majority of Toronto vot-

ers on New Year's Day, 1947 approved the following question:

> Are you in favour of the City acquiring, for the purposes of the civic square, certain lands and buildings within the area bounded by Bay Street, Queen Street, Chestnut

Fig. 11-3. City staff prepared this scheme in 1945. It would have seen a new city hall building on the current site of Nathan Phillips Square, with its back to Lennox's building. [City of Toronto Archives, Series 1188, File 3, PT 3-352-C]

Street and a line approximately 460 feet north of Albert Street and having an assessed value of approximately $2,000,000?

Council left out reference to the courthouse/police headquarters (as well as a possible underground garage) as premature. The feeling was that land acquisition and postwar material shortages would delay any construction for years. But the silence on what might overlook the square was undoubtedly also a hint that the idea of a new city hall for that location was not fully dead.

And so it wasn't. Six years later, in October of 1952, the civic advisory council — a panel of citizens appointed by the city council, and headed by future Governor General Roland

Michener — submitted a report to council on the city hall space problem. The advisory council recommended that a new city hall *and* a new court building be built on the civic square site. The recommended plan (by the advisory council's consulting architects Marani and Morris) called for a completion of the trio of buildings envisaged in John Lyle's 1911 plan (Fig. 10-2). In a conceptual drawing by Marani and Morris that hearkens to Alfred Chapman's 1927 scheme (Fig. 11-2), a replica of the Registry Building is shown on the eastern edge of the site, where it would serve as a courthouse. A modern office tower between the two buildings would serve as both the city hall and police headquarters.

Within a year, the civic advisory council's proposal was out-of-date. In 1953, regional government arrived with the establishment of the Municipality of Metropolitan Toronto; the advisory council had been clear that it had not factored any potential Metro space into its plans. Yet the creation of Metro made the space issue even more pressing. The following year, a Chicago-based pension fund looking to invest its money stepped into the breach. It was backing

Fig. 11-4. When Torontonians voted to acquire the land where New City Hall now sits, council's plan was to build a courthouse, not municipal offices. This scheme for a courthouse and square was prepared by the city's buildings department in 1946. [City of Toronto Archives, Series 1188, File 6, PT 354-C]

Fig. 11-5. This design for a mixed-use municipal and commercial office building was prepared by the Chicago firm of Naess and Murphy and presented to council in 1954. Located on the site of Old City Hall, a grand staircase across Bay Street would connect the building to the new civic square to the west. [City of Toronto Archives, Series 1088, File 1]

a Canadian-American syndicate's offer to build a new city hall for Toronto based on a sale-leaseback arrangement. Under the deal, council would convey the site to the developers, who would build court and municipal offices in the podium of a massive commercial office tower. After renting the space in the $75-million structure for twenty-five years, the city could buy the entire complex back from the developers for $9 million.

The financing of the building was not the only innovative thing about it. The fifty-one-storey limestone structure (eighteen storeys higher than anything else in the city at the time and with more square footage than the Empire State Building) was to be designed by the Chicago firm of Naess and Murphy (Fig. 11-5). With its limestone facade and crowning spire, it had obvious stylistic similarities to the firm's Prudential Building, which would be the tallest building in Chicago when it opened in 1955. Contrary to the civic advisory council's recommendation, the building would not be on the civic square block, but on the site of Lennox's building, which would be demolished. A colossal ceremonial staircase would extend westward from the city hall's second-floor entrance on Bay Street to the new civic square, forming a bridge over Bay Street. In this rather clever way, the city hall could be oriented to the new civic square, and the commercial office building, with its entrances off Queen, could dominate the financial district from the top of Bay Street.

Council rejected the proposal. Although some councillors were opposed to tearing down Old City Hall, and staff had planning and traffic objections, in the end it was undoubtedly the unconventional (and foreign) financing that killed the deal: the very thought, as Mayor Allan Lamport put it, of the deed to Toronto's city hall "sitting in a Chicago safety deposit box." "If anybody's going to build a city hall," said Lamport "it will be the city." By now, the prospect of income from having Metro as a tenant made it feasible for Toronto to go ahead with the city hall project without fancy financing schemes. That, and the economic savings of having its staff in one location, got the ball rolling. City council asked Marani and Morris, the firm that had developed the 1952 plans for the civic advisory council, to collaborate on new plans with two other local firms, Mathers and Haldenby, and Shore and Moffat.

In February of 1955, the three firms presented a model of the proposed new municipal offices and square to the board of control. It showed a modernistic office building at the north end of the site, facing a landscaped square. The council chamber sat in a separate, low-rise structure in front of the tower. The whole complex would be clad in limestone. According to L.E. Shore, the inspiration for the scheme was the new United Nations headquarters in New York (also designed by committee). Shore was a partner in Shore and Moffat, which was seen as the most stylistically progressive of the firms. For architects interested in current design trends, it is easy to see why the modernist U.N. building would have been a compelling precedent. But it seems at least as evident that the design of the council podium, both in its scale and in the row of columns that extended across its front, was inspired by the 1917 Registry Building right next door.

After looking at the model for five minutes, Mayor Nathan Phillips and his fellow controllers expressed disappointment. In the mayor's view, the City Hall looked like "the Grand Hotel with the longest balcony in the world. All it needs is a swimming pool." If the new plans were greeted with a less than enthusiastic response, it was not because of any sentimentality over the current city hall. In response to Metro Chairman Frederick Gardiner's statement that Metro would rather build a new courthouse than convert the current City Hall, Mayor Phillips suggested that Lennox's masterpiece could be torn down to make way for a new hotel. One councillor said that Osgoode Hall should be demolished while they were at it, telling his colleagues, "We should take out these two old crocks."

Mayor Phillips called for an international competition, but the board of control rejected the idea. Instead, it asked the committee of architects to return with detailed plans. These plans, an elaboration of what had been shown in the model, were approved (Fig. 11-6). The proposal seemed to excite no one, except those opposed to it. All classes at the University of Toronto Faculty of Architecture sent a joint letter condemning the proposal, saying it resembled "a funeral home of vast dimensions" and was "a monstrous monument to backwardness." They called for a national competition, or at the very least a panel of three architects appointed by the five schools of architecture in Canada. Frank Lloyd Wright called the plan "sterilization" and a "cliché already dated." Walter Gropius, the founder of the Bauhaus movement, called it "a very poor pseudo-modern design unworthy of the city of Toronto." Toronto voters were similarly unimpressed, defeating the money by-law required to build it in the municipal elections of 1955.

Despite the contemporary criticisms, much of the uproar over the proposed design was stoked by the feeling that such an important commission should have been decided by competition. Today, simply looking at the building on its own merits, the harsher stylistic criticisms of the 1955 proposal seem difficult to understand. The committee-designed city hall proposal was not materially different from other office buildings (also in limestone) designed by at least two of the collaborating firms around the same time, including Marani and Morris's Shell Oil Building on University Avenue, and Mathers and Haldenby's Imperial Oil Building on St. Clair Avenue West, which bears a particular resemblance to the rejected city hall design. Fifty years on, the clean design and quality of materials of those buildings continue to contribute an elegant, if understated presence to the urban fabric that has seldom been duplicated since.

Undoubtedly, the joint city hall design of 1955 would have done the same. But Toronto wasn't looking for understated or

Fig. 11-6. The plan that council wanted to build in 1955, a collaborative effort by Marani and Morris, Mathers and Haldenby, and Shore and Moffat. The Toronto electorate had other ideas. Rendering by Schell Lewis. [City of Toronto Archives, PT344-C-5]

for corporate architecture pressed into public service. As the writer of a letter to the editor of the *Star* put it in 1952 (when the civic advisory council's report was released), the municipal buildings shouldn't merely be "bigger and better versions of the banks on Bay Street … but an expression of a democratic way of life."

No small challenge. Yet one that Toronto would meet before the decade was out.

Chapter 12

NEW CITY HALL

1958 / Built to different plans

THE VOTERS' REFUSAL TO APPROVE a new city hall for Toronto in a question put to the electorate in the December 1955 municipal elections might have been seen as a huge setback for Mayor Nathan Phillips. Phillips had run on a platform of building a new city hall. But he saw the defeat as an opportunity. He had never liked the structure that council had intended to build (Fig. 11-6). Its rejection was his chance to go back to the people with a revised proposal that would correct what he saw as the two flaws that had led the public to reject the plan: price and design.

As far as price was concerned, Metro council's agreement to buy Old City Hall meant that the $4.5-million purchase price for that building could be used to reduce the $18 million required to construct the new building. As for design, council was now recommending an international competition, the approach that Phillips had championed all along. Torontonians gave the revised city hall proposal the green light in December 1956. The city was about to embark on an adventure that would transform its view of itself.

Professor Eric Arthur of the University of Toronto's Faculty of Architecture was appointed professional advisor for the competition. The jury consisted of William Holford from England, Charles E. (Ned) Pratt from Vancouver, Ernesto Rogers from the University of Milan, Gordon Stephenson from the University of Toronto and Finnish architect Eero Saarinen (by then practising in the United States) (Fig. 12-1). Competitors were asked to prepare designs for both the city hall and the new civic square it would front on.

They were given a lot of leeway in approaching the task. The competition conditions, published in September 1957, didn't leave much instruction as to what was wanted in the square, other than that it would be primarily "a landscaped open space of great beauty serving as a forecourt to the city hall, and as an open space for the pleasure of citizens." A place where citizens could sit on benches, listen to music from bands and "stroll between

Fig. 12-1. The judges for the international competition for Toronto's new city hall, pictured among the competition models, April 1958. From left to right: Eric Arthur, Ned Pratt, Eero Saarinen, Ernesto Rogers, Sir William Holford, Gordon Stevenson. [Panda Collection, 58504-2, Canadian Architectural Archives, University of Calgary]

flower beds." While a water feature wasn't mandatory, contestants were asked to "carefully consider" incorporating one into their schemes, to give an illusion of coolness in Toronto's scorching summers. Consideration of shady spots and sunny spots was also recommended, as well as some recognition that the mayor would occasionally greet dignitaries at the entrance to city hall.

Competitors were instructed that the building itself should not resemble "just another office building, hardly differentiated from the commercial structures which surround it." Instead, the design of the building should suggest "government, continuity of certain democratic traditions and service to the community." Despite these ideals, as in any good North American city, symbolic primacy had already been given to the automobile: contestants had to design around the thirteen-hundred-car underground parking garage that had recently been completed beneath the square site.

A deadline of April 18, 1958, was set for submissions. The response could hardly have been greater: 520 entrants, as officially reported, from forty-two countries shipped the required models and drawings to Toronto — enough to pack the 32,000-square-foot Horticultural Building at the CNE (Figs. 12-2a, 12-2b). All models were submitted anonymously, to ensure fairness. By the end of the month, the field was winnowed to eight finalists, one from Canada; four from the United States; and one each from Australia, Denmark and Finland. These short-listed architects were given four months to refine their designs and create larger scale models.

It has become part of the legend of New City Hall that Viljo Revell's winning design almost didn't make it to the short list. Saarinen arrived for the judging a day and a half late. By then, the other judges had already made a list of those entrants that could summarily be rejected. Somewhat saucily, Saarinen asked to view their discards. Among them was Revell's now-iconic design. Saarinen convinced his fellow judges not only that it should be put on the short list, but that it should be the contest winner. The story, recounted by Arthur himself, may help make sense of an incongruity in the committee's choice of finalists: Revell's scheme, with its curving towers, is strikingly different from the seven other finalists, all of which were rectilinear compositions, tending to the low or mid-rise.

Given the iconic status that Revell's building has achieved, there are few more fascinating "also-rans" in unbuilt Toronto than the entrants that might have been proclaimed the winner in the 1958 city hall competition.

The proposal submitted by a team of Harvard students, led by John Andrews of Massachusetts, stood out with Revell's from the rest of the entrants in its exuberant, even flamboyant approach (Fig. 12-3). Centred on a single, five-storey structure, it was quite different from Revell's, but with its undulating roof and slanted, articulated walls, it shared something of its sculptural quality. The team included Macy Dubois, who, along with Andrews, would later relocate to Toronto (a

decade later, Andrews would be lead architect on the Metro Centre proposal, see chapter 6). It acknowledged Toronto as a winter city, proposing not one, but two squares: an open "summer square" in front of the city hall, and a covered "winter square" in the courtyard of the city hall itself. The summer square was actually an oval, surrounded by grass, with a circular pool in the middle. The low, projecting council chamber bridged the summer and winter squares, extending out from the main building, past the paved oval and into the pool.

As the judges themselves acknowledged, a low, rectangular building surrounding a central courtyard was a theme in a number of the runners-up. Toronto architect David Horne proposed a six-storey building with a central courtyard (Fig. 12-4). Perkins and Will of New York proposed a composition that involved a large podium, taking up half the site. On this podium would be four storeys of offices, set on an arcade. The council chamber would be set in the central courtyard of the building (Fig. 12-5). American I.M. Pei (who would later work on the original Eaton Centre proposal: see chapter 4) also proposed a square building with a central court, as did a team led by Minnesota architect Frank Mikutowski (Figs. 12-6, 12-7). At ten storeys, Mikutowski's proposal was the tallest of the fully enclosed courtyard proposals, although a team led by William Hayward of Philadelphia proposed a semi-enclosed plaza encircled by low arms stretching out from either side of a fourteen-storey tower (Fig. 12-8). This left the nineteen-storey submission of Halldor Gunnlogsson and Jorn Nielson of Denmark as the only one featuring a straightforward open square (Fig 12-9).

The placement of trees at the south end of the site was a theme in all the runners-up. In the period when the south side of Queen had yet to be redeveloped, not only would they have provided shade, they also would have shielded the new civic precinct from the down-at-the-heels commercial buildings across the street. John Andrews's double row of

Figs. 12-2a (top), 12-2b (bottom). The response to the competition was overwhelming: enough models to pack the Horticultural Building at the CNE. [Panda Collection, 58504-5, 58504-4, Canadian Architectural Archives, University of Calgary]

Fig. 12-3 (top). The proposal submitted by a team of Harvard students, led by John Andrews of Massachusetts, stood out in its exuberance. It had both a summer square and a winter square. [Panda Collection, 581085-2, Canadian Architectural Archives, University of Calgary]

Fig. 12-4 (bottom). Many of the runners-up were low, rectangular buildings with central courtyards. This six-storey proposal was by Toronto architect David Horne. [Panda Collection, 581080-1, Canadian Architectural Archives, University of Calgary]

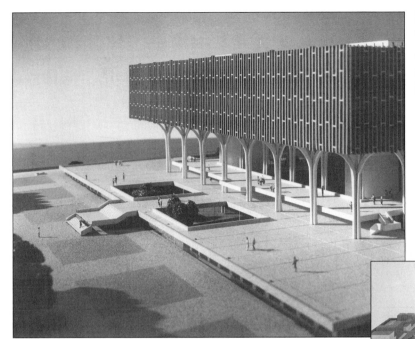

Fig. 12-5. In this design by Perkins and Will of New York, the council chamber would be set in the central courtyard of the building, surrounded by water. [Panda Collection, 581079-6, Canadian Architectural Archives, University of Calgary]

Fig. 12-6. American I.M. Pei was alone among the finalists in not providing for a water feature. [Panda Collection, 581086-1, Canadian Architectural Archives, University of Calgary]

Fig. 12-7. Minnesota architect Frank Mikutowski placed a public library (a required element) in the centre of a reflecting pool, which would surround it like a moat. [Panda Collection, 581083-2, Canadian Architectural Archives, University of Calgary]

Fig. 12-8. A team led by William Hayward of Philadelphia proposed a semi-enclosed plaza encircled by low arms stretching out from either side of a fourteen-storey tower. Monumental steps led to the plaza. [Panda Collection, 581080-4, Canadian Architectural Archives, University of Calgary]

Fig. 12-9. The submission of Halldor Gunnlogsson and Jorn Nielson of Denmark was the only one among the runners-up to propose a straightforward open square. [Panda Collection, 581082-1, Canadian Architectural Archives, University of Calgary]

trees became triple or quadruple rows in the entries of Perkins and Will, Gunnlogsson and Nielson and David Horne. Mikutowski and Pei went even further, dedicating almost half the site to an urban forest.

This approach provided another significant difference between Revell's proposal and those of the other finalists. Plantings in Revell's original scheme were kept to a minimum: his model shows a small blob of indeterminate vegetation just south of the reflecting pool. The judges noted that this feature would have to be augmented and refined as the overall design evolved. Later iterations do show a much larger area of vegetation to the west of a shifted reflecting pool, as well as a smaller planting area to its north (the larger area was reduced in size to accommodate a snack bar and washrooms, while the smaller one became the Peace Garden in 1984). As well, the southern end of the elevated walkway was pushed back, with the result that Revell's design acquired the rows of trees along Queen Street that all the other finalists had.

Revell's walkways were not the only attempt to play with grade (though they were the most distinctive). Andrews's oval "summer square" was in fact sunken. The Mikutowski and Pei entries also had sunken plazas, while the northern half of the Hayward entry had monumental steps leading to a raised plaza.

The public library, which was required to be accommodated in any scheme, was placed outside the city hall building in two of the plans, sited as a freestanding structure on the squares proposed by Horne and Mikutowski. Mikutowski's plan actually had the library in the centre of a reflecting pool, which surrounded it like a moat. The Perkins and Will scheme also used a moat-like feature, but in their case surrounding the council chamber in the central courtyard. In one way or another, water features of various sizes and configurations found their way into each of the prize-winning schemes, save Pei's.

Of all the finalists, Revell's original design was by far the sparsest in detail. Nonetheless, the key elements of the composition we know today were clearly evident: the twin curvilinear towers of differing height (which were, interestingly, flipped between the first model and the second); the freestanding council chamber; the vast, paved square with its reflecting pool set off along the axis of Old City Hall; and the elevated walkway or arcade encompassing the whole. While all the judges appreciated that this was an imaginative and original building that would stand out from the pack of workaday commercial buildings, two of the judges submitted a minority report setting out their reservations. They felt that the building was impractical, and that the blank walls of its towers would not integrate with the surrounding city, perhaps impeding neighbouring redevelopment that might otherwise occur. They also felt that the civic square was too stark.

When Revell's design was announced as the winner in September 1958, Frank Lloyd Wright's view of the composition was blunt: "You've got a headmarker for a grave and future generations will look at it and say: 'This marks the spot where Toronto fell.'" It hardly bears saying, of course: Wright was wrong.

Chapter 13

MISSISSAUGA CITY HALL

1982 / Built to different plans

WHEN THE CITY OF MISSISSAUGA announced a national competition for a new city hall in April 1982, competitors had their work cut out for them. In addition to merely providing new space, the building would have to create a true civic centre out of the Burnamthorpe/Hurontario area, which was typified then as much by empty fields as it was by the Square One shopping mall and some scattered office development. As well, at that point, the City of Mississauga itself was only eight years old, having been created in 1974 through the amalgamation of the towns of Port Credit, Streetsville and Mississauga (the Town of Mississauga itself having been created through the amalgamation of several smaller communities in 1968). The city hall would have to provide a symbolic heart for the new city. These challenges would make any competition for the commission interesting enough. But the Mississauga city hall competition had an additional significance: it was held when the state of architecture itself was in flux. The winning entry by architects Edward Jones and Michael Kirkland is probably Canada's best-known example of postmodern architecture. Because of the status the building has achieved since it opened more than two decades ago, it's particularly interesting to examine the other prize-winning entries, all of which were seen as displaying elements of the emerging postmodern movement.

As with the City of Toronto's city hall competition twenty-five years earlier (see chapter 12), Mississauga was looking for designs for both a city hall and a civic square. The budget was set at $56 million for both. A six-member jury was appointed to judge the results (Fig. 13-1). Its professional advisor and chair was George Baird, a well-known architect and faculty member (and later chair) of the University of Toronto's architecture school. Baird was joined by prominent Toronto architect Jerome Markson and architect Phyllis Lambert, founder and director of the Canadian Centre for Architecture in Montreal. In addition to the

Fig. 13-1. The judges in the Mississauga city hall competition hard at work, September 1982. From left to right, Douglas Kilner, James Stirling, Russell Edmunds, Phyllis Lambert, Jerome Markson (seated, facing away from camera) and George Baird (leaning over table, face obscured). [City of Mississauga]

city's commissioner of planning, Russell Edmunds, and engineer and Mississauga resident Douglas Kilner, the group was rounded out by an international heavy hitter, British architect James Stirling, who had won the Pritzker prize in architecture the year before.

Despite the challenging requirements, the response from the profession was enormous: 246 entries from seven provinces. A slowed economy meant that many firms had the time and resources to devote to such a speculative venture.

Jury chair George Baird has written about the diverse influences evident in the submissions, ranging from mainstream modernism, to modular designs (in the tradition of Moshe Safdie's Habitat 67 in Montreal), to expression-

ism, regionalism and rationalism. Above all, the Mississauga city hall competition became associated with one aesthetic movement in particular: postmodernism. Postmodern ideas — of turning away from the austerity and formalism of modernist design to explore (often tongue-in-cheek) regional and historical influences — were very much in the air. In fact, one of the movement's earlier and most celebrated works, Michael Graves's Portland Public Service Building, had opened in Oregon the same year that Mississauga sent out its call.

Commentators at the time noted a partiality among the jury to the postmodern submissions. Certainly Jones and Kirkland's entry, which was the jury's unanimous choice, was immediately identified with the movement. Unlike the Jones and Kirkland submission, which relied on several distinctly massed structures combined into an asymmetrical composition, the second-ranked submission of Barton Myers Associates took a more unified approach (Figs. 13-2, 13-3). It consisted of what were actually three seven-storey buildings, but they would share a common curved external curtain wall, making the complex appear as an integrated whole. These buildings would occupy the periphery of the site, creating an open courtyard. Four lighting masts would serve a decorative as well as practical function. The form of the building and its materials (granite and limestone) were intended to set it apart from the surrounding commercial buildings.

The third-place entry of the Thom Partnership and Harvey Cowan Architect was similar in many ways to the Barton Myers submission (Fig. 13-4). It too distributed the building

evenly along the periphery of the site in order to create a semi-enclosed square. Instead of a square-shaped plaza within a circular building, however, the Thom-Cowan submission placed the circular element, an arcade, within the square. A clock tower in the northwest corner indicated the ceremonial entrance to the building; the council chamber was contained in a cube protruding into the square, over a reflecting pool.

The fourth-place entry of Michael Brisson configured the public facilities required by the program as buildings surrounding the square, each with its own facade (Fig. 13-5). The centrally located council chamber was placed over the ceremonial entrance to the complex, demarcated by a dramatic, bowed roofline. Mature trees from Mississauga's historical communities would be transplanted to the square, immediately denoting it as a welcoming, public place.

Ground was broken for Jones and Kirkland's winning scheme on May 8, 1984. A little over three years later, the

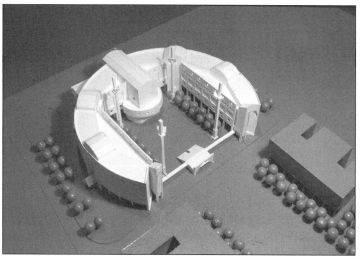 

Fig. 13-2 (left). A model of the second-prize submission of Barton Myers Associates. Unlike the winning scheme, it distributed its built form around three sides of the site to create an open courtyard. [City of Mississauga]. Fig. 13-3 (right). The Barton Myers entry: the main entrance at eye level. [City of Mississauga]

Mississauga Civic Centre (otherwise known as Mississauga City Hall) was officially opened by the Duke and Duchess of York. The building was welcomed by critics and the public and has become the symbolic heart of the city that the competition organizers had hoped for. The competition had been an obvious a success. But, as George Baird has written, architectural competitions serve a purpose beyond choosing winning buildings, namely "to bring together for full consideration the evident talents and preoccupations of architects across the country, at a given historical moment." From that perspective too, the Mississauga city hall competition continues to count as an obvious success.

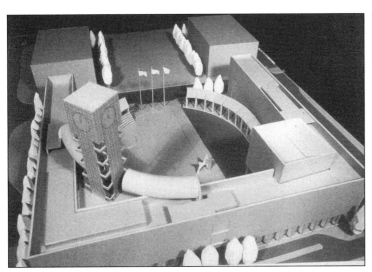 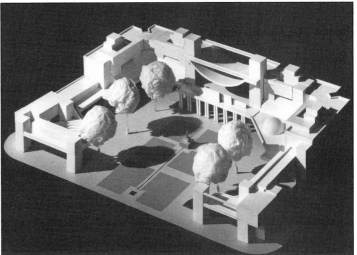

Fig. 13-4 (left). The third-prize entry of the Thom Partnership and Harvey Cowan Architect. [City of Mississauga]. **Fig. 13-5 (right).** The fourth-prize entry of Michael Brisson. [Bob Brisson]

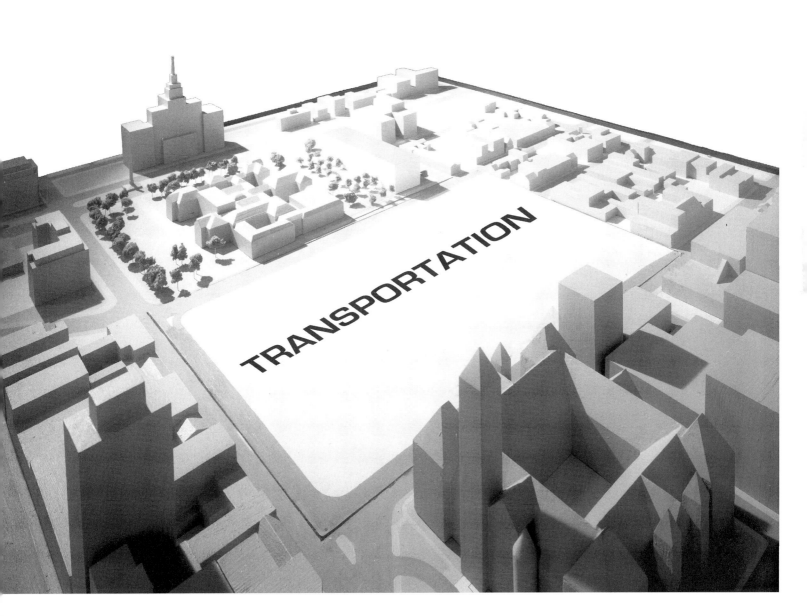

Chapter 14

TORONTO AND GEORGIAN BAY SHIP CANAL

1858 / Unbuilt

NEWMARKET CANAL

1908 / Partially built

ANYONE WHO'S BEEN IN BUMPER-to-bumper traffic on Highway 400, trying to head up to cottage country on a summer afternoon, would probably like the idea of the Toronto and Georgian Bay Ship Canal. Think of it: you get in your boat on the Humber River, and take a leisurely sail north till you reach your cottage dock in Lake Simcoe, Lake Couchiching or Georgian Bay. What could be more civilized?

It sounded like an attractive idea in 1855 too, but for entirely different reasons. In the 1850s, what we now call the Midwest was opening up in a big way. Chicago was growing by leaps and bounds, and railways were bringing it and other Great Lakes ports the produce, minerals, timber and other raw materials of the expanding frontier. From there, shipping access to New York and the Atlantic Ocean was possible via the Welland or Erie Canals. But both required a southward diversion through Lake Erie. If a direct connection could be made between Lake Huron and Lake Ontario, with its access

to the St. Lawrence River, it would save a significant amount of time. And, even in the 1850s, time was money.

With this thought in mind, in September of 1855, a group of businessmen from Ontario, Illinois and New York got together in Toronto to explore the possibility of constructing a canal between Toronto and Georgian Bay. It wasn't a new idea. In the 1840s, local landowner and builder Rowland Burr twice walked the route in furtherance of his advocacy of the scheme. And in 1846, Kivas Tully (Fig. 8-1) surveyed the route for an interested client. But in the minds of the businessmen meeting in 1855, this was an idea whose time had now come. They determined that the immense trade developing from the northwest demanded "the immediate construction of a canal between the Upper Lakes and Lake Ontario … from Lake Huron to Lake Ontario at Toronto or its vicinity." In 1856, the Toronto and Georgian Bay Ship Canal Co. was incorporated. Kivas Tully was appointed chief engineer, charged with the task of surveying the area and reporting on the feasibility of the concept. Tully travelled the route with consulting engineer R.B. Mason of Chicago in November 1856.

The two men made their final report two years later, Mason analyzing the business case for the proposal and Tully focusing on the construction aspects. For his part, Mason concluded that, even with its $22-million construction costs, the canal would more than pay back its investment. The northwest was exploding, and was destined to keep growing. The market for a Georgian Bay canal, which Tully estimated would shave over four hundred miles off the current Chicago to New York shipping route, would keep growing with it.

From an engineering perspective, Tully felt that the concept, although challenging, was eminently feasible. He recommended a route that would lead from the Humber to the Holland River, through Lake Simcoe's Kempenfelt Bay to the Nottawasaga River, and from there into Georgian Bay (Fig. 14-1). He rejected outright a Don River route in the south, due largely to issues of harbour depth and increased length. In the north, however, he provided for three alternatives, one of which used the Severn River as the upper outlet (instead of the Nottawasaga) and two of which connected the Humber and Nottawasaga directly, without passing through Lake Simcoe.

Even though Tully's recommended route was the most practical of the lot, that was a relative proposition. It would still require the construction of eleven locks with an average lift of just under twelve feet. At the highest point of the route, the canal would have to be two hundred feet deep, which the engineers admitted would probably be the largest and most expensive canal cut yet undertaken. Even so, they concluded that if construction were to start soon, the canal could be in operation by 1865. But the numbers — whether they related to dollars or feet — just never made sense. The scheme

continued to find advocates even decades on (later becoming the "Huron and Ontario Ship Canal") but a ceremonial groundbreaking in 1859 was about as far as it got.

———————

Eventually, of course, there *was* a Lake Ontario to Georgian Bay connection, but it was via the Trent and Severn Rivers, not the Humber and Nottawasaga. By 1904, it was just about nearing completion. That's when the federal Member of Parliament for York North, William Mulock (Fig. 14-2), floated the idea of extending the Trent system, with a canal from Lake Simcoe to Newmarket and Aurora. Mulock proposed using the Holland River — just as Kivas Tully had recommended a half century earlier.

Resurrecting this portion of Tully's scheme was an idea that Mulock had most likely been thinking about for some time. How these speculative musings became the political and engineering fiasco known as "Mulock's Madness" is recounted by James Angus in *A Respectable Ditch*, his history of the Trent-Severn Waterway. The catalyst was a train ride that Mulock shared with Newmarket mayor H.S. Cane. The mayor, who also happened to own the town's major industrial concern, was complaining that railway shipping costs had got so bad, he was thinking of moving his operations to Georgian Bay. That year, the Grand Trunk Railway, which had a near monopoly in Ontario, had increased its freight rates by 50 percent.

It was then that Mulock described his idea for an extension of the Trent canal down to Newmarket and beyond. The way Mulock saw it, the canal would provide needed competition for the railway. As an added bonus, it was sure to bring an influx of tourists, in the form of vacationing Torontonians

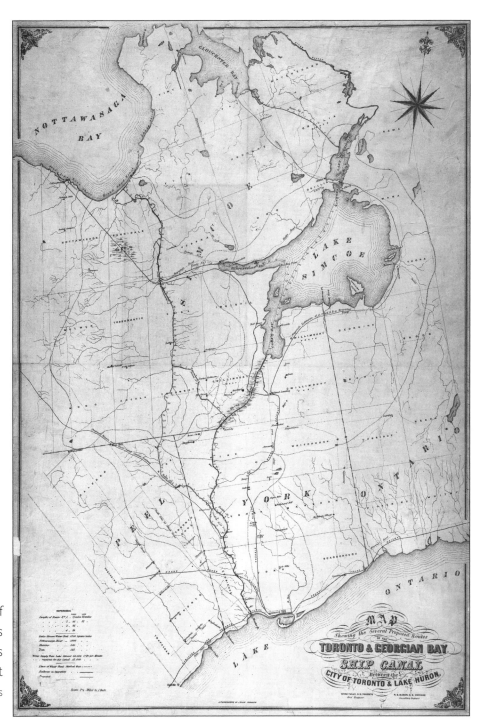

Fig. 14-1. This 1858 map shows the route of the Toronto and Georgian Bay Ship Canal, as surveyed by Kivas Tully and R.B. Mason. At its highest point, it would have required a cut two hundred feet deep. [Library and Archives Canada, n0043038]

Fig. 14-2. Sir William Mulock (left) and Sir Wilfrid Laurier. The member from York North convinced the Liberal prime minister to back the construction of a canal that would become known as "Mulock's Madness." [City of Toronto Archives, Fonds 1244, Item 583]

who would flock to Newmarket in order to cruise up the new canal to Lake Simcoe.

After this chance conversation, the ball got rolling quickly. On September 10 a meeting of interested persons was held in Newmarket with some three hundred people attending. Two weeks later, initial surveys of the proposed route were made, and the Trent Valley Canal Extension Association was formed to press the cause in Ottawa. With a general election looming in November, it would not have been lost on the Liberal Mulock that championing this obviously popular proposal might be a good strategy as he looked to maintain his seat against his Tory rival.

At Mulock's urging, Prime Minister Wilfrid Laurier met with a delegation of fifty-nine local leaders to hear their arguments in favour of the Newmarket canal. Although federal bureaucrats had advised against pursuing the scheme, the direction from their political masters was clear: make it work. The plan they came up with consisted of three sections. The first was a simple dredging of the five-mile stretch of the Holland River between Lake Simcoe and Holland Landing. The second stretch, connecting Holland Landing and Newmarket, required the construction of four locks, three dams, swing bridges and a dock and turning basin in Newmarket. The final stretch, between Newmarket and Aurora, was not planned until 1908. It required five additional locks.

The scheme looked great on paper. The problem, as the government engineers knew, was that there wasn't enough water to make it work. They estimated there would be sufficient water to keep the canal operational only two months of the year, during the spring runoff. But the Newmarket

Fig. 14-3. Lock Two of "Mulock's Madness" as it appears today. Newmarket's ghost canal never saw a single ship.

Canal, born of politics, was sustained by politics. Mulock resigned his seat in 1905 to take an appointment to the bench (he would later become chief justice of the Supreme Court of Ontario, and would serve as chancellor of the University of Toronto until his death at 100 in 1944). Mulock's resignation left the Liberals facing a by-election at the end of the year. It was no time to say "no" to the canal-seeking people of York North.

Although the Liberal candidate won the by-election, it was only by 149 votes. Obviously what was needed in York North was more canal spending. Tenders for the first stretch of the canal were let even before the chief engineer's final report was submitted in September 1906. A general election on the horizon in 1908 guaranteed still more construction.

Work on the stretch of canal between Holland Landing and Newmarket — with its multiple locks, dams and swing bridges — began in the spring of 1908 (Figs. 14-3, 14-4, 14-5). However, the concern about the lack of water had still not been addressed. The fix the government settled on underscored better than anything ever could how little sense the Newmarket canal actually made: water would be pumped the ten miles from Lake Simcoe to Newmarket, and then sent *back* to Lake Simcoe again in the canal. The newspapers and the opposition had a field day. Yet construction continued, actually picking up speed in the months leading to the general election of 1911.

When the Liberals lost that election, the Newmarket Canal's days were numbered. Work on the canal was immediately suspended and then halted for good. The right-of-way for the canal had been purchased from Lake Simcoe to Newmarket, all the locks and three swing bridges built, a turning basin completed, and 80 percent of the dredging completed. Still, it made more economic sense to abandon the plan — into which over $800,000 had been sunk — than complete it. For, even completed, the canal would need constant staffing and repair, all for the benefit of some pleasure craft and

Fig. 14-4 (left). The concrete walls of the lock's holding area, now filled in, poke up through dry earth. Fig. 14-5 (right). The machinery of an abandoned swing bridge is concealed today under a modern pedestrian bridge.

the occasional lumber scow. It simply didn't make sense, even apart from the lack of water.

The dredged portion of the Holland River between Holland Landing and Lake Simcoe was ultimately incorporated into the Trent-Severn, and in 1924 the government filled in much of the work done in the Newmarket stretch for safety reasons. But evidence of "Mulock's Madness" is still there, a nearly-completed ghost canal whose forgotten and decaying structures emerge occasionally along the course of the Holland River as it wends its way from Newmarket.

It's comforting to know — just in case those Grand Trunk freight charges ever get out of hand again.

Chapter 15

PRINCE EDWARD VIADUCT

1910/Built to different plans

WITH THE GROWTH OF suburban development east of the Don in the late nineteenth and early twentieth centuries, it became ever more apparent that a new connection across the Don Valley would be needed north of Gerrard Street. The need became pressing when Riverdale joined the city in 1889, and was underscored with the additional annexation of East Toronto in 1909.

Given its importance and visibility, it's hard to imagine the city today without the Prince Edward Viaduct, more commonly known as the Bloor Street Viaduct. But Torontonians voted against its construction three times — in 1910, 1911 and 1912 — before finally approving the expenditure necessary to build it in 1913. This reticence may not have been a bad thing: if any of those earlier referendums had succeeded, there would be a very different viaduct connecting Bloor and Danforth today.

In planning the viaduct that Torontonians were originally asked to approve, city engineer C.H. Rust recommended a straight route, directly connecting Danforth Avenue with Bloor Street (which, because of the Rosedale Ravine, then ended at Sherbourne Street). This direct connection would be made with a single, mile-long bridge crossing the Don and running a considerable distance through the Rosedale Ravine. Parliament Street would be continued northward on its own bridge in order to connect with the new viaduct, resulting in an elevated "T" intersection.

This plan may have made east-enders happy, but a lot of other Torontonians were strongly opposed. Rosedale residents were against the scheme because of the traffic it would bring within eye- and earshot of their quiet neighbourhood. The Guild of Civic Art and the Civic Improvement Committee (see chapter 3) opposed it because of its impact on the picturesque Rosedale Ravine. And people across the city were of the view that the extensive bridgework required was simply too expensive, especially since the area north of the Danforth (which was not yet part of the city) wouldn't be contributing a cent to the construction costs.

Alternatives were considered. One involved extending Bloor northward through Rosedale via Dale Avenue. Another involved extending it southward via Howard Street. The Rosedale Ravine would still have to be crossed with either alternative, but it would be at a right angle, significantly reducing the length of the bridging required and, thus, its cost and physical impact. But Rust was steadfast in championing a direct route: in his view, a major thoroughfare should not bend, and Toronto needed one great avenue that would traverse the entire city in a straight line, from the extreme east to the extreme west.

Although council adopted Rust's recommendation, the by-law to spend the money on the viaduct was voted down in the municipal election of 1910. When the proposal was put on the municipal ballot again in 1911 (municipal elections were held yearly — on New Year's Day no less), once again it was rejected. Undaunted, the city took the matter to the voters a third time, in 1912. The local press reported on January 2, 1912, that this time, finally, the viaduct had been approved. Two days later, it turned out that there had been a counting error. The viaduct had been defeated again. In the two days when it appeared to have passed, a number of south Rosedalians announced that they intended to sell their homes.

Soon after the last viaduct defeat, Mayor George Geary called a public meeting on the matter. Although there seemed to be general support for the concept of a viaduct, the divisive issue was the route. A general consensus emerged at the meeting favouring a compromise between the straight-line approach that had been voted down and the Howard Street route (Fig. 15-1). This compromise had been devised by John Lyle (Fig. 15-2), consulting architect to the Civic Improvement Committee, and was recommended in a special report of the committee released in October 1911, a month ahead of its final report.

Lyle's ingenious solution was to construct a terrace on the south end of the Rosedale Ravine on which to extend Bloor Street. Few people now probably even think of this stretch of Bloor between Sherbourne and Parliament as being part of the viaduct. And probably most would assume that it is built on naturally occurring tableland. But the fact is that it is just as artificial (if not as visible) as the heroic bridge over the Don. It's also the piece of the viaduct that made the whole thing politically viable.

Lyle's approach resulted in a route that was four hundred feet shorter than the Howard Street proposal, and without the massive expropriation it would have entailed. Moreover, it was only two-hundred-and-fifty feet longer than the straight-line approach. The bridged intersection with Parliament required by the straight route could be avoided, as could the intrusive bridgework in the Rosedale Ravine. Although there was still a one-hundred-foot deviation southward, as the Guild of Civic Art had pointed out in earlier championing the Howard Street proposal, most travellers coming from the east would be intending to head downtown in any event, making this deviation a potential timesaver if anything.

Support continued in some quarters for the straight route (the *World* remained unconvinced by what it had derided as the "wiggle-waggle," "wibble-wobble," and "jiggle-joggle" approach of a "crooked plan," and even Old City Hall architect E.J. Lennox felt that abandoning the straight-line scheme would be a mistake) but a committee appointed by the mayor to report on the matter recommended that Lyle's solution be adopted. Council officially did so in September 1912. On New Year's Day, 1913, Toronto voters finally approved the $2.5 million needed for the viaduct's construction.

In the meantime, Rust, who had been such a stalwart champion of the straight route, had been replaced by R.C.

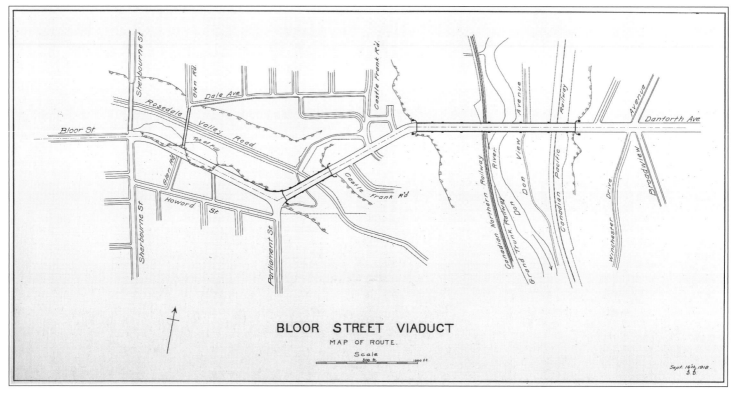

Fig. 15-1. The route finally chosen for the Prince Edward Viaduct, named after the future Edward VIII, who officially opened it. Architect John Lyle's proposal of extending Bloor Street on an embankment north of Howard Street was the design solution that finally made the entire project politically viable. [City of Toronto Archives, Series 372, Sub-series 10, Item 878]

Harris (who was also given the title of commissioner of public works). This change undoubtedly smoothed the way for the abandonment of the straight route. It also resulted in another significant change in the viaduct plans. Rust had been a proponent of an all-concrete structure for the Don section of the viaduct, believing it to be cheaper in the long run (since steel requires regular painting). Harris was vehemently opposed to concrete, however. He felt that the heavier concrete bridge would be unsuited to the shale base of the Don Valley.

The concrete interests responded with an intensive lobbying campaign. They had the support of the Guild of Civic Art, which felt that a concrete bridge would be more aesthetically pleasing (see Fig. 15-3). In February 1913, when Harris officially recommended to the city's board of control that a steel structure be built on concrete piers, Alderman Rowland presented the board with a drawing of a concrete design commissioned from the American engineering firm Hedrick and Cochrane (Fig. 15-4). Despite this last-minute intervention, both the board of control

Fig. 15-2. Architect John Lyle (foreground), shown here in 1895, while working at the Atelier Paul Blondel in Paris, having finished his studies at the École des Beaux-Arts. [Archives of Ontario, C33-2-0-0-1]

Fig. 15-3. This elaborate design by L. G. Mouchel and Partners Limited (Hennebique Ferro-concrete) illustrates why the Guild of Civic Art felt that concrete bridges for the viaduct would be more aesthetically pleasing than steel bridges. The subway platforms under the roadway are not visible, being completely enclosed. [City of Toronto Archives, Series 372, Sub-series 10, Item 187]

and later city council adopted Harris's recommendation for a largely steel structure. On a subsequent vote in April, however, and following continuing lobbying from concrete contractors, council agreed to a compromise: in the bid documents for the Don section of the viaduct, council specified that it preferred a steel superstructure, but left it open to bidders on the project to tender on an all-concrete bridge. If bidding on the steel option, contractors were to supply quotes based on a design supplied by the city (with architectural detailing by consulting architect Edmund Burke). If tendering on the concrete option, contractors had to supply their own designs.

When the bids were opened in October 1914, there were as many qualifying concrete bids as steel: five of each.

Fig. 15-4. The all-concrete proposal that was a calculated challenge to the recommendations of City Works Commissioner R.C. Harris. It was designed by the engineering firm of Hedrick and Cochrane. The American firm had designed a similar structure for Dallas, Texas, that was touted at the time as the longest concrete bridge in the world. [City of Toronto Archives, Series 372, Sub-series 10, Item 63]

What's more, the lowest concrete bid, at some $850,000, was almost $148,000 less than the nearest steel bid. In a normal tendering process, this would have settled the issue. But the problem, of course, was that the steel and concrete bids were on different bridges. And each concrete proposal was itself unique. It was like comparing apples with several varieties of concrete oranges.

To put an end to the matter, council asked the city engineer's department to prepare a report recommending a course of action. The Ontario Concrete Association responded with a full-page newspaper ad listing the advantages of concrete over steel. According to the association, they were numerous: a concrete bridge would be quieter, safer and more aesthetically pleasing, could be built more quickly and more cheaply — and

Fig. 15-5. This concrete design, by the Toronto engineering firm James, Loudan and Hertzberg, was actually the lowest bid in a tender call for the Don section of the viaduct. Council rejected it in favour of a steel-arched design. [City of Toronto Archives, Series 372, Sub-series 10, Item 189]

with Canadian materials. The association's ad was illustrated with the design of the lowest bidders, by the Toronto firm James, Loudan and Hertzberg (Fig. 15-5).

When city staff reported back to council in December 1914, they continued to recommend a steel viaduct. After an acrimonious debate of four hours (in which one councillor called Commissioner Harris a bookworm with a prejudice against concrete), the mayor forced the matter to a vote. Council awarded the tender for the Don section in steel to Quinlan and Robertson of Montreal.

The now "crooked" steel viaduct was to have one more change over what had been proposed in 1912: lower decks on the bridges over the Don and Rosedale sections were added to accommodate future subways. This idea had originated in a 1910 report prepared for the city by an American firm of transit consultants, Jacobs and Davies. In debating the proposal that went to the electorate in 1912, council had considered making provision for a subway, but decided that the additional $300,000 price tag couldn't be justified. When construction tenders went out in 1913, however, bidders were asked to provide two quotes, one that included a subway deck and one that didn't. In the end, of course, the lower decks were provided for. And half a century later, in 1966, they would finally fulfill their planned function when the Bloor-Danforth line opened.

That is, at least in the Don section. Although the bridge over the Rosedale section was also supplied with a lower subway deck, the bend in the tracks required to use it was considered too sharp, so the TTC built its own bridge over the Rosedale Valley from Castle Frank, leaving the lower subway deck of the Rosedale section stranded and forgotten.

Chapter 16

HAMILTON NORTHWEST ENTRANCE

1927 / Built to different plans

I N 1917 THE PROVINCIAL GOVERNMENT opened a two-lane, concrete highway between Toronto and Hamilton (later known as Highway 2, it still enters Toronto as Lake Shore Boulevard). The Toronto-Hamilton Highway carried a huge increase in traffic once the Great War ended. As the western terminus of this new route, the City of Hamilton was determined to make a good impression on the influx of visitors it would bring, holding an architectural competition for a gateway that would be "the most beautiful in America." The winning scheme, never fully realized, led one rhapsodic *Toronto Star* reporter to predict that when the work was finished, "thousands of people will come every evening from Toronto to visit it and deplore the fact that their own city fathers did not dream so splendid a dream."

York Street in the west end of Hamilton got its name in the early nineteenth century because it was literally the street to what was then York (just as Kingston Road and Dundas Street in Toronto lead to their respective namesakes). The new Toronto-Hamilton Highway connected with York Street over Burlington Heights, a high sandbar separating Hamilton Harbour from a marshy area known as Cootes Paradise. A two-lane bridge across the heights spanned the Desjardins Canal, which had provided early water access to Dundas. It was a stunning location, with views of the city, Lake Ontario and Cootes Paradise. Dundurn Castle, the palatial estate of nineteenth-century politician and businessman Sir Allan Macnab, dominated Hamilton Harbour to the south.

Despite its natural beauty, similar to Toronto's own waterfront, the area had been marred by railway tracks and ramshackle development. Hamilton alderman Thomas B. McQuesten had been an advocate of cleaning up the area when the highway was in the planning stages, but nothing came of it. A decade later, an application to put a billboard along the highway at Burlington Heights again drew attention to the area's neglect. McQuesten was no longer on council, but as a member of Hamilton's Board of Parks Management, he was still in a position to do something. The board, which was a semi-autonomous authority, had been very active in acquiring parkland properties, transforming Hamilton with its City Beautiful vision. Now it set its sights on Burlington Heights. It got what it wanted. In March 1927, the city transferred title.

The parks board brought in professor Eric Arthur of the University of Toronto's School of Architecture to provide his views on how the board should deal with the area. Arthur, who thirty years later would be technical advisor on the Toronto city hall competition (see chapter 12), advised holding a competition for the Hamilton site. The jury would be Arthur himself, Hamilton architect W.P. Witton and Toronto

city surveyor T.D. LeMay. Prizes were set at $2,000, $1,000 and $500. In addition to a new bridge across the canal, the Board of Parks Management was looking for a complete landscaping treatment for the area, including proposals for attractions and facilities such as "a pavilion, a large gasoline station, tea houses, etc." Entrants were not given entirely free reign, however: the board made it clear that it did not want "to see a tourist camp incorporated into the scheme."

When the February 1928 deadline arrived, twelve submissions were received. The three prizes all went to Toronto firms. In first place was the plan submitted by Wilson, Bunnell and Borgstrom, engineers and landscape architects. Carl Borgstrom, who was acknowledged as the group's lead,

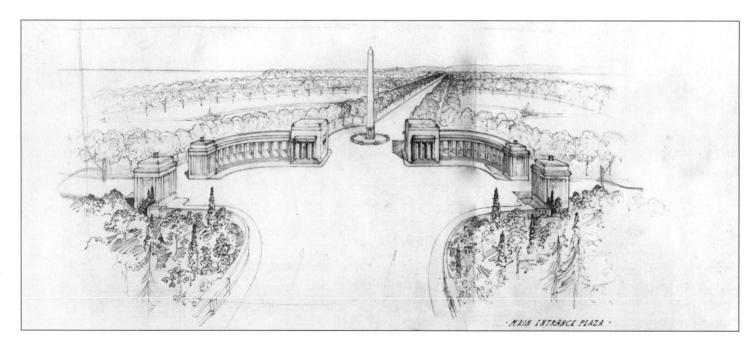

Fig. 16-1. This grand plaza would have greeted drivers heading into Hamilton on the new Toronto-Hamilton Highway. By the team of Wilson, Bunnell and Borgstrom, it was part of the first-place submission for the Hamilton northwest entrance competition. [Royal Botanical Gardens]

had received his landscape training in his native Sweden. The defining feature of the Borgstrom plan was its lowering and widening of the heights. The result would be a broader boulevard than otherwise could have been achieved on the narrow ridge that divided the harbour and Cootes Paradise. Borgstrom also called for the construction of a secondary road along the lakeshore. The jury was impressed by the Borgstrom team's innovative and practical approach to the traffic issues. As far as architectural treatment, however, the Borgstrom scheme lacked the grandeur and panache of some of the other entrants. One exception was its western entrance plaza, which featured a seventy-one-foot obelisk that would greet travellers heading in from Toronto (Fig. 16-1). An obelisk also featured in the submission of Chapman and Oxley, but on the eastern end of the precinct, in front of Dundurn Castle (Fig. 16-2).

The second-place winners were the husband-and-wife team of Howard and Lorrie Dunnington-Grubb. Well known as landscape planners, the Dunnington-Grubbs had designed the new Lawrence Park subdivision in Toronto. They had also prepared the plans for another major Board of Parks Management Project, the sixty-four-acre Gage Park, which had just been completed. Although the jury appreciated their architectural proposals, including an art gallery overlooking the harbour, it felt that their scheme was weaker in its solutions to the transportation issues.

Fig. 16-2. A drawing prepared by the Toronto firm of Chapman and Oxley shows a traffic circle at the southern end of the new entranceway. In addition to demarcating the approach to the new bridge, it would have provided a grand entrance to Dundurn Castle, shown here with landscape improvements suggested by the firm. [Archives of Ontario, C23, A-7, project 264]

In third place was architect John Lyle (Fig. 15-2). As consulting architect to Toronto's Civic Improvement Committee, and having devised the route that was adopted for Toronto's own Bloor Street Viaduct (see chapters 3 and 15), Lyle was no stranger to the problems of town planning in general and road planning in particular. Although he had made his reputation in Toronto with commissions such as the Royal Alexandra Theatre and Union Station (on which he was a collaborator), he was actually a native Hamiltonian and had designed a fountain in Gage Park for the Board of Parks Management. The judges were impressed by Lyle's bridge, which was truly monumental (Fig. 16-3). A massive arch would span the Desjardins Canal. Four pylons flanking the arch would be joined along the road-

way by colonnades. Between the columns of these colonnades, Lyle proposed the installation of ten statues of great Canadians. This suggestion was in keeping with his growing search for a national expression in Canadian architecture.

The Board of Parks Management had reserved the right to take the best elements of any of the submissions and, in the end, that is what it did. It proceeded with Borgstrom's broad boulevard on a lowered causeway. Borgstrom was hired to do the landscaping work, although in council's inevitable call for economy, his grand plaza was deleted. In 1930, Lyle, whose bridge design had been a standout, was hired as consulting architect on the architectural treatment of the bridge. The high-level bridge that resulted (later named the Thomas

Fig. 16-3. John Lyle's monumental bridge drew the approval of the jury. Lyle would be hired as architectural consultant for the bridge that was ultimately constructed, incorporating elements of this design into it. [Royal Botanical Gardens]

Fig. 16-4. An aerial view of the Hamilton northwest entrance as constructed. The niches in the massive pylons of the high-level bridge were meant for statues of famous Canadians. They remain empty to this day. [Archives of Ontario, C 33-1-0-23]

B. McQuesten High Level Bridge) was also diminished from Lyle's initial proposal. The decision to use steel-span construction meant the loss of his massive arch. His colonnades also disappeared. In the end, what Lyle proposed were four freestanding pylons; their link to his original design was perceptible, but they were much simplified. Apart from any fiscal considerations (even these pared-down pylons had barely survived council's cost-cutting scrutiny), the modified design reflected the more modern aesthetic that Lyle had been exploring in the intervening years. He still retained a spot for his great Canadians, however; now reduced to four, the statues would stand in niches in the pylons themselves. The niches sit empty to this day, despite the occasional call to fill them with statuary (Fig. 16-4).

In contrast to its effect on many private sector projects, the Depression actually hastened work on the northwest entrance. A scheme that was initially mooted for completion in time for Hamilton's centenary in 1946 became a relief project, officially opening in June of 1932. It marked the end of an era of remarkable achievement for Hamilton's Board of Parks Management. In addition to initiating the northwest entrance redevelopment, since 1927 the board had quadrupled the city's parkland holdings, preserved in perpetuity many wildlife areas, attracted McMaster College away from the University of Toronto and provided it with a Hamilton campus, begun to build the Royal Botanical Gardens and undertaken the construction of Civic (later Ivor Wynne) Stadium in anticipation of the first British Empire Games in 1930. Not a bad five years.

McQuesten remained on the Board of Parks Management until his death in 1948, but in 1934 he would expand the scope of his public service when he became a member of the provincial parliament, serving as minister of highways (among other portfolios) and as chairman of the Niagara Parks Commission until 1943. In those roles, he oversaw the development of the Niagara parks system, and spearheaded the construction of the continent's first limited access expressway, the Queen Elizabeth Way between Toronto and Niagara Falls. Its bypass of Burlington Heights meant time savings for Torontonians heading to Niagara and the United States, but it also meant that generations of them would no longer routinely see one of McQuesten's other great legacies, the Hamilton northwest entrance.

Chapter 17

ISLANDS TUNNEL
1935 / Partially built

DEBATE ABOUT THE NEED TO construct a "fixed link" to the Toronto islands has been a recurrent feature of the city's history. Any number of proposals have come and — invariably — gone. But a 1935 plan to construct a tunnel under the western gap was different from the others: they actually started to build it.

Given how tantalizingly close the islands are to the mainland — especially at the western gap — it's no surprise that by 1935, various schemes to provide a link between the islands and the mainland had been considered (Fig. 17-1). In 1894 (two years after the introduction of electric streetcars), streetcar service was proposed to the island via a swing bridge across the western gap. Plans prepared three years later by the Harbour Commission's engineer, Kivas Tully (Fig. 8-1), showed a variation on this proposal, with the streetcars crossing the western gap in a tunnel instead of a bridge. A plan by the city's parks commissioner in 1909 kept the tunnel, but replaced the streetcars with automobiles.

While the proposals were intriguing, two developments in the early years of the twentieth century would eventually lead to shovels actually being put in the ground. First, in 1913 the federal government had agreed to spend $800,000 on the construction of two moveable bridges to the islands, one across the eastern gap and one across the western gap. This commitment was in support of a $20-million plan for the entire lakefront prepared by the Harbour Commission. Although the money never materialized, some twenty years later local politicians had still not forgotten the commitment to provide it. The second development that ultimately led to tunnel construction happened ten years earlier: in 1903 the first successful power flight was reported by the Wright Brothers.

It was the dream of an island airport that finally provided the hard-nosed rationale that would make a fixed link to the islands a "necessity." In the 1920s, seaplanes were using the Toronto Harbour and, by 1929, airmail service between

Fig. 17-1. An aerial shot across the western gap. Given how close the islands are to the mainland, it's no surprise that there have been many proposals for bridges and tunnels over the years. This photograph was taken to chronicle construction that began on a tunnel to the islands in 1935. [Toronto Port Authority Archives, PC1/1/11181]

Toronto and Buffalo commenced, again using amphibious planes (the service was discontinued in 1931). That same year, Toronto city council gave the Harbour Commission funds for preliminary work on an island "air harbour" across the western gap. A fixed link to the mainland was considered an integral part of any airport plan. A 1934 report prepared for the Harbour Commission recommended a tunnel instead of a bridge, however. The view was that, although a tunnel would be more expensive initially to construct, over the long run, it would be less expensive to operate; a lift bridge would require staff and would have to be opened six to seven thousand times a year. At a time when ship traffic was expected to increase significantly (the rebuilt Welland Canal had recently opened), this was more than an inconvenience: with a lift bridge there was always the possibility of a maritime collision, a hazard that a tunnel eliminated.

In February 1935 Mayor James Simpson went to Ottawa to meet with the minister of public works, H.A. Stewart, to try to get federal funds for the project. Two months later, the government included $1 million for the tunnel project in a bill that allocated money for various relief works across the country. The government wanted the bill to receive royal assent before the Easter recess, but the tunnel was harshly criticized by Liberal members of the House, who called it "a tunnel to a summer resort." They wanted money spent on slum clearance, an idea that had been advocated the previous year in a report by Ontario's lieutenant governor, Herbert Bruce. After seven hours of debate, the bill failed to clear committee. When the House resumed sitting in May, a Liberal motion to reallocate the tunnel money was ruled out of order, and the bill finally passed.

The ride wasn't any easier at city council. City staff were of the view that if the tunnel were built, it would result in pressure to allow automobile traffic on the islands, which would be incompatible with its role as a public playground. It was a well-founded fear: plans prepared in April 1935 already showed the tunnel linking up with a "Boulevard Drive" on the island, part of a forty-five-mile ring road around the city that the Harbour Commission had been championing since 1921. And then there was the money issue. The Harbour Commission informed council that the federal government would not tender the contract for the tunnel until assurances had been received that the city would approve some $425,000 of additional funds, $119,000 for paving and ventilation in the tunnel and an additional $305,000 to be spent by the commission in developing the airport. Moreover, the city would be responsible for the tunnel's ongoing maintenance.

Councillor Sam McBride (Fig. 17-2) argued that on these terms, the federal government's $1-million gift was actually an unending liability for the city. His research showed that municipal airports across North America were money-losers. And anyway, he warned council, only "murderers and millionaires" travelled by air. The debate at council was acrimonious, going into the early hours of the morning. But when a vote was finally taken at 2:30 a.m. on August 8, the tunnel got council support by a vote of fifteen to seven.

Things moved relatively quickly from that point. Tenders were received the next month and a construction contract was signed in October. The tunnel would be 1327.7 feet long, including approaches, and have an interior width of fifty-five feet, four inches. Forty feet of that would be taken up by roadway, with additional provision for two seven-foot sidewalks. From the ceiling of the tunnel to the top of the road would be fourteen feet (Fig. 17-3). Work began almost immediately and proceeded quickly. Underground utilities were moved out of the way on the mainland, the channel was dredged and steel piling and crib bedding were installed in the channel as part of a temporary coffer dam to keep water out of the work area. Most dramatically, the sea wall on the northern part of the western gap was broken as the first step in digging under the lake bed (Figs. 17-4, 17-5).

Fig. 17-2. Samuel McBride, whose election as mayor in 1936 ensured the Toronto islands tunnel project would stay dead. [City of Toronto Archives, Series 1057, Item 3517]

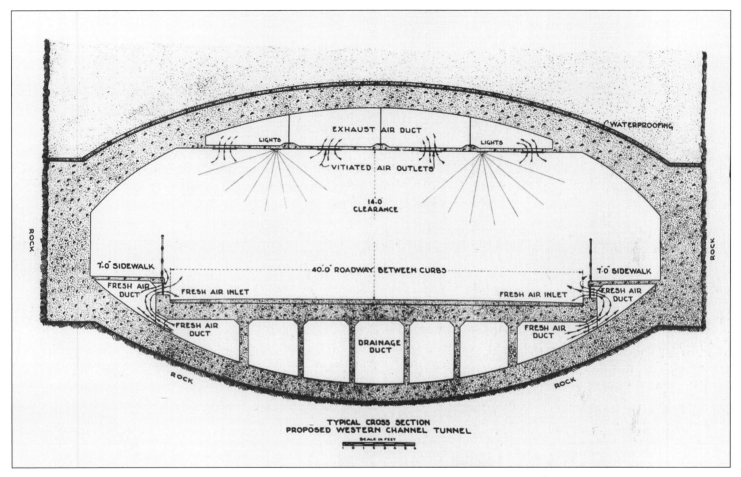

Fig. 17-3. A cross-section of the tunnel shows accommodation for vehicular and pedestrian traffic. A conduit below the road bed would carry utilities from the mainland to the island. [Toronto Port Authority Archives, PC1/1/11180]

But on October 14, 1935, R.B. Bennett's Conservatives were defeated by William Lyon Mackenzie King's Liberals. The party that had opposed the project was now the government. The events that followed were inevitable. On the evening of Tuesday, October 29, a telegram was sent by the new federal minster of public works, J.A. Cardin, ordering the work suspended (as part of a review of all major contracts signed by the previous government). Work carried on till noon the next day, when the city's commissioner of public works, R.C. Harris, relayed the stop-work order to the construction site. The city's board of control voted to send Mayor Simpson to Ottawa to persuade the government to reverse its decision, but it was futile. In the last week of the year, the federal government officially notified the contractor that the

Fig. 17-4 (top). Work on the islands tunnel began and ended in the fall of 1935. This photograph is stamped October 15, 1935, eleven days before the federal government sent a telegram ordering that all construction be stopped. [Toronto Port Authority Archives, PC1/1/11136]. Fig. 17-5 (bottom). This shot shows the breaks made in the seawall of the western gap during tunnel construction. In the background is Maple Leaf Stadium, which had been built by the Toronto Harbour Commissioners in 1926. Demolished in 1968, it lives on only in the name Stadium Road, near Bathurst Quay. [Toronto Port Authority Archives, PC1/1/11194]

contract had been terminated. A few days later, on New Year's Day 1936, Samuel McBride defeated Simpson for the mayor's job. His opposition to the tunnel had been a very public part of his platform. The tunnel project was truly dead. The holes that had been made in the north wall of the western channel were filled in August 1936.

The Harbour Commission had warned that if a tunnel wasn't built, the airport project would also have to be shelved. But the island airport was up and running by 1939. Access was by ferry.

Chapter 18

QUEEN STREET SUBWAY

1946 / Partially built

FORTY-SIX FEET BELOW STREET LEVEL, underneath the Queen subway station, there is an area the public never sees. An inconspicuous door on the concourse level of that station leads to this cavernous concrete space, 288 feet long and fifty-two feet wide. It was built at the same time as the Yonge line, between 1949 and 1952, at a cost of a half million dollars, but has never been used for its original purpose. It's not a bomb shelter, or some massive storage space, but the shell of the planned City Hall subway station. A fascinating anachronism, City Hall station was the first and only construction undertaken on the abandoned Queen subway line (Figs. 18-1a, 18-1b).

In 1944, the Toronto Transit Commission began planning in earnest for the expected boom in postwar traffic by establishing a rapid transit department. From the start, the TTC anticipated that both a north-south line and an east-west line would be needed, with Yonge and Queen — which had the busiest streetcar lines in the city — chosen as the routes. Although both were initially conceived as streetcar subways (that is, streetcar lines in which the streetcars would run underground for at least part of their route), the ultimate decision saw the Yonge line proposed as a heavy-rail subway from Union Station to Eglinton. The Queen line continued to be planned as a streetcar subway that could be converted to heavy rail service later if demand warranted. It would run in its own right-of-way between Trinity-Bellwoods Park and Logan Avenue. For most of the route, this right-of-way would be in an open trench, generally behind the buildings fronting on the north side of Queen, but the section between University Avenue and Church Street would be located in a tunnel. The Queen line would serve as a trunk line for other streetcar lines that would feed into it from the east and west (Figs. 18-2, 18-3). The decision to construct the Queen line as a streetcar subway is still evident in the shell

Figs. 18-1a (left), 18-1b (right). An unassuming door leads to the shell of what would have been City Hall station on the Queen Street subway line. [James Dawson]

of City Hall station: it is noticeably higher than the stations built on the Yonge line at the time, and its platforms are lower than those of a normal subway station, designed for easy access to streetcars.

On New Year's Day 1946, Toronto voters approved the TTC's rapid transit scheme by a margin of ten to one. Work began on the Yonge line three years later. At the official opening ceremonies in March 1954, the chair of the TTC called

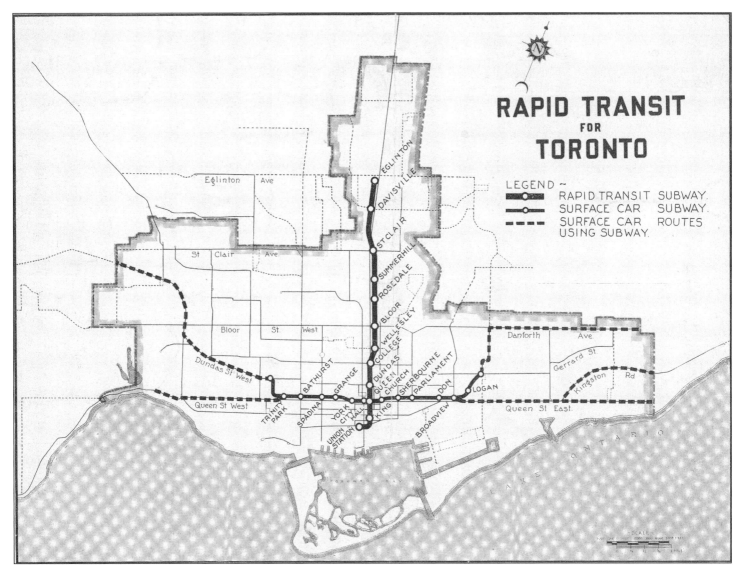

Fig. 18-2. The plan for Toronto's rapid transit system that was overwhelmingly approved by voters in 1946. [City of Toronto Archives, Series 836, Sub-series 2, File 50]

for an immediate start to construction on the Queen Street line, but the TTC began to re-evaluate the wisdom of the line almost immediately. By 1956, it was clear that the city's midtown had become a major new area for growth, a fact that was reflected in the overcrowded Bloor-Danforth streetcar line. The TTC was now of the view that the logical alignment for the new east-west line was on Bloor and Danforth, between Keele and Woodbine. A University Avenue spur would provide additional integration between this new line and the busy Yonge line (although there is no "ghost station" under Osgoode station on the University line, supports under it were engineered to accommodate the future Queen line).

Metro planners rejected this straight Bloor-Danforth route. They wanted a "U"-shaped alignment: starting at Keele, the line would dip south at Christie, roughly following a Grace-Gorevale alignment until it hit Queen Street. From there it would continue east on a Queen Street alignment until it reached Pape Avenue. From Pape, it would again head north, to Danforth, following that street to Woodbine. In many ways, Metro's "U" proposal was an update of the 1944 Queen Street subway plan. An acrimonious political battle ensued over which plan would triumph, with the straight Bloor-Danforth route championed by TTC chair (and former Toronto mayor) Allan Lamport, and the "U" plan backed by the Metro chairman, Frederick Gardiner. Ultimately, Gardiner acquiesced to the straight alignment, which was later endorsed by the Ontario Municipal Board. As a result, the subway deck of the Prince Edward Viaduct would finally be put to use (see chapter 15). The old positions clearly died hard, however. When the new Bloor-Danforth line opened in February 1966, Toronto Mayor Phil Givens called it a mistake.

Despite the opening of the Bloor-Danforth line, the Queen line was far from dead. The year service started on Bloor-Danforth, the city's traffic director called the need for the Queen line urgent. For its part, Toronto city council pushed the Queen subway as an alternative to expressway construction, specifically the Crosstown Expressway (see chapter 20). The line was shown on the 1966 Metro official plan and, by this time, was envisaged as a full subway from Greenwood in the east to Ronscesvalles in the west (Fig. 20-1), but the plan stated that further studies would be required to determine its "complete validity." Neither the TTC nor Metro's planning department was of the view that a full subway was warranted yet: in 1967, the Queen streetcar line carried only three-quarters of the volume that the old Bloor streetcar line had carried in rush hour, and 67 percent of what it had carried all day. As a result, in 1968, the TTC ranked a Queen line as its third rapid transit construction priority, after the extension of the Yonge line between Eglinton and Sheppard, and the construction of the Spadina line, north from St. George. The mayors of North York, Scarborough and York questioned even that ranking for the Queen subway, calling for an Eglinton line instead.

The Queen line's low priority became apparent in 1969, during the construction of what would later be the Sheraton Centre across from New City Hall. City council had asked the TTC whether it made sense to dig a tunnel along Queen between Bay and University at the same time the hotel was being built, for eventual use in the subway. The TTC's response was that if that kind of money was available, it should be used instead to extend the Yonge line from Sheppard to Finch. The Queen line had now become the TTC's fourth rapid transit priority. Even for those who championed a downtown east-west line, there was the growing feeling that times had changed since 1946, and the line should be farther south than Queen Street. Apart from the fact that the Queen line would be only a mile and a quarter south of the Bloor-Danforth line, with the Eaton Centre development now officially cancelled (see chapter 4), all the major office proposals, such as the Toronto-Dominion Centre, Commerce Court,

Fig. 18-3. A westbound streetcar on the Queen line emerges from the tunnel west of University Avenue into an open trench north of Queen Street. The tower of Old City Hall is in the distance. [City of Toronto Archives, Series 648, File 80, Item 14]

and First Canadian Place (then in the planning stages) were on King Street. Not to mention the massive Metro Centre proposal south of Front Street (see chapter 6). Regardless, in October 1973, the TTC approved, in principle, construction of the Queen line from the Humber to Greenwood, at an estimated cost of $400 million. The provincial government, which was expected to pay for 75 percent of the new line's construction costs, said it was not committing to anything until it saw the results of a joint provincial-Metro review of Metro Toronto's transportation needs, then being carried out.

The Metro Toronto Transportation Plan Review released its analysis of proposed subway additions in January 1974 and its final report the following year. It concluded that studies to date had not made out a need for the Queen line. It said that one of the benefits that had been touted in support of the subway, diverting passengers from the busy interchange of the Yonge and Bloor lines, could likely be met by other means, such as an underground streetcar system or by rapid transit in the Don Valley (which the Ontario government was then proposing to build). Interestingly, the report also said that a planned extension of the Bloor line west from Islington to Kipling should be re-evaluated, as a major rationale for that extension had been to allow for the construction of a new subway yard to serve the Bloor line (the Greenwood yard was to be commandeered to serve the new Queen line).

By this time, Toronto city council, which had always been a booster of the Queen line (often in the face of suburban opposition) had its own reasons to oppose it. Another subway in the downtown core wasn't compatible with the office decentralization then seen as desirable. Beyond that, part and parcel of the Queen subway project, certainly in the 1960s, was the removal of the King, Queen, Dundas and Carlton streetcar lines (it was also assumed by the city's traffic planners that after the streetcars were gone, a one-way street system could be introduced into the downtown core). By the mid-seventies, there were those who felt that even the loss of the local service provided by the Queen streetcar alone would not be a fair trade-off. When Metro's new official plan was approved in 1980, it didn't contain a Queen Street subway. But even if the city's planning maps no longer show the route on which it was to be the central hub, City Hall station remains, still waiting to be of service.

Chapter 19

A VERTICALLY SEPARATED CITY

1959 / Partially built

TORONTO IS FAMOUS FOR ITS extensive downtown PATH system, connecting fifty buildings in an ever-expanding underground network that starts south of Front Street and pushes north past Dundas. But if planners in the 1950s and 1960s had had their way, it might have been the cars, not the people, travelling underground.

There had long been isolated examples of pedestrian bridges and tunnels in Toronto, such as the connection made between Union Station and the Royal York Hotel when the hotel opened in 1929. By the 1950s, however, cutting-edge city planning required a wholesale approach to separating pedestrian from vehicular traffic. It was no longer seen as adequate simply to provide roads for cars and sidewalks for pedestrians; the ideal was actually to get the vehicular and pedestrian traffic totally separated, either in different precincts, through pedestrian malls (called horizontal or "precinctual" separation) or — the preferred solution for the space age — onto different levels entirely (vertical separation).

The choice of Viljo Revell's design for the new city hall and civic square in 1958 (see chapter 12) provided the specific impetus for Toronto's exploration of pedestrian and vehicle separation. Revell's elevated walkways were envisaged as a defining element of the square, like Bernini's colonnade around St. Peter's Square; they were not planned as the first step in an integrated elevated walkway system (or "plus-15" system, so named because of the number of feet between the walkways and road). Even so, the walkways and the creation of the vast new pedestrian area that was the square itself got council to thinking. In 1959, it asked the city's planning board to prepare a report proposing solutions to what it saw as the growing conflict between pedestrian and auto traffic in the downtown core.

The board's report was entitled *The Pedestrian in Downtown Toronto*. In it, the board canvassed examples from other cities of the three main approaches to solving the separation issue: overhead walkways, underground pedestrian tunnels and mid-block pedestrian malls (which might or might not be enclosed). The board recommended a mixture of all three approaches in achieving pedestrian separation in Toronto, without getting into too many specifics about how any of them might be employed. A fourth approach, putting the cars underground, was floated a few years later when *Canadian Architect* asked five design professionals to collaborate on a plan for central Toronto for an article that ran in the August 1962 issue. Full vertical separation figured prominently in their scheme, with automobiles shown in underground tunnels on both Yonge and Queen Streets. The aim continued to be to relieve congestion, both for cars and pedestrians.

What might have seemed no more than a far-out exercise in theoretical planning was actually picked up by the planning board the following year in its *Plan for Downtown Toronto*. It called for mid-block, surface pedestrian malls parallel to Bay and Yonge, but concluded that ultimately even these would not be enough to solve the increasing problem of pedestrian congestion. Although the report did not recommend one approach over another, it clearly favoured putting vehicles underground. It was a radical proposal to be sure, but the *Plan for Downtown Toronto* acknowledged that "a major undertaking of this sort is not likely to be carried out until conditions make it imperative, certainly not before 1980" (Fig. 19-1).

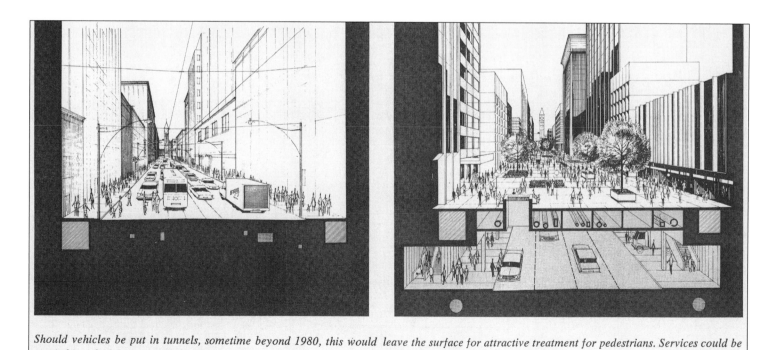

Should vehicles be put in tunnels, sometime beyond 1980, this would leave the surface for attractive treatment for pedestrians. Services could be carried in a deck between the two levels.

Fig. 19-1. 1963's *Plan for Downtown Toronto* predicted that sometime after 1980, automobiles would have to be put in tunnels in the downtown core. [City of Toronto Archives, Series 10, item 162]

Although the *Plan for Downtown Toronto* was adopted in principle by city council, the concept of putting cars underground seems not to have had a serious life beyond the pages of the plan itself. Perfunctory attempts were made to give Toronto at least a partial plus-15 system in the first half of the 1970s by having developers work them into new projects. When the Four Seasons-Sheraton hotel opened across from City Hall in 1972, it featured a connection to the Nathan Phillips Square walkways, as did the new Holiday Inn north of City Hall, which opened the same year. Two extensions of the system eastward from the latter building failed to materialize, although large glassed areas on the second-level terrace indicate where the connections would have been made. Symptomatic of the city's ambivalence to a plus-15 approach, when it had called for proposals to redevelop the lands on which the Four Seasons-Sheraton was later built, a link to the City Hall walkway was merely to be "considered," whereas underground connections were required to the City Hall and the Richmond Adelaide Centre (whose below-ground shopping concourse was the first designed specifically in anticipation of an interconnected system). An elevated walkway planned from the Colonnade north across Bloor Street failed to materialize and, down at the waterfront, a system of elevated walkways that got a start with connections north and west from the Harbour Castle Hotel was never extended as planned (Fig. 19-2).

In its 1974 report, the Core Area Task Force recommended against the creation of new elevated walkways, which it saw as generally "dull and disruptive." In an era when Yonge Street was being closed down in the summers as a pedestrian

Fig. 19-2. The Harbour Square condominiums were intended to have an elevated pedestrian connection north across Queen's Quay. It was part of an extensive system planned for the entire area.

mall, citizens were more interested in taking back the streets from cars than in handing them over entirely. Even so, the weather protection offered by the expanding underground system was irresistible. While the protection it offered would also have been available in an enclosed plus-15 system, such as those in Calgary and Minneapolis, Toronto had something that that those other winter cities didn't: a subway. In Toronto, it was the ability to access the subway while keeping dry and warm that assured the popularity of an underground pedestrian system. The concurrent development of a network of shops and restaurants added to the attraction. By the 1990s, Toronto actually had official plan policies prohibiting new overhead walkways and encouraging the demolition of existing ones. But the PATH system continued to grow.

In the end then, the 1963 *Plan for Downtown Toronto* got it right and wrong. Forty-five years after the plan was written, there is substantial vertical separation in the downtown core, but its expansion isn't driven by traffic congestion. And it's not the cars that are in the tunnels.

Chapter 20

SPADINA EXPRESSWAY

1962 / Partially built

ON HIS LAST FULL DAY IN OFFICE — February 7, 1985 — Premier Bill Davis delivered a legal document to Toronto Mayor Art Eggleton. It was a ninety-nine-year lease from the province to the city — for a strip of land three feet deep by 750 feet long — an oddly shaped property for anyone to be interested in. But, as they say, with real estate it's location, location, location. And the location of this three-foot strip was highly significant: on the south side of Eglinton Avenue, right below where the William R. Allen Road — a.k.a. the Spadina Expressway — comes to a halt. The provincial government had killed the Spadina project back in 1971, against Metro Toronto's wishes, and much to the City of Toronto's relief. The city's three-foot strip was meant to thwart any attempts that Metro might make to push it farther south. While the conveyance was mostly of symbolic importance, it was an important symbol: a nail in the coffin of an expressway that had caused fifteen years of division.

The Spadina Expressway was a Metro undertaking, but the idea of a major road into downtown Toronto from the northwest predated Metro's founding. It was contentious from the beginning. As early as 1947, the City of Toronto had envisaged a northern extension of Spadina as a means of easing traffic congestion. But the concept of a road continuing through the Cedarvale and Nordheimer ravines was opposed by the Township of York. A planned widening of Spadina up to St. Clair got no farther north than Dupont. In the first year of its creation, the new Metro government began actively planning the Spadina extension, which had now evolved into a controlled-access expressway. The Township of North York lost no time in getting expropriations going for the northern portion of the right-of-way.

During this period, the Spadina Expressway was still seen as a relatively low priority, secondary in importance to the Don Valley Parkway, the Gardiner and the east-west subway line. Even so, it formed an integral part of the expressway system set out in Metro's 1959 official plan. The plan envisaged

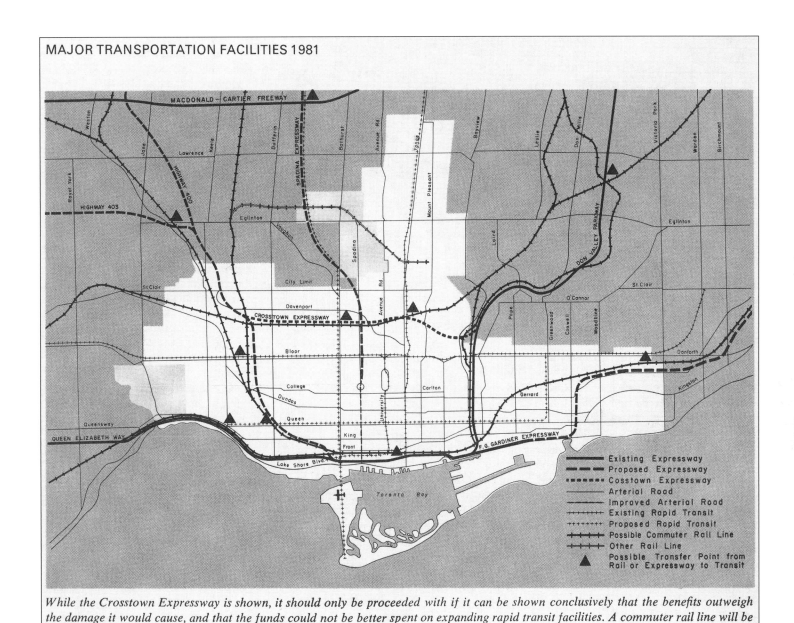

MAJOR TRANSPORTATION FACILITIES 1981

Legend:
Existing Expressway
Proposed Expressway
Cosstown Expressway
Arterial Road
Improved Arterial Road
Existing Rapid Transit
Proposed Rapid Transit
Possible Commuter Rail Line
Other Rail Line
Possible Transfer Point from Rail or Expressway to Transit

While the Crosstown Expressway is shown, it should only be proceeded with if it can be shown conclusively that the benefits outweigh the damage it would cause, and that the funds could not be better spent on expanding rapid transit facilities. A commuter rail line will be in operation along the lakeshore from Hamilton to Dunbarton by 1967.

Fig. 20-1. This map from a 1966 City of Toronto planning study shows the outer and inner expressway system proposed for Toronto. Although the Spadina, Scarborough, Crosstown and Richview expressways would be cancelled, they have left behind ghostly vestiges. [City of Toronto Archives, Series 10, Item 418, Page 49]

two rings of expressways, one surrounding the downtown core, and one surrounding Metro as a whole (Fig. 20-1). The Gardiner would form the common southern element of both. The outer ring would consist of Highway 27 in the west, the Scarborough Expressway in the east, and Highway 401 in the north. The inner or "circumferential" ring would consist of an extension of Highway 400 down to the Gardiner (via Christie and Grace) in the west, the Don Valley Parkway in the east and, to the north, something called the Crosstown Expressway, which would connect the 400 extension and the DVP along a Dupont-Roxborough route. Like the Richview Expressway farther west (which would connect the 403 with the 400 extension), Spadina would function as a radial link between the outer and inner rings. Starting at Wilson, it would connect the 401 and the Crosstown. Among this criss-crossing web of highways, Spadina was unique in that a subway line, an extension of the University line, was part of the scheme.

Although Spadina was fine as a line on a map, the political problems associated with it meant that council was happy enough to defer its actual construction. When the first Metro report was released on the proposal in 1954, York residents had been outraged at the prospect of losing eighteen acres of Cedarvale Park. The memory of their reaction lingered; when an update to the report was prepared two years later, Metro council voted not to release it, with Metro Chairman Frederick Gardiner concluding that to do so would "stir up a dandy lot of trouble." But by the end of the decade, the construction of the Yorkdale shopping mall — which would have frontage on the new expressway — meant that the issue couldn't be avoided any longer. In 1959, the province had approved a clover-leaf intersection at Spadina and the 401, but before it would start construction, it wanted an assurance from Metro that the Spadina Expressway would actually be built. A reasonable request for an interchange that ended up covering 150 acres and costing $14 million.

The time had come for Metro to fish or cut bait. It decided to do both. Although studies had been prepared showing the Spadina Expressway extending all the way south to the Gardiner, when council finally approved construction, in December 1961, it was only to Lawrence Avenue. Based on strong opposition from the City of Toronto, the Crosstown Expressway was taken off the table altogether. Even with these concessions, the council debate leading to the approval of this truncated "baby expressway" lasted fourteen hours, and more than seventy ratepayers groups voiced their opposition. The Ontario minister of highways, W.A. Goodfellow, was not impressed. In January 1962, he advised Metro that the province wouldn't build the 401 interchange unless the expressway was approved at least as far south as Bloor. Metro complied. On March 6, 1962, it voted $73,689,000 for the construction of the Spadina Expressway to Bloor, and $80 million for a rapid transit line. The Township of York, the Village of Forest Hill and ratepayers' groups officially opposed the project at a subsequent Ontario Municipal Board hearing, but to no avail.

In December 1966, the first leg of the expressway, from Wilson Heights north of the 401 south to Lawrence Avenue, was officially opened. The portion down to Eglinton was expected to be open by 1971, with the entire thing finished by 1983 (later expedited to 1975). The portion of the expressway that had proven most contentious so far, the radial stretch connecting the expressway to Spadina Road through the Cedarvale and Nordheimer ravines, had yet to be built, although a promise to tunnel through the park had helped to mute some opposition. But the neighbourhoods south of St. Clair, which were starting to organize against the looming threat, had yet to be dealt with. A headline in the Telegram in June 1966 must stand as one of the most understatedly prescient headlines in Toronto history: "Expressway fight below St. Clair predicted."

The southern portion of the expressway had unique problems. After the cancellation of the Crosstown Expressway, there had never been a satisfactory explanation of what would happen to the five thousand cars per hour that that would be dumped into the downtown core. And beyond the traffic infiltration issue, there was the damage that would be caused to downtown neighbourhoods like the Annex by the very presence of the three-hundred-foot-wide expressway itself. South of Bloor, the four lanes of the Spadina would somehow (planning studies were still being done) merge with the four lanes of the existing street, drastically altering a vibrant commercial district. Whatever solution was chosen, mass expropriation would be necessary. By 1969, over four hundred houses had already been demolished for the northern part of the route, and Metro had started expropriating the 173 properties it would need within the City of Toronto itself.

In May of 1969, Metro council re-named the expressway north of Bloor in honour of retiring Metro Chairman William R. Allen (see Fig. 4-1), who had succeeded Frederick Gardiner as Metro chairman in 1962. But it was still the same beast. An anti-expressway coalition calling itself SSSOCCC, or Stop Spadina Save Our City Coordinating Committee, was formed in October 1969 to step up the fight. Chaired by University of Toronto professor Allan Powell, SSSOCCC brought students, academics, ratepayer groups and business people together in common opposition to the project, which became an issue in the 1969 municipal elections (Figs. 20-2, 20-3). Urban theorist Jane Jacobs, who had recently moved to the city from New York, gave intellectual leadership to the movement, and a book setting out the planning and economic arguments against the proposal, *The Bad Trip*, by David and Nadine Nowlan, became a local bestseller in early 1970. At the same time, Ontario's highway minister, George Gomme, rejected the argument of

Fig. 20-2. Stop Spadina Save Our City Co-ordinating Committee (SSSOCCC) conducts a protest march in front of Casa Loma. The expressway would have plunged past the landmark along Spadina Road. [Clara Thomas Archives and Special Collections, York University, Toronto Telegram Photograph Collection, ASC04295]

some expressway advocates that Metro was obliged to complete the highway to Bloor because of its 1962 deal with the province over the 401 interchange. He said that Metro could stop the expressway wherever it wanted. Even North York council, which had steadfastly pushed for the highway, was now divided. A tipping point had been reached.

This renewed opposition came at a time when the money originally budgeted for the expressway was running out. The cost was now estimated at $220 million, almost three times what the OMB had approved. South of Lawrence, the roadbed down to Eglinton was ready to be paved (Fig. 20-4), and a 1,500-foot-long ditch had been dug in Cedarvale Park. If work was to continue, Metro would need to go back to the OMB to get permission to incur the extra debt. After a sixteen-day hearing, the board approved the spending on the extension in a two-to-one decision released in February 1970.

Fighting to the last, the expressway's opponents shifted their focus to the provincial government, asking the cabinet to overturn the tribunal's decision. The province had decided to stay out of the Spadina debate, so the prospects of getting the OMB's decision overturned didn't look good. But 1971 brought a new premier, Bill Davis, and a surprising announcement. On June 3, 1971, Davis informed the legislature that cabinet had completed its review: the expressway was dead. In a speech that was widely quoted, Davis said, "If we are building a transportation system to serve the automobile, the Spadina Expressway would be a good place to start. But if we are building a transportation system to serve people, the Spadina Expressway is a good place to stop." He acknowledged that the government was going against the wishes of the elected Metro councillors, but concluded, "I am confident that if the people of the Toronto of tomorrow were consulted, they would give overwhelming approval to the decision their government has taken today."

Fig. 20-3. SSSOCCC protesting at Spadina and Dupont. [Clara Thomas Archives and Special Collections, York University, Toronto Telegram Photograph Collection, ASC04294]

Despite Davis' strong words, in 1976 Metro continued the expressway south to Eglinton, albeit as a four-lane "arterial" (a 1971 Davis plan to have Buckminster Fuller design housing for the right-of-way between Eglinton and Lawrence had been quietly abandoned, see chapter 5). The City of Toronto had been unsuccessful in its attempts to get an injunction against the construction, but it could later take some comfort in the fact that land swaps between Metro and the province prevented the expressway from going south of Eglinton. In 1983, in exchange for the province constructing the southern extension of the 400 to Eglinton (which became Black Creek Drive), Metro agreed to convey its Spadina right-of-way south of Eglinton to the province. The province leased it back to Metro for ninety-nine-years, on the condition that the land could not be used for an expressway. As late as 1988, Metro planners were still calling for completion of the expressway (three-foot strip and provincial lease conditions notwithstanding), but the party was over, not only for the Spadina Expressway, but for all new expressway construction in the city. Within a decade Metro itself would be history.

Still, the ghosts of the unbuilt portion of the Spadina Expressway haunt its former right-of-way to this day: the windowless Spadina facade of U of T's New College (why look out on an expressway?); the lawn in front of the Toronto Archives on Spadina north of Dupont (ready for its highway); and Ben Nobleman Parkette at Eglinton and the Allen (made from left-over right-of-way). There are other unbuilt bits of Metro's 1959 expressway system scattered throughout the city: the empty Richview right-of-way north of Eglinton between Martingrove Road and Royal York Road; the interchange between the DVP and Bloor Street (built for the Crosstown); and the concrete supports of the demolished eastern Gardiner, turned into street sculpture at Leslie and Lake Shore. Remnants all of a future overtaken by changing times.

Fig. 20-4. The right-of-way for the Spadina south of Lawrence. After the cancellation of the expressway, it was eventually completed as an arterial road down to Eglinton. [Clara Thomas Archives and Special Collections, York University, Toronto Telegram Photograph Collection, ASC04392]

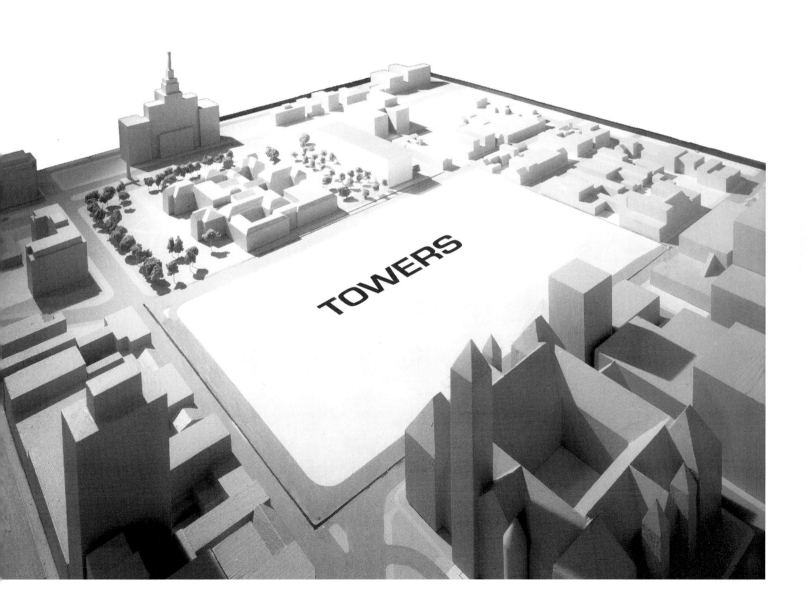

Chapter 21

TORONTO TOWERS

1927 / Unbuilt

BANK OF NOVA SCOTIA BUILDING

1929 / Built to different plans

ALTHOUGH THE CORNER OF KING and Bay has been Toronto's quintessential business address for over 150 years, development in the area was particularly active during the boom decade of the 1920s, leaving a legacy of some of the city's greatest commercial buildings. None was more ambitious than Toronto Towers. Yet even in the overheated economy of the era, there was a limit to how much new office space the city could absorb, and Toronto Towers was history even before the collapse of the economy. The Bank of Nova Scotia building, by contrast, had solid backing and a ready lead tenant in the bank itself. Unlike other projects "temporarily" cancelled after the market crash, architect John Lyle's head office building was actually built after the Depression (and the Second World War) had ended. Indeed, after the architect himself had died.

On November 25, 1927, the *Toronto Daily Star* reported that the city's property committee had granted permission to exceed the 130-foot height limit in the downtown core for three new towers — ranging in height from 280 to 530 feet — in the block north of King, east of Bay. As further details emerged, it became clear just how exciting the new development would be. In what was the largest real estate transaction in the city's history, the King-Adelaide Corporation had assembled a parcel stretching between King and Adelaide, taking up the middle third of the block bounded by Yonge and Bay. The company proposed building a new street through the middle of its holdings, connecting King and Adelaide, to be called Toronto Towers Street. A massive forty-storey tower would occupy the west side of the new street, rising from a fourteen-storey podium that would step down to twelve storeys on both Adelaide and King (Fig. 21-1).

The eastern side of Toronto Towers Street would be taken up by two buildings. The first was a nine-hundred-room, twenty-nine-storey hotel, to be called the Brock, which would

Fig. 21-1. The massive "Toronto Towers" development between King and Adelaide. Designed by Charles Dolphin, the $30-million project included three towers and what would have been the forerunner to the PATH system. Two weeks after the project received city approval, its promoters announced an even more ambitious scheme. [Toronto Public Library; after *The Contract Record and Engneering Review*]

occupy the north half of the site, fronting Adelaide. That site was then home to the Grand Opera House, and had been purchased from the widow of Ambrose Small, the impresario who had vanished eight years earlier in one of Toronto's most infamous unsolved mysteries. Oddly, it was announced that the hotel would contain a small chapel or shrine to Mr. Small. A pipe organ (which, one assumes, was to be salvaged from the theatre) would dominate the hotel's lobby from an organ loft. The other building on the east side of the site was described only as a "bank tower"; it would face King. The entire project was projected to cost $30 million, an astronomical sum in 1927. But H.F. Williams, spokesman for the consortium undertaking the development, told the press that a Chicago firm of real estate appraisers had sent eleven men to Toronto to prepare a report on the project, which concluded that it was viable. Williams said that site clearance would definitely begin by the end of the year.

In planning the three buildings, architect Charles Dolphin (who would later design the Postal Sorting Station, now incorporated into the Air Canada Centre) anticipated Toronto's PATH system by forty years. In Dolphin's plans, a grand staircase would lead from the street level lobby of the hotel to a basement concourse containing shops and restaurants. The concourse would connect with the new bank on King. From there, the concourse would continue westward to Toronto Towers. In this way, explained the architect, tenants of the office buildings could reach the hotel's restaurants and facilities "dry shod," and hotel guests could similarly avoid the weather in reaching their cars in the office building's 704-space underground parking lot.

Less than two weeks after Toronto Towers received municipal approval, its publicist revealed an extension of the scheme — "an even more ambitious project than the one that created such a stir when announced a few weeks ago." A syndicate represented by Mr. Williams had optioned almost all the properties on Temperance Street between Yonge and Bay, and planned to redevelop it into "the highest class shopping district on the continent," anchored by a new three-thousand-seat theatre. In one of the more unlikely utterances in Toronto's planning history, Mr. Williams enthused that "Temperance Street is to become the Rue de la Paix of Toronto."

After rumours of delays, in April 1928 it was announced that the Toronto Towers project was "definitely in abeyance," and that the King Street options held by the developers had expired. The usually effusive Mr. Williams admitted that the project's backers had failed to secure financing for the office tower. Even so, he said that the hotel portion of the development would proceed immediately. By then, however, the syndicate's option on the Grand Opera House had also expired. The cancellation of the Temperance Street project seems to have been a given; it simply wasn't mentioned again.

In May of 1928, the *Toronto Daily Star* reported that comedian John Dooley incorporated a Toronto Towers joke into his "burlesque wall papering act" in Earl Carroll's Vanities at the Princess Theatre. So ended the saga of Toronto Towers: from braggadocio to burlesque in less than a year.

———

Although the Depression spelled the end for most office projects still in the planning stage at the time of the crash, the Bank of Nova Scotia office building that stands at the northeast corner of King and Bay is a fascinating example of a project that was delayed by the Depression — and by the world war that followed it. Delayed, in fact, by a generation. Completed in 1951, the Bank's King and Bay headquarters has a vestigial sort of pre-war art deco feel to it. This should come as no surprise: the building was actually designed in 1929–30

by John M. Lyle (Fig. 15-2), but constructed twenty years later under the supervision of different architects to modified versions of Lyle's plans.

The Bank of Nova Scotia had moved its head office from Halifax to Toronto in 1902, but lacked a first-rate location and structure. The opportunity to acquire both occurred in 1929, when the bank bought the King and Bay property from the Canada Life Assurance Company. Canada Life had long had its headquarters there, and had considered rebuilding at that location earlier in the decade. In 1920, architect W.F. Sparling had prepared plans for the insurance company for the site; his building was described as a $2.5-million, thirty-nine to forty-storey skyscraper (Fig. 21-2). With a central tower facing King Street, rising straight up from a massive base, the building resembled New York's Woolworth Building, then the tallest skyscraper in the world. Undoubtedly, Sparling's design would have made an impressive statement for the company. But the opportunity to move to the prestigious University Avenue, which was slated to be extended southward from Canada Life's new Queen Street site to Union Station (see chapter 3), proved irresistible (Figs. 21-3a, 21-3b).

The trade journal *Construction* announced in November 1930 that work would start on the bank's new building in the spring. The journal noted that plans were still in the preliminary stage, but that the bank was believed to be planning a twenty-five-storey building costing around $7 million. Demolition of the site would commence around April 1, once Canada Life had moved to its new head office. The following

Fig. 21-2. The Canada Life Assurance Company planned this tower for the northeast corner of King and Bay in 1920. Before the decade was over, however, it would sell the land to the Bank of Nova Scotia. [Clara Thomas Archives and Special Collections, York University, Toronto Telegram Photograph Collection, ASC04290]

Figs. 21-3a, 21-3b. Canada Life's building at Queen and University, with its quirky weather beacon, has become a landmark in Toronto. These drawings show concepts that were considered for the building, including a contemporary design that presents quite a different face from the beaux arts design that was settled on. [Archives of Ontario, C 292-1-0-305, K-605]

Fig. 21-4. This 1930 perspective shows architect John Lyle's design for the Bank of Nova Scotia's headquarters at King and Bay. The scheme would be put to use two decades later. [Scotiabank Group Archives]

month, *Construction* found hope in the bank's plans despite the massive downturn in the economy, concluding that "In this huge undertaking which will tower approximately 30 storeys the Bank of Nova Scotia gives us unmistakable evidence of a well-founded faith in the future of the Dominion."

Despite *Construction*'s hopefulness, 1931 brought only a worsening economy, not a new tower for the Bank of Nova Scotia. Nonetheless, the bank did show faith in the future as Lyle's office continued to work on the design for the bank in anticipation of eventual construction (Fig. 21-4). Lyle had already designed a number of buildings for the bank, including its original head office in Halifax. But, in his words, this was the "Big Job," a chance to apply his principles of a Canadian style in architecture to a Canadian skyscraper.

The outbreak of war again delayed the project. In 1945, the bank decided to proceed with its plan. Unfortunately, Lyle died in December. In 1946, the bank contracted with the Toronto firm of Mathers and Haldenby, working with Beck and Eadie (a firm formed by two of Lyle's assistants who had worked on the project with him from the beginning). Lyle's essential massing was retained, as was the accent on verticality that architectural historian Geoffrey Hunt has identified in the original plans: buttress-like piers extending from the base up the tower, and rising in a sheer ascent before the building terminates in setbacks toward the upper stories. The decorative elements that Lyle had planned for the building, however, were greatly simplified: anything curved, angled or arched was straightened, with stark bas-reliefs of Greek gods at the top of the tower base substituting for the grillwork, carvings, finials and statuary of the original plan. The result is a building whose two-decade evolution is discernable on its face.

Chapter 22

EATON'S COLLEGE STREET

1928 / Partially built

I N 1869, IRISH IMMIGRANT TIMOTHY Eaton opened a dry goods store at Yonge and Queen. It employed four clerks and had a street frontage of twenty-four feet. Just shy of sixty years later, the T. Eaton Company Ltd. announced construction of the world's largest department store at Yonge and College — part of one of the planet's largest buildings.

The College Street project had its genesis in the years before the First World War. By that time the Eaton's Queen Street store had become a Toronto institution. But the Eaton's board of directors, chaired by Timothy's successor Sir John Eaton, was convinced that the city's central shopping district would eventually be pulled northward as the city expanded. And it wanted Eaton's to be at the heart of it: Carlton Street.

For it was on Carlton, and not College, that Eaton's intended to build its new flagship store. With this goal in mind, agents for Eaton's went on a massive buying spree in 1910,

in one three-day period, purchasing over 75 percent of the land in the two blocks north of Carlton between Yonge and Church. The speed was necessary in order to get deals signed before neighbours could talk with each other and figure out that a massive land assembly was underway — which would inevitably drive up prices. For the same reason, all the purchases were handled through agents, and the involvement of Eaton's was a closely guarded secret. So much so that the land became known as the "Mystery Block." In 1912 the Toronto *World* become privy to the contents of architectural plans held up at customs; it announced that it was Eaton's that had been buying in the Yonge / Carlton area, and that it would be building a ten-storey building. This report had to compete with other speculation, however, including that the land had been bought by the CPR for a new railway terminal (with a six-thousand-foot-long tunnel connecting it to the CPR's tracks at Summerhill). Despite the *World*'s speculation over the role of Eaton's, the company's ownership was not confirmed until its College Street store was set to open twenty years later.

Even before the start of the Great War, Eaton's had acquired the block on the south side of College between Yonge and Bay, and now planned to build its store on the western site (although this fact too remained a closely guarded secret until 1928). The centrality of this new location had won out over earlier concerns that down-market Terauley Street (later the northern continuation of Bay Street) would not provide an appropriate frontage for a first-class department store. In 1915, the federal government's war-time request that no large building projects be undertaken put construction on hold, although in the years immediately following, Eaton's continued to plan and seek municipal approvals for an eight-storey building that could later be increased to fifteen storeys. As for the original Carlton Street block, Eaton's offered it to its old Queen Street rival, Simpson's, in the belief that proximity was good for both of them. Simpson's declined, opting instead to expand its existing Queen Street operations westward. (Eaton's continued to bank the land, but would have no trouble finding other purchasers once its College Street plans were known: among other buildings, Maple Leaf Gardens and the Toronto Hydro Building would eventually rise on the surplus Carlton lands. See chapter 24.)

Finally, in July 1928 — almost twenty years after its initial three-day land rush — Eaton's announced its plans to build a seven-storey, 600,000-square-foot building on the College Street site. Illustrations in the daily newspapers showed essentially the building we know today as College Park. This news alone was considered significant. Then, in November, Eaton's made an astonishing announcement: the College Street structure announced five months earlier, and now beginning to be built, would be just the start of a phased development that would even-

tually fill the entire block between Yonge and what was now called Bay, stretching from College south to Hayter. The result would be one of the largest building complexes in the world, with over four million square feet of space, including almost three million square feet of retail sales space. Only Rockefeller Centre, then in the planning stages, would have been bigger. Anticipating this later development, the first phase of the complex would now extend along its full College and Yonge Street frontages, albeit in truncated one- and two-storey form.

When completed, the project would be dominated by a 670-foot, thirty-two-storey tower (Figs. 22-1, 22-2a, 22-2b). Ross and Macdonald of Montreal, in conjunction with the Toronto firm of Sproatt and Rolph, were the architects. During the same period, this team was also working on the Royal York Hotel and, indeed, one can see a kinship between the completed hotel and the unbuilt Eaton's tower — in massing and roof treatment — the former's chateau chimney substituting for the latter's terminating beacon.

There can be no doubt that Eaton's genuinely intended to build a tower. For one thing, it actually bought the Manitoba quarry where the building's Tyndall limestone was quarried, in order to ensure an adequate future supply. And the foundations for a tower were constructed: in 1981, the development of the College Park underground garage necessitated the removal of sixteen foundation pillars, each ten feet in diameter, extending thirty feet down to bedrock — all under a one-storey building. Even so, the plans remained vague at best. In September 1929 it was reported that the department store was considering moving the tower from the centre of the complex. The idea now was that it would be pushed northward, so that it would rise from the College Street facade. Although the tower as originally planned appeared imposing in the perspective circulated the previous year, it must have become apparent

Drawing of Proposed New Store
of The T. Eaton Co. Limited, Toronto

In block bounded by Yonge, College, Bay and Hayter Streets, as it will appear when complete.

The erection of this great structure will cover a period of years.

DIMENSIONS are

Yonge St. frontage . 500 ft.   Bay St. frontage . . 506 ft.
College St. frontage . 661 ft.   Hayter St. frontage . 664 ft.
Height of tower . 670 ft.
Section indicated in foreground now under construction.

Fig. 22-1. This card was produced by Eaton's in November of 1928 to announce the 670-foot tower that would eventually rise from its College Street location, then under construction. [Archives of Ontario, F 229-162-0-323; used with permission of Sears Canada Inc.]

that because of its location in the centre of the site, the tower as proposed would all but disappear for people actually standing outside the new building. Modifications to the steel work in the first phase were undertaken so that this shift could be accommodated. Internal company correspondence suggests that indeed, the entire building had been over-engineered to accommodate a tower for which little more than an eye-catching drawing and model had been prepared.

Wherever the tower was to end up, the Depression spelled an end to any thoughts of its near-term construction. Originally, the idea had been to move all Toronto operations to College Street. The later decision to keep the Queen Street operations open, however (partially for fear that College would be too far for lunchtime purchases by downtown office workers) removed any imperative to continue the College Street scheme. Certainly no work appears to have been done in furtherance of it. Even internal

Figs. 22-2a (left), 22-2b (right). Two earlier perspectives by the architectural firms of Ross and Macdonald and Sproatt and Rolph. The firms were collaborating on the Royal York Hotel at the same time. The similarities are evident. [Archives of Ontario, F 229-500-2-57; used with permission of Sears Canada Inc.]

suggestions of completing the building to seven storeys on the full site went nowhere. After the Second World War, the city's prestige retail area did move northward, as Eaton's had anticipated. But it was to Bloor, not College Street. The awe-inspiring scheme announced in 1928 was a dead letter. Today, the truncated pilasters on the southern portion of the Yonge Street facade give silent testimony that this is a building awaiting a future that will never come.

While one can lament the loss of the grand Eaton's tower, the building we are actually left with remains one of Toronto's architectural highlights. Its dignified "modern classic" facades and spectacular art deco interiors, culminating in the seventh-floor Round Room and Auditorium (now operated as the Carlu, after their designer, Jacques Carlu) are an irreplaceable contribution to the urbanity of the city. This is apart from the legacy of the improvements to the public realm made possible by the land assemblies of Eaton's: the widened streets and sidewalks all around the new store (in the case of Carlton, extending even east of Church), the straightening of the Bay/College

Fig. 22-3. An early plan for the first phase of the Eaton's College Street store. Ultimately the bulk of the complex was shifted to the northeast corner of the site. The project never got beyond its initial phase. [Archives of Ontario, F 229-500-2-57; used with permission of Sears Canada Inc.]

intersection, and the removal in 1931 of the half-block jog between College and Carlton to create a continuous east-west street. These too are a significant physical legacy of a project that lives mostly in imagination.

Chapter 23

VICTORY BUILDING

1929 / Partially built

BAYVIEW GHOST

1959 / Partially built

TWO BUILDINGS, STARTING OUT LIFE thirty years apart, gained notoriety not as finished works but as unfinished shells. For almost eight years in Depression-era Toronto, the abandoned husk of a nineteen-storey skyscraper served as concrete evidence of the economic devastation of the Depression, and a daily reminder that despite the lyrics of the song, happy days were not here again. At the end of the booming 1950s, it wasn't lack of money that left the Hampton Court Apartments — better known as the "Bayview Ghost" — half-finished throughout the 1960s and 1970s, but lack of agreement, a twenty-two-year stalemate between the landowners and the municipality.

Both buildings spent years as deserted hulks, but their stories had very different endings.

Construction started on the Victory Building at 80 Richmond Street West in the summer of 1929. A number of office buildings had risen in the downtown core in the previous few years, but the Victory Building stood out from the pack. It would be the first air-conditioned rental office building in the country. And, unlike most skyscrapers of the era, its frame would not be of structural steel, but of reinforced concrete. In fact, at twenty-six storeys, it was promoted as the tallest "all-concrete" structure in the British Empire. The exterior styling was as up-to-date as the engineering. The building's architects, Baldwin and Greene, had designed two other recently constructed downtown towers, the Central Building, at Richmond east of Bay, and the Concourse Building, at Adelaide and Sheppard. Both were unabashedly modernistic, but the Victory Building would be the jazziest of the lot (Fig. 23-1). Twenty storeys rising straight up from the street, the upward thrust of the building emphasized by the grouping of the windows into vertical columns. These columns of windows were

OCCUPY THEATRE SITE

This is an architect's perspective, drawn by Colonel E. L. Thomson of the Victory building, which is now in course of construction at 80 Richmond St. W. This 26-storey skyscraper will cost two million dollars. The unusual design is by Baldwin and Greene, architects, and is based on a conception by Henry Falk, builder of many of Toronto's downtown structures.

separated by piers of tan brick. From the twentieth floor, the piers would step back to create a dramatic ziggurat, providing a distinctive and modern crowning element, reflected in the ziggurat design on the cast concrete panel above each window.

Construction progressed quickly. Within four months, the concrete frame had reached the nineteenth floor. But the stock market crash changed everything. As the economy cratered, few ventures would have had a dimmer outlook than a speculative office building offering 125,000 square feet of high-end commercial space, especially since at least six new office buildings had opened in the financial district in 1929 alone, making an unprecedented amount of space available in a drastically shrunken market. Within a month of Black Tuesday, it was obvious that work had stopped. The developer's spokesman admitted only to a slowdown. The problem, he told the press, was that the Victory Building was actually *too* successful. Construction had progressed so quickly that it had got ahead of the timetable on which the mortgage lender was committed to advance funds. Work had simply slowed down so it could get back in line with the planned construction schedule. The building would be ready for occupancy by spring 1930. Advertisements seeking investors told a different story (Fig. 23-2).

January 1930 saw an official halt to all work on the project. Nineteen storeys of concrete structure had been completed, with brickwork finished up to the seventeenth floor. But there was simply no money to continue. And so the Victory Building sat (Fig. 23-3). An announcement almost two years later that a new developer would complete the building

Fig. 23-1. A rendering of the original design for the Victory Building, as published in the *Toronto Daily Star*. The upper six floors, with their dramatic ziggurat effect, would never be built. But the ziggurat design is reflected in panels that can be seen on the building to this day. [Toronto Public Library]

came to nothing. By the spring of 1932, the city architect was concerned that the scaffolding and wooden forms on the abandoned project had become a safety hazard. With the original venture insolvent, the job of making the site safe fell to the city. In 1933, a trustee stepped in to try to sell the structure on behalf of the shareholders and mortgagee, but no satisfactory offers were received. Nor were there offers in 1934 or 1935.

Finally, in 1936, seven years after work had ceased, the building was sold in a court-approved sale for a reported $110,000 (plus $5,000 to pay off the construction liens). The new owner's plans were to add an additional four floors, resulting in twenty-three storeys in total. It ended up costing $800,000 to complete the structure. Even so, the building topped out at only twenty storeys, not twenty-three — much less the twenty-six that had been planned when construction began. The ziggurat motifs above the windows are there to this day, but the Victory Building never did get the art deco crown they were meant to reflect. Still, it was open to receive tenants on April 1, 1937 — the first new office tower since the start of the Depression. And at that point, that was victory enough.

———

In October 1959, thirty years after construction started on the Victory Building, a permit was issued for a structure that would become a contentious landmark in the Don Valley for the next twenty-two years. The building was the first half of a planned $1.5-million apartment complex to be known as the Hampton Court Apartments. Here was modern living. With its location on a crest west of the Don Valley Parkway and the Bayview Extension, residents of the 210-unit complex would

Fig. 23-2. By the time this advertisement seeking investors ran in the *Globe and Mail*, in December 1929, all work had stopped on the Victory Building. [Toronto Public Library]

Fig. 23-3. The Victory Building, shown in this photograph from 1936, was touted as the tallest all-concrete building in the British Empire when construction began in 1929. Its nineteen-storey shell sat unfinished for seven years. [City of Toronto Archives Series 372, Sub-series 1, Item 1410]

enjoy wide-open views from their balconies overlooking the valley. There would even be a pool and a putting green.

At least that was the plan. To say that not everyone shared in the vision would be an understatement. Six days after the permit had been issued, East York council resolved not to supply services to the site, and asked the province not to approve the plan of subdivision required for the project. Council's view was that the land was intended for a greenbelt and the permit had been issued in error. Residents of the adjacent Governor's Bridge neighbourhood, at the eastern edge of Rosedale, were vehemently opposed to the introduction of the apartment buildings into their low-density area and kept effective pressure on the borough not to back down.

The building's owners went ahead with construction anyway. But with the uncertainty over municipal approvals, work stopped by the end of 1960, leaving a white-brick, seven-storey shell of a 105-unit apartment building (Fig. 23-4). In 1961, East York council re-zoned the land for single-family housing. The borough's reeve blamed Metro for the whole Bayview Ghost fiasco, alleging that Metro had caused confusion by designating the land as parkland, but then redirecting the route of the Bayview Extension for the purpose of making the parcel more developable. Ratepayers' call for a judicial inquiry into the matter were rendered practically moot when the Ontario Municipal Board refused to consider East York's re-zoning of the site until the legality of the existing construction had been sorted out. The board referred the matter to the Court of Appeal for a ruling. The problem was, the municipality and the landowners couldn't agree on a statement of facts to put before the court. So there was no ruling from the court, and the OMB held the zoning matter in abeyance. The project was now in legal as well as physical limbo.

Years passed. Diefenbaker, Camelot, the British Invasion, the Centennial celebrations, Trudeaumania, men on the moon and Watergate all came and went. The Bayview

Fig. 23-4. The Bayview Ghost sat in legal limbo for twenty-two years, becoming an accidental landmark in the process. [City of Toronto Archives, Series 577, Item 114]

Ghost continued to haunt its site overlooking the valley. Then, in 1975, new developers came with a different proposal, for 2,500 units in two twelve-storey apartment buildings, plus an additional 1,200 townhouse units. Needless to say, the prospect of 3,200 units wasn't particularly saleable with a municipality and ratepayers that had been outraged at the prospect of 105. Instead of the re-zoning requested, in 1979 the landowners got a special by-law ordering demolition of the Bayview Ghost and special provincial legislation backing up the by-law.

In 1981, a county court judge ruled that East York could demolish the twenty-two-year-old landmark, but had to do so at its own expense. By then the OMB had approved 444 units for the site, which was later reduced to sixty-six by the Ontario cabinet. With that number, which presumably made no one particularly happy, the matter had essentially been resolved. East York Mayor Alan Redway swang the first pass of the wrecking ball on October 30, 1981, in a ceremony marking the start of demolition. The timing was perfect for the banishment of a ghost: the day before Halloween.

Chapter 24

TORONTO HYDRO TOWER

1931 / Partially built

TORONTO HYDRO'S TEN-STOREY head office building at 14 Carlton Street has served as the company's headquarters for over three quarters of a century (Fig. 24-1). Praised when it opened in 1933 as "one of the outstanding architectural achievements of recent years," Chapman and Oxley's limestone structure still conveys an austere vigour that seems particularly suited to the headquarters of an electrical utility. Although it has suffered some indignities (art deco grillwork was removed from its first-floor windows), as architectural historian Patricia McHugh has written, "Even today's glassy towers are little match for the smoothness of its meticulously laid limestone face, sleekly graced with moderne bas-reliefs and four female heads peering down precipitously over the sidewalk …"

Chapman and Oxley were a natural choice to design the building. They had a solid record of public commissions at the Canadian National Exhibition (see chapter 28), and had recently been retained to design the new Queen's Park Crescent addition to the 1914 Royal Ontario Museum building that backs onto Philosopher's Walk (interestingly, the building they produced for the ROM would also feature four downward-gazing figures, though smaller, just above the main entrance). More important, in the previous few years, the firm had shown itself adept at cutting-edge skyscraper design, with a number of towers in the downtown core. For Toronto Hydro, this last fact would have been particularly important, because it was a tower that the company set out to build at Carlton and Yonge.

When the Toronto Hydro Electric Commission became interested in the Yonge/Carlton intersection as the site for its new headquarters in 1930, the stock market had already crashed. As a public body, however, Toronto Hydro went ahead with its construction plans as a relief project, purchasing the land from Eaton's in 1931 (see chapter 22). Apart from the traffic benefits, the realignment of College and Carlton into a continuous east-west thoroughfare that year had the decided

Fig. 24-1. The head office of the Toronto Hydro-Electric Commission occupied a commanding site at Yonge and Carlton. The building as it stands today was intended as the base for an art deco skyscraper. [City of Toronto Archives, Fonds 1231, Item 1662]

advantage of placing Hydro's new lot at the termination of a newly created vista, when one looked eastward from College. At the heart of what was shaping up as Toronto's new prestige commercial district — Eaton's had opened its College Street store the year before, and Maple Leaf Gardens would open by year's end — it would be the perfect place for an office tower.

Although the company took an optimistic stance in 1930 when it decided to build, by the time construction actually started in 1932, even a monopoly couldn't avoid the devastation of the Depression. In 1931, Hydro's revenues dropped

for the first time ever. In 1932 it actually ran a deficit of over $300,000, a figure that reached almost half a million dollars in 1933. As a result, when tenders were let in the summer of 1932, it was for a ten-storey building. The building was engineered, however, so that a twenty-storey tower addition could be added later.

Certainly Toronto Hydro was not the only landowner in the area abandoning or scaling back its building plans because of the economy. There was no longer talk of an Eaton's tower across the street, and two other towers planned for the area, a fourteen-storey office tower on Yonge south of Carlton and a new office tower for the Canadian Bank of Commerce on the northwest corner of Yonge and College never materialized. Even the more modest buildings in the area that actually got built are often scaled-back versions of their intended selves: the three-storey Alcazar Hotel at Jarvis and Gerrard (now the Econo Lodge) lost four storeys from drawing board to realization, and the Monetary Times Building at Church and Gerrard (now part of Ryerson University) lost two. Farther west, the new Ontario Hydro head office on University Avenue, which had been announced as a twenty-storey tower at the same time that Toronto Hydro's building was announced, opened its doors as a mere six-storey building in 1935. In contrast to the Toronto Hydro Building, however, an additional ten storeys would be seamlessly added a decade later (Fig. 24-2). (This wouldn't be the last time Ontario Hydro would modify its building plans on University Avenue. See Fig. 24-3.)

Looking at Alfred Chapman's design for the Toronto Hydro Building, you wouldn't know that anything more was intended. But Chapman himself felt that those imposing female heads, a horizontal motif that served to cap off the building as constructed, appeared "somewhat abruptly terminated" outside their ultimate context. Likewise "[t]he long hall to the elevators, which at present would seem to be a defect in the plan, will, it is hoped, find its full justification and reason in the next extension of the building." As Chapman explained that extension, the existing building would be enlarged northward at its current height toward Wood Street. This expanded structure would form the base for a tower that would thrust twenty storeys upwards, resulting in a thirty-storey landmark structure. The tower would not span the whole of the existing Carlton facade, but would be set back to the east and west, rising from the area demarcated by those heads — a motif which itself would be repeated on the tower. In this way, the general massing of the building would seem

Fig. 24-2. Sproatt and Rolph's Ontario Hydro Building on University Avenue (now the Princess Margaret Hospital) was also scaled back because of the Depression. After the war, an additional ten storeys would be added. Note the intention in this drawing (never carried out) to eradicate the beaux arts facade of George W. Gouinlock's original Ontario Hydro building to the south. [Archives of Ontario, C 292-1-0-333, K-605]

Fig. 24-3. This design for Ontario Hydro's final head office building at University and College was announced in September 1968. By Gordon S. Adamson and Associates and Shore and Moffat and Partners, it differs radically from the building that opened in 1975, by Kenneth R. Cooper. [Clara Thomas Archives and Special Collections, York University, Toronto Telegram Photograph Collection, ASC04287]

consistent with that of Chapman and Oxley's 1929 Toronto Daily Star Building on King Street West, demolished to make way for First Canadian Place (Fig. 24-4).

The Yonge/College/Carlton intersection didn't become Toronto's new high-rent business location, of course. Eaton's closed shop on College in 1976 and Maple Leaf Gardens has sat silent since 1999. But the Toronto Hydro Building (now the Richard R. Horkins Building), still serves as the head office of Toronto's hydroelectric utility all these years later. Those four female heads continue to look down on Carlton as they have done since 1933, waiting for the sisters that, in Alfred Chapman's vision, would make it all come together.

Fig. 24-4. Chapman and Oxley's Toronto Daily Star Building (demolished) gives an indication of what might have arisen on Carlton Street. [City of Toronto Archives, Series 1057, Item 2037]

Chapter 25

WILLOWDALE TELECOMMUNICATIONS TOWER

1966 / Unbuilt

YOU'RE SIPPING A GLASS OF PINOT grigio, enjoying a gourmet lunch. It's a clear day, and you can see Niagara Falls in the distance — one of the advantages of dining in the revolving restaurant high atop Toronto's landmark telecommunications tower.

You know, the one in Willowdale.

It may seem bizarre now, but for several years in the 1960s this was a future that a lot of people assumed was imminent. A future that would see Yonge and Sheppard, and not the waterfront, as the site of Toronto's famous tower.

To understand the origins of the idea, you have to place yourself back in North York when the idea was first proposed. In 1966 the municipality had finally shed its township status, with its rural connotations, and become a borough, now undeniably part of Metropolitan Toronto. It had grown from a conglomeration of villages to the fourth-largest municipality in the country, with almost 383,000 residents. By 1966, North York had spent a number of years as the country's fastest-growing municipality, with 1965 seeing thirty thousand new residents, the largest number yet. In each of the last several years, an average of four thousand new apartment units had been added to the municipality's housing stock. Yorkdale, the country's largest shopping centre, had opened in 1964. York University, which had become independent from the University of Toronto in 1965, was busy developing five hundred acres of fields into a modern new campus at Steeles and Keele. It was an era of unbelievable growth, transformation and possibility. But, despite all this development, North York had no focal point, no "there" — something the planners were calling a "metropolitan subcentre," but everyone else was calling a downtown.

Earlier in the decade, North York's planners had realized that merely serving as a bedroom community for the City of Toronto was not ideal. The hundreds of thousands of people who lived in the township should be able to benefit from the urban experience — its arts, culture and commerce — without

Fig. 25-1. North York reeve (and later mayor) James Service. He believed that nineteen acres of surplus cemetery land in Willowdale could become the heart of a high-density downtown, served by the subway. [Clara Thomas Archives and Special Collections, York University, Toronto Telegram Photograph Collection, ASC04393]

having to head to downtown Toronto. In 1963, the township's staff prepared a plan for a new downtown. A sports stadium, community college, government buildings, shopping centre and apartment buildings would line both sides of a two-mile stretch of Yonge Street in Willowdale, between Sheppard and Finch. The Yonge Street location made sense, since it was expected that after the completion of the Bloor-Danforth subway, the Yonge line would be extended northward to Sheppard and beyond.

The idea of a civic centre for North York was championed wholeheartedly by James Service when he became reeve in 1965 (Fig. 25-1). Growth was an undeniable fact, and Service was a firm believer that North York should welcome it and direct it. In February of 1966, consulting planners John B. Parkin Associates presented a conceptual plan to council for a $600-million civic centre redevelopment in the Yonge-Sheppard area. Liking what it saw, council commissioned the firm, along with Murray V. Jones and Associates, Ltd. (who would also work on the Metro Centre and Harbour City plans, see chapters 6 and 7) to prepare a detailed study. The planners' first task was to confirm that the Yonge Street corridor (and not some other spot, such as Don Mills or Yorkdale) was the right place for a new downtown. If they decided it wasn't, no further work would be done.

With the Yonge location a go, North York paid $2.3 million for 18.8 acres of land west of Yonge, between Sheppard and Finch in September 1966. It was an unused part of the York Memorial Cemetery. On this surplus cemetery land, Mayor Service (the title "reeve" had disappeared with township status) envisioned the development of modern high-rise apartment and office buildings, hotels and theatres. A place that would have "the real excitement of the city," a downtown "where the average Mrs. North York can forget the drudgery of being a housewife." Not everyone shared the vision. Some councillors questioned whether a downtown would really

develop one-and-half miles north of the 401. A scheme that Service said could be compared to Trafalgar Square, Rockefeller Centre or the newly opened Nathan Phillips Square, critics derided as "cemetery square."

A year later, in October 1967, the Parkin-Murray group presented the second part of their study. In what was described as a "hush-hush" meeting with civic politicians and bureaucrats, the firms submitted plans for a modern, high-density city centre. In their scenarios, Willowdale's population would increase by sixty thousand people, and twenty thousand new jobs would be added to the area. In addition to theatre-auditoriums, an art gallery/museum and a non-denominational community church, the plan contained two signature elements, which had been retained from the conceptual schemes that had been shown to council the previous year. The first was a city hall that straddled Yonge Street. Cars driving on Yonge would actually drive under the building, which would be five or six storeys high. The second signature element would rise on the west side of Yonge as a companion to the new city hall: a soaring telecommunications tower. The tower was described for planning purposes as being between six hundred and thirteen hundred feet high, but accompanying drawings and contemporary press coverage assumed a structure that would be one thousand feet high. It would have a revolving restaurant at the seven-hundred-foot level, with three hundred feet of antenna on top of that. With these two landmark structures, its new board of education building and a civic square, North York would finally have a city centre worthy of the name. Joined by residential and commercial high-rises over the next twenty years, the result would be a downtown as modern as tomorrow (Fig. 25-2).

While North York would presumably build its own city hall, it did not intend to get into the telecommunications business. The idea was that the tower would be built on a portion of the land that the borough had bought from the

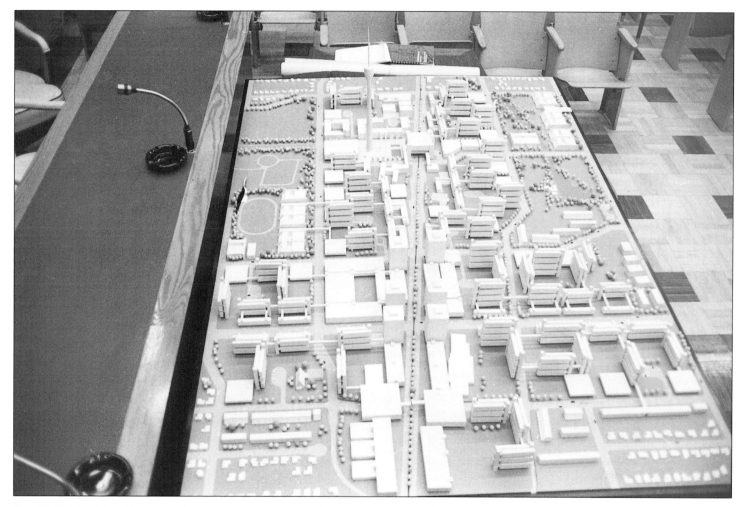

Fig. 25-2. North York's planned downtown was as modern as tomorrow. Cars would drive under the new city hall, which would straddle Yonge Street. Rising beside it would be Metro Toronto's landmark telecommunications tower. [Clara Thomas Archives and Special Collections, York University, Toronto Telegram Photograph Collection]

cemetery, which would be leased out to the tower's builders. The builders would sub-lease space to ten radio and six television stations, including what the newspapers referred to as "Ontario's proposed new educational TV system" — TV Ontario. Bell Canada was being courted as chief tenant, but it

needed to move in by May 1970. With this timeline in mind back in 1966, immediately after Parkin's conceptual plan had been presented to it, council had cleared an early hurdle by obtaining Ontario Municipal Board approval for a long-term lease by the borough of the land on which the tower would be built. In February 1968, the consultants released their final plan. The telecommunications tower that had been leaked in the "hush-hush" meeting of the previous year continued to be central to it. Projected to cost $6 million, construction was expected to begin in 1969 in order to achieve a 1971 completion date.

In July of 1968, the *Toronto Daily Star* was reporting that a syndicate headed by Bell and the CBC was looking at constructing the tower. The problem was, said the newspaper, it was also looking at other sites in Metro, including what would later be known as the Metro Centre site, then being actively planned (see chapter 6). North York alderman Murray Chusid called the tower plan "pie in the sky." But Mayor Service remained confident: "If it's pie in the sky then he'll be eating it in the sky, in the revolving restaurant on the tower." The prospect of that happening became more distant when the CBC announced that it preferred the Metro Centre location. Still, Service remained optimistic that the national broadcaster would come around, touting the fact that the North York tower could be ready sooner and cheaper (a million dollars and two years had now been dropped from the completion forecast). By January 1969, the CBC had confirmed its choice of the Metro Centre location (see Fig. 6-4), but North York continued to forge ahead with its plans, choosing a development consortium from among twelve proposals and passing the necessary zoning by-laws. The zoning was approved by the OMB in March, despite the objections of ratepayers' groups who feared that the tower would spark redevelopment in the area — which is exactly what it was intended to do.

A year later, work had still not started, and the plans continued to morph. In February, the North York planning board approved a "slim" fifty-nine-storey office building, three storeys higher than the TD Tower, then Metro's tallest. It would be topped by a four-hundred-foot telecommunications mast. A revolving restaurant was still planned, now at the 740-foot

mark. In August, the developer proposed to add a hotel, shopping centre, high-rise apartments and other uses to the mix. The telecommunications tower had gone from being the point of the exercise, to merely an add-on. Eventually, it disappeared entirely as the project fizzled.

When North York council again looked at developing its civic centre three years later, construction had already started on what would become the CN Tower. North York's new consultants concluded that the 1960s plans had been too grandiose. Not only was there no talk of a telecommunications tower, the consultants felt that, in fact, none of the new civic buildings should be over six storeys, and that monumentality in the area was to be avoided. Although the high-density node that James Service envisioned in 1966 has subsequently come to pass, there's no trace of the space-age telecom tower that was meant to be the start and centre of it all. That portion of the plan, at least, continues to remain an ephemeral vision, broadcast from an imagined future.

Chapter 26

BAY-ADELAIDE CENTRE

1988 / Built to different plans

FOR FIFTEEN YEARS, A PARCEL OF land on Adelaide, just east of Bay, was the site of a six-storey structure that Torontonians affectionately called the "stump" (Fig. 26-1). The stump was actually part of an elevator shaft. Along with an 1,100-car underground parking garage, it was all that was ever built of the original proposal for the Bay-Adelaide Centre, an imposing fifty-seven-storey office tower cut down by the recession of the early 1990s. While the stump came to be regarded as an innocuous curiosity, the building it was meant to be part of was probably the most contentious development proposal of the 1980s construction boom.

The story of the Bay-Adelaide Centre began when the Hudson's Bay Company acquired Simpson's department stores in the late 1970s. Markborough Properties, the Bay's real estate arm, began assembling land to the south of the Queen Street Simpson's store, in the area bounded by Bay, Yonge, Richmond and Adelaide. By the late 1980s, it had assembled three development parcels over three separate blocks. With development partner Trizec Equities, it sought approval for a fifty-seven-storey, 1.7-million-square-foot office tower on Adelaide Street, on the block directly north of the new sixty-eight-storey Scotia Plaza. Though not as tall as that tower, the granite and glass Bay-Adelaide Centre — designed by the same architects, the Webb Zerafa Menkes Housden Partnership — would still have cut a distinctive figure on the skyline, with gabled facades capped off by a peaked roof and spire. North of the tower, between Temperance and Richmond, the developers proposed a ten- to twelve-storey office building (Fig. 26-2). Smaller buildings would incorporate historic facades on Yonge Street, resulting in a complex of nearly two million square feet of new commercial space, a place where over six thousand people were expected to report to work each day.

Because the developers were seeking a landmark building, they proposed to redistribute the density that was permitted

Fig. 26-1. For fifteen years, the "stump" occupied the site of the Bay-Adelaide Centre, becoming a Toronto landmark in the process. This view is from Temperance Street. Test panels for the building's granite and glass curtain walls can be seen affixed to the back of the National Building, on the far right, just above the final lamp post.

Fig. 26-2. The original proposal for the Bay-Adelaide Centre. The project was shelved indefinitely when the bottom fell out of the office market. [WZMH Architects]

over their holdings to allow for the construction of the fifty-seven-storey tower on the southernmost parcel. Without the redistribution, they would have been limited to twenty-five storeys. They also wanted to build only office and retail space, but the by-law required that some residential space be developed as well. Council was agreeable to granting these concessions, but at a price. The developer had to preserve the historic Yonge Street commercial buildings and the Simpson's store at Yonge and Queen, extend the PATH system through the site to the Sheraton Centre, via Simpson's, dedicate a half-acre park and $5 million to build it (the result was Cloud Park off Richmond Street) and place Simpson's Richmond Street truck loading bays underground. Finally, in addition to the provision of daycare facilities and the standard requirements for things like public art and street improvements, the city required the developer to provide a site for 561 units of social housing (or its monetary equivalent). The developer met this last requirement by giving the city the Sears warehouse on Mutual Street (it would later become the Merchandise Lofts after the city flipped it as part of a subsequent deal).

Council considered the Bay-Adelaide Centre's final approvals at a special meeting in October 1988. It was a rough ride. There had been growing dissatisfaction among some councillors and the public with the "bonusing" approach by which the city granted extra height and density to developers in exchange for public benefits such as social housing. Two other prominent developments of the 1980s office boom, BCE Place and Scotia Plaza, had resulted from this process but, by the time the Bay-Adelaide Centre came along, criticisms of "let's-make-a-deal" planning were getting serious traction. As a result, council debate on the Bay-Adelaide Centre went till three o'clock in the morning. Although the development was ultimately approved (in council's last act before the November municipal elections), the matter was far from settled. It became a lightning rod for opposition to the status quo in the planning process. And there was a lot of lightning. A grass-roots anti-development movement called Reform Toronto endorsed a slate of seven candidates in the election, five of whom won office. The incoming council now had a majority of so-called reform councillors intent on changing the planning approvals system. A review of the Bay-Adelaide Centre was top of their list.

The new council hired an independent consultant to report on the bonusing aspects of the Bay-Adelaide approval. The report concluded that the city's planning process had not been abused in the Bay-Adelaide deal and that, in fact, the developer would have to provide about $80 million in benefits to the city in order to secure additional building rights worth between $63 and $74 million. With council satisfied, construction on the complex began in 1989, but a new threat to its completion was gaining strength: the worsening recession and the collapse in the office rental market it brought. In 1991, with the six storeys built and with structural steel and the building's sapphire-brown granite already purchased, Markborough and Trizec put construction on hold for two years. Finally, in August 1993, with an office vacancy rate in the city of 18.6 percent, they announced they were postponing the project indefinitely. The package of benefits that had been required under the bonusing agreement was the city's to keep, however.

Five years later, in 1998, the project was re-launched, with a different development consortium. WZMH Partnership stayed on as architects, and gave the building a major update (Fig. 26-3). The general massing was the same, although the building was now forty-five storeys, and there was no more ten-storey north tower. Fins of South American granite would emphasize the tower's verticality. Despite a planned 2000 opening, the failure to find a lead tenant put the project into abeyance once more.

Another eight years would pass before the next re-launch. In 2006, new owners Brookfield Properties announced that the Bay-Adelaide Centre was on again, but this time in an entirely reconceived form. Brookfield had acquired two older office buildings on Bay Street, achieving the Bay frontage that earlier versions of the project had lacked (despite its name). WZMH Partnership's new plans would see a fifty-storey, 1.1-million-square-foot tower at Bay and Adelaide, incorporating Chapman and Oxley's 1926 National Building. The Richmond-Temperance site, where the ten-storey building had been proposed in 1988, would contain a hotel-condo building. Longer-term plans called for the construction of a third tower on the eastern end of the Adelaide frontage. The three buildings would surround an urban plaza, roughly at the site of the demolished stump.

In July 2006, in a ceremony reminiscent of the one at the Bayview Ghost twenty-five years earlier (see chapter 23), Mayor David Miller took a ceremonial swing at the stump with a sledgehammer. It marked the start of demolition. After fifteen years, the stump would finally be developed: into open space.

Fig. 26-3. The 1998 proposal. [WZMH Architects]

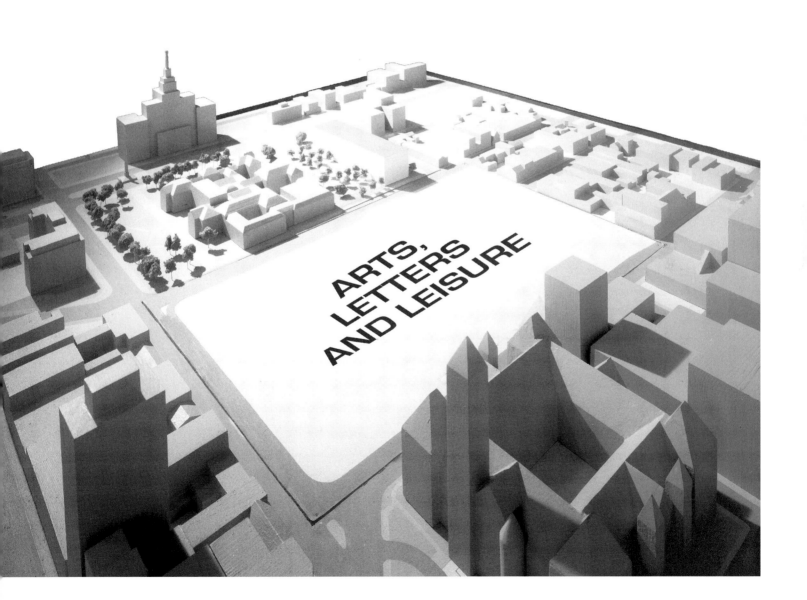

Chapter 27

UNIVERSITY OF KING'S COLLEGE

1829 / Built to different plans

SOME OF THE MOST BEAUTIFUL buildings in the city are on the University of Toronto campus. But perhaps none is more ambitious than the buildings that were proposed for Ontario's first university, the University of King's College. The story of King's College is a fascinating tale of how a small colonial town of three thousand people planned to build a university that would not have been out of place in the imperial capitals of Europe.

The central character in the story and the driving force behind the University of King's College was Rev. John Strachan, Anglican rector of the Town of York (Fig. 9-1). As early as 1815 he had written on the need for improved education in the province, including the need for a university. By 1827, after visiting England, Strachan had obtained a royal charter for Upper Canada's new university, the University of King's College. To fund his new school, Strachan was able to secure from the government a land endowment and a yearly grant of £1,000. With this financial backing in place, the college council could proceed to the next step, finding an appropriate site for the university and planning the buildings that would be built on it.

They first considered a site near the Humber River. It is intriguing to speculate on how the city's subsequent development might have differed had the Humber site not been deemed "insalubrious" by medical men, because the site that was chosen instead — the area now bounded by Bloor and College — has been shaped by the presence of post-secondary institutions ever since. Especially since part of the ultimate land grant included a tract for a grand boulevard stretching south from the building site (approximately where the provincial legislative buildings now stand) down to Lot Street (now Queen Street). This "Queen Street Avenue" or "College Avenue" as it was also called, would, of course, later become University Avenue, a fitting ceremonial approach when the legislature moved to the King's College site in the 1890s.

English architect Charles Fowler was retained to design the campus for the new building. In his book, *A Not*

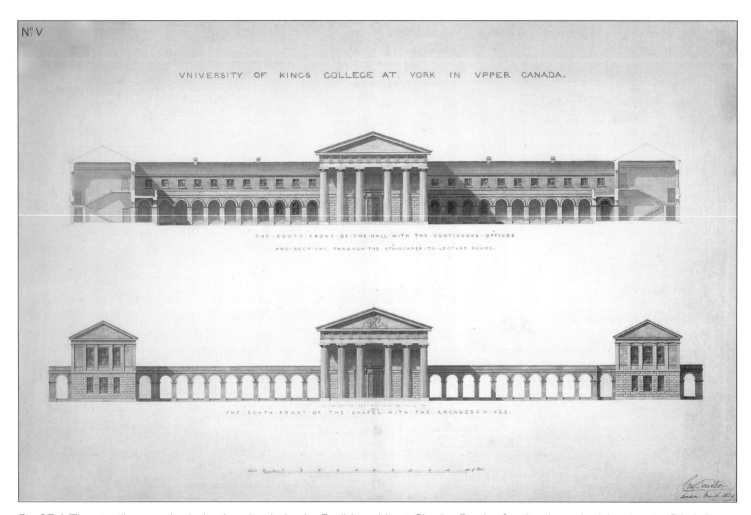

Fig. 27-1. The startling neoclassical university design by English architect Charles Fowler for the tiny colonial outpost of York. It was to sit on the site of the current provincial legislative buildings. [Archives of Ontario, C 11-438-0-1,{411}]

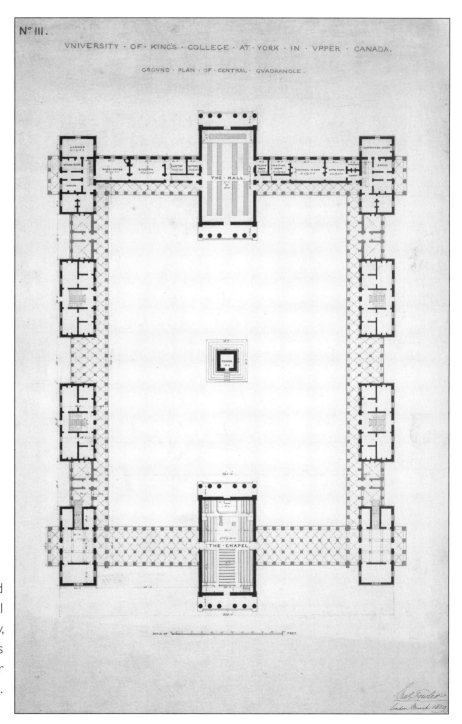

Fig. 27-2. The Anglican chapel enjoyed pride of place at the head of the central quadrangle. The full plan included secondary, open quadrangles on either side of this central quadrangle, as well as a semicircular range of professors' houses to the north. [Archives of Ontario, C 11-438-0-1,{411}]

Unsightly Building: University College and Its History, architectural historian Douglas Richardson provides the definitive account of King's College and its startlingly grand building plans. Richardson notes that Fowler and Strachan were friends, making it probable that the cleric and the architect discussed the project when Strachan was in London securing the charter. At the time, Fowler was working on London's Covent Garden Market. His King's College proposal bore a resemblance to this neoclassical project. "What Fowler offered," writes Richardson, "was in the current taste, a Neo-Classical forum of the intellect … on a scale fit for St. Petersburg" (Fig. 27-1).

The plan centred on a large quadrangle, formed by ten buildings connected by a cloister. Although Strachan's university would be open to men of all denominations, it would be an Anglican institution, whose professors would all subscribe to the Anglican faith. Fittingly, the proposed building scheme was dominated by an Anglican chapel. Across the quadrangle from the chapel, the highly symmetrical plan called for a large assembly hall of equal size (Fig. 27-2). Between these two principal spaces, a bell tower would provide a focal element for the academic community (Fig. 27-3). Outside the central quadrangle and facing it on the east and west would be two, three-sided, open quadrangles. These were likely meant to provide student accommodation. To the north, a semicircular arcade would connect residences for professors and enclose a fourth quadrangle space.

In addition to the neoclassical design, Fowler provided a neo-Gothic alternative (Fig. 27-4). Although Gothic style would become the default choice for new academic and government buildings later in the nineteenth century, it would have been a cutting-edge recommendation for a new public building in 1829.

Whether neoclassical or Gothic, it was an ambitious scheme for such a tiny colonial outpost. It was impossibly ambitious, in fact. But Fowler can be forgiven. He had never actually seen the building site. For that matter, he had never been to Upper Canada at all and would have had little idea of the colony's needs or means. The entire plan was conceived from his studio in London in what Richardson characterizes as an "abstract exercise in taste."

When Sir John Colborne became governor of Upper Canada in 1829 he put a halt to any college construction until secondary education in the province had been improved and until changes to the university's charter were made. The strictly Anglican nature of the charter (all professors had to be members of the Church of England) had proven highly contentious. Work continued on the grounds, however, and Belgian-born landscape architect André Parmentier, who during this period was practising in New York, was retained to provide the landscaping plans. In 1835, architect John Howard (who seventeen years later would design the waterfront Walks and Gardens plan for the city, see chapter 2) offered Colborne a plan for the college that was even more fantastic than Fowler's (Fig. 27-5). Howard had recently immigrated to Upper Canada from England; the King's College design was part of a series of proposals for public buildings he produced at the time for his new hometown, including a guild hall, lunatic asylum and government house. Each was more grandiose than the next. And none of them was built.

When construction did begin on King's College, it was to the designs of still another architect. In 1837, Toronto architect Thomas Young had been commissioned to adapt Fowler's plans. He replaced Fowler's four quadrangles with a single, larger quadrangle made up of four unconnected ranges of buildings, also in a neoclassical style. Construction was delayed by the Rebellion of 1837, and the political fallout from it, and by the scandal following the discovery that the college's finances had been misappropriated. In

Fig. 27-3. The bell tower was the focal point of the central quadrangle. [Archives of Ontario, C 11-438-0-1,{411}]

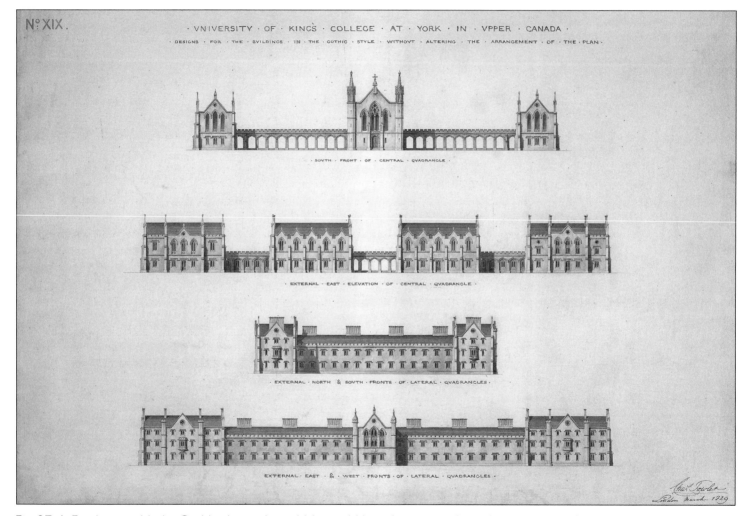

Fig. 27-4. Fowler provided a Gothic alternative, which would have been a cutting-edge suggestion for a public building in 1829.
[Archives of Ontario, C 11-438-0-1,{411}]

Fig. 27-5. John Howard's plan of 1835 was even more ambitious than Fowler's — and even more impractical. [Toronto Public Library]

June of 1842, with John (now Bishop) Strachan present, Lieutenant Governor Sir Charles Bagot laid the first stone for King's College, fifteen years after Strachan had returned from London. The building, a student residence, was in the southeast corner of what is now Queen's Park. It was intended as one of three pavilions in the southernmost range of the college.

The residence building was completed in 1843, but sat empty for two years. There were no funds remaining to build the central building that would have contained the dining and cooking facilities needed for a residence. In 1848 Strachan resigned as president and the following year the college was secularized as the University of Toronto. In 1851 Young was again retained (following a design competition) to prepare scaled-back plans for buildings for the new University of Toronto that would be incorporated into his completed King's College student residence.

They would never be built. In 1853 the United Province of Canada expropriated what would become Queen's Park in order to build parliament buildings. As things turned out, Ottawa was chosen as the site for the parliament but, by then, King's College, both the concept and the building plan, were finished. Young's ill-fated King's College building became the University Lunatic Asylum in 1856, but even this use was

Fig. 27-6. What was built of King's College. It is shown here being demolished to make way for Ontario's new parliament buildings. [Archives of Ontario, F 4436-0-0-0-58]

discontinued after the Provincial Lunatic Asylum on Queen Street was expanded in the late 1860s. King's College sat empty and neglected until 1886, when it was demolished to make way for Ontario's new parliament buildings (see chapter 8). Pictures taken during its demolition show a truly handsome and imposing structure (Fig. 27-6). It is easy to agree with Douglas Richardson when he writes that, had Young's entire program been built, it "would have provided Toronto with university buildings unmatched in North America."

Chapter 28

CNE FIFTY-YEAR PLAN

1920 / Partially built

1971 CNE MASTER PLAN

1971 / Partially built

THE PRINCES' GATES AT THE Canadian National Exhibition have become the recognized symbol of the annual fair — and a true Toronto landmark. Although the gates are impressive in their own right, they are merely the most visible vestige of a grand plan for the CNE from the 1920s that became known as the "Fifty-Year Plan."

Founded in 1879 as an agricultural fair, by 1920 the CNE had become a showcase of industrial and manufacturing marvels as well, achieving the status of the world's largest annual fair. What was needed now were fairgrounds that would do justice to the CNE's new mandates and stature, and provide a permanent rival to any fairground in the world.

The first order of business under the plan, prepared by the Toronto architectural firm of Chapman and Oxley at the request of the CNE's Plans Committee, was a major expansion of the fairgrounds themselves, both to the west and to the east (by some 1,300 feet, over to Strachan Avenue), as well as

to the south. Since the exhibition grounds bordered on Lake Ontario, the southern extension was to be accomplished by filling. On the reclaimed southern land, "Boulevard Drive" (the current Lake Shore Boulevard), would be built, providing a new connection between the city's downtown and its expanding western suburbs. This proposed lakeshore promenade had, in modified form, been part of earlier plans by the Harbour Commission.

The plans underwent several revisions, but a constant component remained monumental entrance gates on the eastern end of the fairgrounds. These triumphal gates would open to an entrance plaza that was 1,300 feet long and 225 feet wide. Two new streets would branch from the new entrance plaza, one from the north and one from the south, each continuing westward across the fairgrounds. The plaza itself would terminate in a planned "Empire Court," consisting of a semi-circle of exhibition buildings, dominated by the British building. The architect Alfred Chapman had suggested the

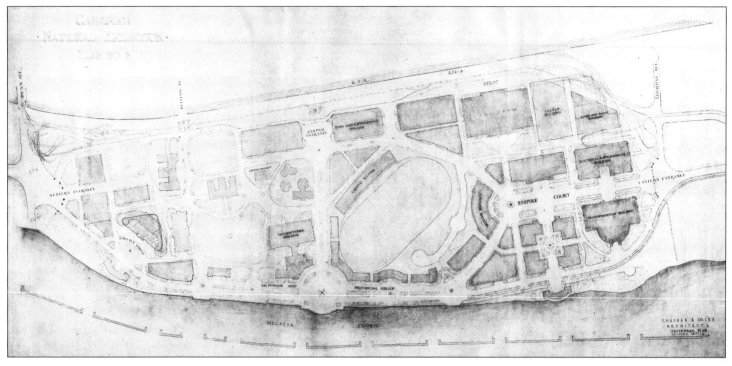

Fig. 28-1. The original concept for the eastern entrance of the CNE, showing the Empire Court that the new entrance gates would open onto. [Archives of Ontario, C 18, Acc. 48506]

idea of an Empire Court in 1924 after visiting the British Empire Exhibition at Wembley in 1924 (Fig. 28-1).

The monumentality of the new entrance plaza gave an indication of the type of building that was projected for the expanded and rationalized fairgrounds. The World's Columbian Exposition, held in Chicago in 1893, had long since set the bar for fair architecture and planning. Its precedent of classically inspired planning and architecture, with monumental yet festive buildings, was continued at subsequent World's Fairs, including the Pan American Exposition held in Buffalo 1901. The CNE's Fifty-Year Plan would fit Toronto's fairgrounds solidly in this tradition.

The Plans Committee's goal was to erect larger, grander and more permanent buildings that could serve as showcases for a number of exhibitors, grouped by theme. Although the buildings would develop over time, they were intended to have "the feeling of an organic whole." Since the Ex is a summer event, the use of courtyards, where practical, would allow exhibits in sheltered buildings, while keeping visitors close at all times to natural light and fresh air. Moreover, the punctuation of the buildings by courtyards would serve to break up what otherwise might be monotonously vast interior expanses (Fig. 28-2).

The CNE constructed several buildings according to the scheme. The Coliseum and the Pure Food Building both opened in 1922, followed two years later by the Province of

Fig. 28-2. A view of the central courtyard for Chapman and Oxley's proposed Automotive Building. Courtyards were a recommended feature for the larger exhibit buildings contemplated for the fairgrounds. [Archives of Ontario, C 18, Acc. 48506]

Ontario Building (touted at the time as the first step in a re-located Empire Court, it ended up being the last). In April of 1927, construction began on the new eastern gates, now officially named the Princes' Gates in honour of Edward, the Prince of Wales, and his brother George, who opened them together that August (Fig. 28-3).

The Fifty-Year Plan contemplated that, immediately upon entering the Princes' Gates, visitors would be flanked by two new massively scaled buildings, the Automotive Building and the Electrical and Engineering Building. The Plans Committee felt that both buildings should be built at once, in order to create a significant enough attraction to draw the CNE's visitors from their accustomed haunts and into the new eastern portion of the grounds. An examination of Alfred Chapman's original designs for both buildings illustrates how well they would have complemented the exuberance and heroic scale of the Princes' Gates.

The Automotive Building would comprise two floors, measure almost five hundred by four hundred feet, and contain a large centre court and two smaller courts (Figs. 28-4a, 28-4b). The Electrical and Engineering Building would be roughly as long as the Automotive Building, which it would face, but some one hundred feet shallower. Eight small court-yards would provide ventilation and, if required, light (Fig. 28-5). The breathtaking centrepiece of the Electrical and Engineering Building would be the Electric Tower (sometimes referred to as the Hydro Tower), rising 180 feet from the fifty-six foot base of the main building. The tower would face a main entrance court, and house a model "electrical home," theatre, restaurant and tea room (Fig. 28-6) .

The *Star Weekly*'s 1923 description of this never-built tower gives some indication of the landmark it would have become:

> And surmounting this building will be one
> of the features of the whole Exhibition,

the Hydro Tower, just one blaze of glorious light day and night. The tower will be one hundred and eighty feet high, built in delicate yet massive proportions, studded with myriad electric lamps of great power, with reflectors and mirrors and moving patterns, leaping up in the sky to bear witness to Canada's power development.

Although the Electric Tower at Exhibition Place would have been grand, it would not have been the first such tower in the area. The centrepiece of the 1901 Pan American Exposition in Buffalo had been a 375-foot-tall, illuminated "Electric Tower" surmounted by an angelic "Goddess of Light." This precedent would surely have been in Chapman and Oxley's minds in proposing their scheme for the Electrical and Engineering Building in Toronto (a "Tower of Light" would also become the centrepiece of the Philadelphia World's Fair in 1926).

In the end, the tower that the *Toronto Daily Star* had predicted would be a highlight of the fair fell victim to economics. The Electrical and Engineering Building was to be financed based on the commitments of exhibitors to sign long-term leases. While there was interest enough to proceed, savings needed to be found. In 1928, when it was announced that the building would be ready for that season's fair, the Electric Tower was nowhere to be seen in published plans. In its place was a two-hundred-foot obelisk, surmounted by a gilded figure, "typifying electrical power." In the end, under pressure from the city's board of control to reign in costs, even this shadow of 1923's Electric Tower fell to the bean-counters' pens.

The Electrical and Engineering Building was to be the last building designed for the fair by Chapman and Oxley. Although the Automotive Building, which followed it the next year, was sited according to their master plan, its architect was chosen as the result of an open competition. The pared-down

Fig. 28-3. The Princes' Gates were built in 1927 to commemorate the diamond jubilee of Confederation. They played an important part in the new monumentality that was planned for the entire CNE. [Archives of Ontario, C 18, Acc. 48506]

moderne structure that resulted was a distinct architectural break from the Princes' Gates and the Electrical and Engineering Building — and even more so from the increasingly distant worlds of Chicago in 1893 and Buffalo in 1901.

It's 1971, fifty years after the creation of the CNE's Fifty-Year Plan. A time when the CNE directors of 1920 would have expected the park's new custodians to be toasting them as they looked out at the magnificent results of their grand and far-sighted scheme.

But members of the Metro planning and parks departments were not toasting the work of that earlier generation. In fact, they did not like what they saw as they looked at

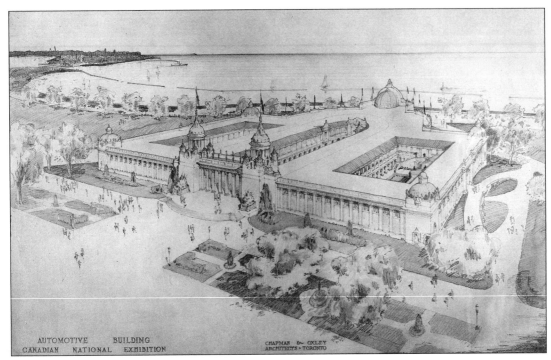

AUTOMOTIVE BUILDING
CANADIAN NATIONAL EXHIBITION

CHAPMAN & OXLEY
ARCHITECTS ~ TORONTO

Figs. 28-4a (top) and 28-4b (bottom). Two views of Chapman and Oxley's massive Automotive Building. The plans were not used. The CNE opted to hold an open competition instead. [Archives of Ontario, C 18, Acc. 48506]

AUTOMOTIVE BUILDING
CANADIAN NATIONAL EXHIBITION

CHAPMAN & OXLEY
ARCHITECTS ~ TORONTO

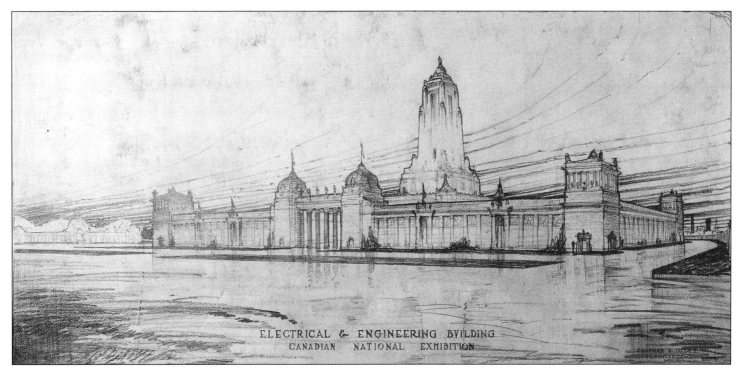

ELECTRICAL & ENGINEERING BVILDING
CANADIAN NATIONAL EXHIBITION

Fig. 28-5. A 1923 drawing of Chapman and Oxley's Electrical and Engineering Building. The last building designed for the CNE by the firm, it was built without its planned Electric Tower. [Archives of Ontario, C 18, Acc. 48506]

Exhibition Place in 1971. Where some may have seen a culturally and architecturally significant conglomeration of buildings on historic fairgrounds, they saw buildings that were hopelessly dated, "functionally obsolete." And when they looked a little farther, across Lake Shore Boulevard, they saw Ontario Place under construction. The way of the future, first revealed at Expo '67, was emerging from Lake Ontario, and it was all domes and pods on stilts.

The view was that the CNE's prognosis in this new world was poor. The remedy was outlined in a 1971 document jointly prepared by the Metro parks and planning departments titled *Proposals for the Rehabilitation of Exhibition Park.*

According to that document, what was needed was a major rethinking. Get rid of the midway. Move it off the grounds, preferably to Coronation Park, just east of the fairgrounds. Plan the grounds around themed areas, three of which — the Winter Fair Complex, the Trade Show Complex and the Sports Complex — would encircle the "Great Central Place," the heart of which would be a vast, concrete plaza known as Canada Square (Fig. 28-7). Tear down fourteen major structures (basically any pre-war building not used for the Royal Winter Fair), including the Bandshell, Automotive Building, Electrical and Engineering Building, Dufferin Gates, International Building and Ontario Government Building. For structures spared the wrecker's ball, "the exterior appearance and landscaping of these buildings should undergo extensive renewal…" And everything should be connected by an elevated minirail system.

Metro council adopted the report, with the proviso that the midway would be retained, and that Exhibition Stadium would not be demolished for the creation of the Great Central Place until a new off-site stadium had been built elsewhere. This latter amendment put a definite crimp in the master plan, which stated that, "the character of the development and activities of the Great Central Place of Exhibition Park will in the final analysis determine whether or not it is possible to restore the park

Fig. 28-6. The Electric Tower, "just one blaze of glorious light, day and night."
[Archives of Ontario, C 18, Acc. 48506]

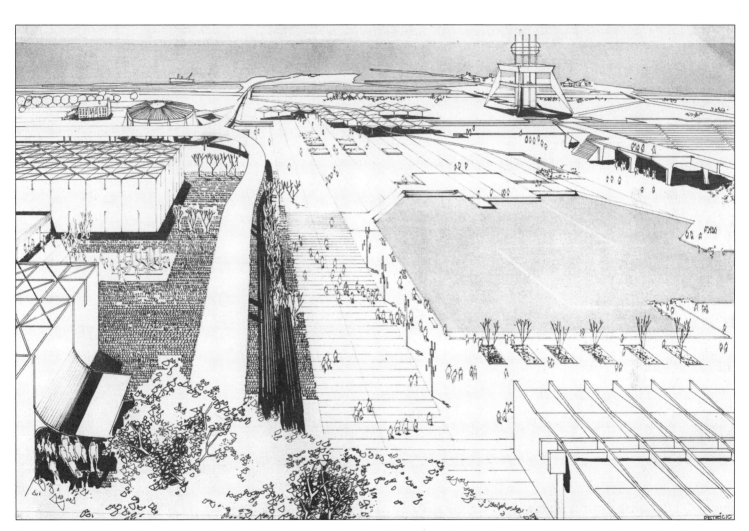

Fig. 28-7. The "Great Central Place" of the 1971 CNE master plan. The plan called for the demolition of fourteen major structures. In this illustration, the Stanley Barracks (in the upper left) is the only familiar building left standing. [City of Toronto Archives, Series 10, Item 617]

as a major institution in the life of Metropolitan Toronto." To quote the song, when Metro council decided in 1974 to retain and expand Exhibition Stadium for major league baseball, the 1971 master plan's great beginning had seen its final inning.

Although *Proposals for the Rehabilitation of Exhibition Park* had a short tenure as active policy, at least one of its proposals came to fruition. In 1972 the Electrical and Engineering Building, which the report had singled out as being in poor structural condition and under-used, was demolished (Fig. 28-8). Although the 1971 plan called for the space to

be occupied by a new "Provinces' Pavilion," it was replaced with a parking lot. The plan did admit that the statuary that surmounted the building's colonnade (by sculptor Charles D. McKechnie) was "intrinsically interesting" and that "the reuse of these statues in the landscaping and decoration of other parts of the park is highly appropriate and desirable." Today you can see some of these fragments — the debris of a collision between 1920's Fifty-Year Plan and 1971's *Proposals for the Rehabilitation of Exhibition Park* — in the Heritage Court of the Direct Energy Centre.

Fig. 28-8. The beaux arts Electrical and Engineering Building was an uncomfortable fit with the hippy era. In 1967 its ornate facade and statuary were entirely (if temporarily) covered in order to turn it into the "with-it" Century of Progress Building. It spent its last three years as the "Young Canada Building." [CNE Archives, Alexandra Studio Collection]

Chapter 29

ST. MICHAEL'S COLLEGE

1929 / Partially built

I N 1929 ST. MICHAEL'S COLLEGE AT the University of Toronto had an ambitious idea: tear down every building on its campus between Bay Street and Queen's Park Crescent and construct a breathtaking neo-Gothic complex patterned after Princeton University.

The college had grown substantially since its founding by the Basilian order of priests in 1854. Since 1910, when St. Mike's had become an arts college at U of T, the number of its students registered at the university had grown from 37 to 272. As well, in 1929 the college was embarking on a significant new academic venture in opening the Institute of Medieval Studies, which would require new space in appropriate buildings. Finally, although the college had purchased land in 1919 to expand eastward, the city took that land only two years later for the northern extension of Bay Street. In conjunction with the litigation with the city that followed, the firm of Sproatt and Rolph prepared plans showing a complex of new college buildings immediately to the west of St. Basil's

Church (Fig. 29-1). At the time, Sproatt and Rolph were designing new buildings for Victoria College next door (Fig. 29-2), but the St. Mike's drawings were likely prepared on behalf of the city, in order to show that the land that the college was left with was suitable to meet its expansion plans.

There was another reason why the time had come for new buildings. When the administrators at St. Michael's compared their current physical plant with the impressive new structures of the other U of T colleges, they found it decidedly lacking. College fundraising materials of the period highlighted this relative deficiency, attempting to draw on denominational pride by contrasting pictures of the new buildings at Victoria College and Trinity College with an unflattering snapshot of the back of an old St. Mike's building. By this time, St. Mike's had been able to use the compensation it had received from the city over the Bay Street transfer to assemble additional lands west of its existing campus, eventually acquiring the entire block from Bay Street to Queen's Park Crescent. It could

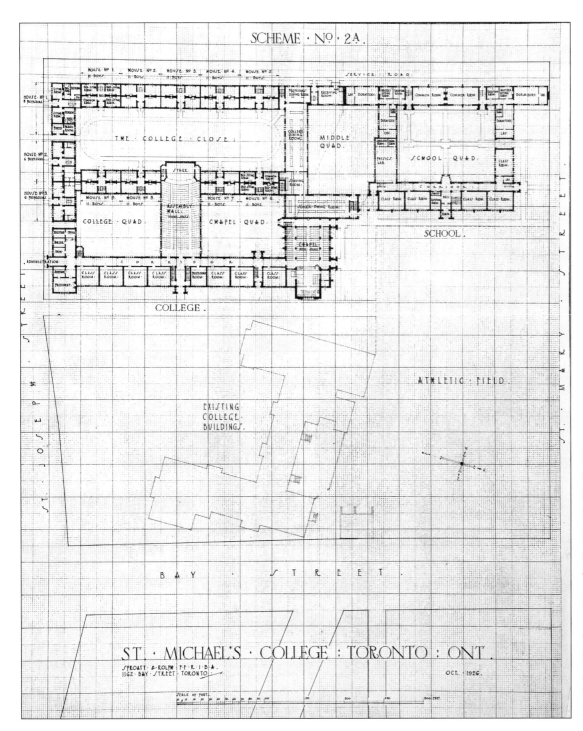

Fig. 29-1. These plans for new St. Michael's College buildings were drawn up by the firm of Sproatt and Rolph after the city's extension of Bay Street thwarted the college's plans to expand eastward. Later, St. Mike's would acquire lands on Queen's Park Crescent, proposing an entirely new campus based on Princeton. [Archives of Ontario, C 292-1-0-325, K-605]

Fig. 29-2. Sproatt and Rolph's drawings for new buildings for Emmanuel College on Queen's Park Crescent. The chapel would replace the one in Victoria College's 1892 neo-Romanesque building, which would have been demolished. [Archives of Ontario, C 292-1-0-306, K-605]

now expand westward toward the University of Toronto and the university's other colleges.

The college hired Toronto architect A.W. Holmes to plan its new campus. Holmes had made a career of designing Roman Catholic church buildings throughout southern Ontario, including three for the Basilians, the most recent being the Basilian-run Holy Rosary Church on St. Clair

Avenue, west of Bathurst (1926–27), which Holmes considered his masterpiece (albeit an unfinished masterpiece: to this day it lacks a planned tower). Although Holmes had proven himself adept at a number of styles, for the St. Michael's commission there was little doubt that Gothic would prevail. Gothic remained the style of choice for collegiate buildings, as recent construction across the University of

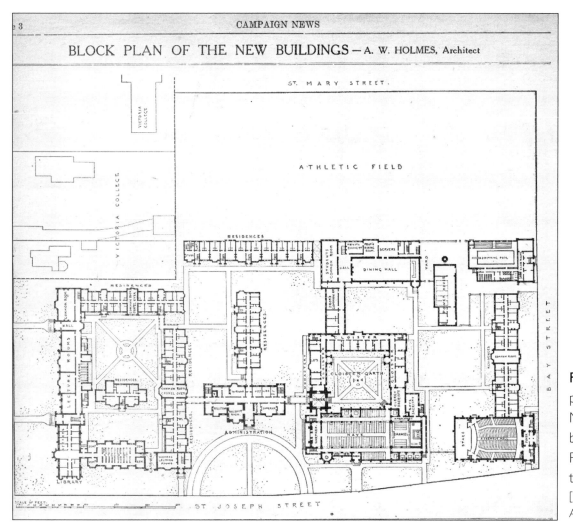

Fig. 29-3. The proposed campus complex for the new St. Michael's College stretched between Bay and Queen's Park Crescent, longer than the facade of Union Station. [University of St. Michael's College Archives]

Toronto campus — such as Trinity College, Hart House and Emmanuel College — had shown. Moreover, the St. Mike's 1850s buildings were Gothic as well, and the college consciously sought to provide a stylistic link to them (even as it planned their demolition). Finally, Holmes and the college staff had taken a tour of Midwestern and eastern American universities, concluding that the breathtaking collection of Gothic buildings at Princeton University (by Ralph Adams Cram, who had earlier been hired to design the new plans for the unfinished St. Alban's Cathedral, see chapter 9) was the best example of buildings suited to "the needs and ideals" of St. Mike's.

Holmes treated the newly assembled St. Michael's site as a greenfield. All existing buildings, including St. Basil's, the original 1856 collegiate church (and the oldest building on the U of T campus) would be removed. In their place he planned a rational, collegiate Gothic complex built around a series of quadrangles. An open quadrangle on St. Joseph Street would serve as the college's main entrance. An administrative building reached by a semi-circular driveway

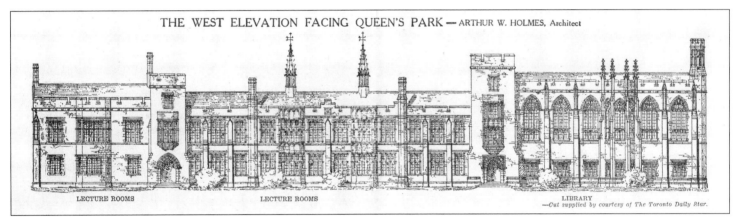

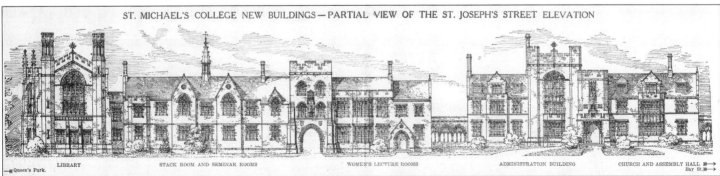

Figs. 29-4a (top) and 29-4b (bottom). A view of the Queen's Park Crescent façade of the new college and a partial view of the St. Joseph Street facade. The tower of the chapel, which would have dominated the complex, is not shown. [University of St. Michael's College Archives]

would be flanked to the west by the library building and to the east by a new collegiate church. The church's tower would dominate the St. Joseph Street facade, which would stretch 860 feet between Queen's Park and Bay Street, longer than the facade of Union Station (Figs. 29-3, 29-4a, 29-4b). In addition to these amenities, there would be residence accommodation for five hundred students (out of a total planned enrollment of one thousand), as well as lecture rooms, a dining hall, a theatre/assembly hall and athletic building containing a pool. A large athletic field would take up the campus's northern border.

The fundraising campaign kicked off on June 3. Its goal was to raise $3 million over eighteen months: half for the new buildings and half for a permanent endowment for the college. The event was noted in the local press, and appeals were made to alumni and among the Catholic faithful at the parish level. On June 3, 1929, $3 million seemed like a reasonable, if ambitious, goal. But after the stock-market crash of October 29, the goal might as well have been $3 billion. The bottom line was clear: there would be no Princeton on Queen's Park Crescent.

Holmes did ultimately produce two buildings for St. Michael's. The Teefy/Fisher/More complex fronting on Queen's

Fig. 29-5. A drawing of the 1935 complex, essentially as it would be built. The tower and adjoining building to the right were never constructed, although a blank wall over the entrance to Teefy Hall continues to anticipate the tower's arrival. [University of St. Michael's College Archives]

Park Crescent was completed in 1935–36, containing classrooms, residences and the Institute of Medieval Studies. Brennan Hall, at the top of Elmsley Place, was constructed in 1938 to house common rooms and dining facilities. Perhaps indicative of the changed mood of 1930s Canada as much as the changed financial situation of St. Mike's, these buildings are in an earlier, more austere Gothic style than had been proposed in 1929, mirroring much more closely the college's pre-Confederation buildings. Indeed, an alternate version of the Queen's Park complex in this sparser style shows the north and south wings joined by a cloister and gate consciously modelled on architect William Hay's never-completed 1856 scheme for the original college buildings.

Although the placement of Brennan Hall and its dining facilities is roughly consistent with the dining hall shown in Holmes's 1929 plan, it seems unlikely that by 1938 there remained any serious contemplation of a southward expansion toward St. Joseph Street; certainly there is nothing in the building to indicate that this was anticipated. As a result, the five late-Victorian houses on Elmsley Place — buildings that were considered tear-downs by the college when it purchased them in the 1920s — have become an integral part of the college's campus. A 1935 perspective drawing of the Teefy/Fisher/More building, essentially as it would be built, shows the tip of St. Basil's spire peeking above the treetops, acknowledgement that by that time no one thought that the college's original building would be going anywhere soon (Fig. 29-5).

The 1935 drawing does indicate a longer-term vision, however, an extension of the new Queen's Park complex along St. Joseph Street. In the drawing, the Queen's Park and St. Joseph Street buildings are joined by a sturdy, square tower. When St. Mike's did finally build on St. Joseph, almost twenty years later (and fifteen years after Holmes's death), it was not to the 1935 plans. Nonetheless, you can still see evi-dence of those plans today. A windowless expanse stretching up from the entrance to Holmes's Teefy Hall marks the site of the architect's planned tower. A 1937 bird's eye map of the entire U of T campus that hangs in the Hart House Map Room shows the college completed to the artist's interpretation of Holmes' 1935 plans. Both are enduring physical reminders of the unfulfilled vision of the "New St. Michael's College."

Chapter 30

ST. LAWRENCE CENTRE

1962 / Partially built

I N THE EARLY 1960S, MUNICIPALITIES across the country began work on "centennial projects," civic improvements undertaken to celebrate the hundredth anniversary of Confederation. Toronto was no different. It decided to build the St. Lawrence Centre for the Arts, an entire district of theatres, schools, museums and art galleries in an arc from Yonge and Front to Richmond and Jarvis. What actually got built fell far short of that dream: a single theatre on Front Street, opening three years too late for Canada's big party.

The St. Lawrence Centre for the Arts was first proposed in a booklet released by the City of Toronto's planning board in October 1962. The impetus for the idea was the opening of the 3,500-seat O'Keefe (later Hummingbird, now Sony) Centre in 1960. The city's planning board was of the view that Toronto lacked an artistic "centre of gravity," and felt that the O'Keefe could serve as the southwestern anchor of an entire new arts campus for the city. While the O'Keefe may have

provided a local stimulus, the idea tapped into two larger movements then current in city planning: urban renewal (that is, the wholesale demolition and rebuilding of "blighted" downtown areas); and the "arts centre," a campus of theatres and cultural buildings. In this way, the St. Lawrence Centre proposal closely mirrored two other projects then under construction, Place des Arts in Montreal and New York's Lincoln Centre. Indeed, the arcaded buildings in the planning board's model were reminiscent of Manhattan's now-iconic buildings (Fig. 30-1).

The plan, developed with Raymond Moriyama as consulting architect, involved two areas. The first consisted of the blocks bounded by Church, Jarvis, Front and Richmond. Everything in those blocks, save the St. James's Cathedral buildings and St. Lawrence Hall, would be demolished. To the east of the cathedral, (the area that is currently St. James's Park) a precinct for arts schools such as the National Ballet School would be developed. South from that block, between

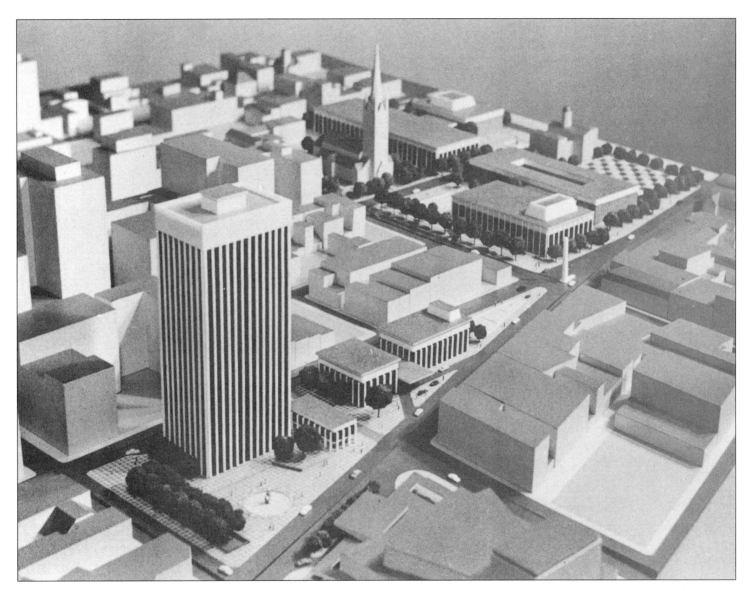

Fig. 30-1. In 1962 the Toronto planning board released this plan for the St. Lawrence Centre, a multi-block district of theatres, schools, museums and art galleries that would serve as the cultural "centre of gravity" for the city. [City of Toronto Archives, Series 10, Item 162, Page 47]

King and Front, would be an art gallery, lecture rooms, and a new market building behind a refurbished St. Lawrence Hall. St. Lawrence Hall itself would be turned into a museum. A 1,500-seat theatre would also occupy this block, at the northeast corner of Front and Church.

The second area dealt with in the plan was the triangular parcel defined by Yonge, Wellington and Front. The western half of this block (west of Scott Street) was owned by O'Keefe Breweries. Incorporating plans that had already been explored by O'Keefe (Fig. 30-2), an office tower — which could accommodate arts organizations, among other tenants —would occupy the western portion of this site. It would be pushed back toward Wellington in order to allow for a plaza facing Front Street, across from the O'Keefe Centre. A restaurant would occupy the plaza as well. On the eastern side of Scott, a repertory theatre and small concert hall would be built.

The board suggested that the St. Lawrence Centre could be undertaken as a centennial project, and the St. Lawrence Centre Foundation was created to explore the proposal. In February 1964, city council gave the foundation the authority to develop the plan as Toronto's centennial project. Council got even more ambitious, changing the name of the foundation to the Toronto Arts Foundation, and expanding its centennial-project mandate to include a $6.3-million expansion of the Art Gallery of Toronto (now the Art Gallery of Ontario) and a $1-million refurbishment of Massey Hall.

Given the magnitude of the plan, it might have been an appropriate project for all the municipalities in Metro to jointly get behind. But each of them (including some that wouldn't live to see 1967, like New Toronto and Mimico) had its own project. The plan's ambiguity didn't help matters. It came off as a space in search of a program, as the broad mix of uses swelled with talk of planetariums and a high school for the arts. The CBC, which badly needed new headquarters,

was actively courted. It was interested, but was not about to abandon plans to move to Don Mills (where it had already bought land) based on what its general manager described as an "airy-fairy" project that was "on again and off again."

The ambivalence the CBC sensed in the city's support for the project was real. Early in 1965, council decided that it would be too expensive to create a museum in St. Lawrence Hall. In May, concerned about the cost of a new $2,225,000 parking garage that had been added to the mix (to be built east of the O'Keefe Centre), the council was prepared to ditch the rest of the St. Lawrence Centre scheme as well. After a debate that lasted till eleven in the evening, the centre was saved only on the understanding that it would not delay any other projects in the city's capital works budget. Hardly a ringing endorsement. Especially when, even with that proviso, the project was saved by only a one-vote majority. At this point, the program consisted of the restoration of St. Lawrence Hall, the Art Gallery of Toronto and Massey Hall upgrades, a new 850-seat theatre and 750-seat "town hall," and an arts facilities building that would be shared by the Canadian Opera Company and the National Ballet for rehearsals, set-making and administration.

The city's financial contribution to the project was conditional on the Toronto Arts Foundation raising $4.8 million from the public. In June 1965, after raising less than $1 million, the foundation admitted defeat. Having had lukewarm support from council, the lack of public response could hardly have come as a shock. With the O'Keefe Centre only five years old and the Royal Alexandra recently refurbished, there were those who questioned why Toronto needed more downtown live theatre space at all. If there were good answers, they weren't effectively conveyed to the public. A poll of Metro residents showed that 17 percent were "pleased" to see the project fail, and 46 percent were indifferent. Of those, many had never even heard of it. Council again re-affirmed its

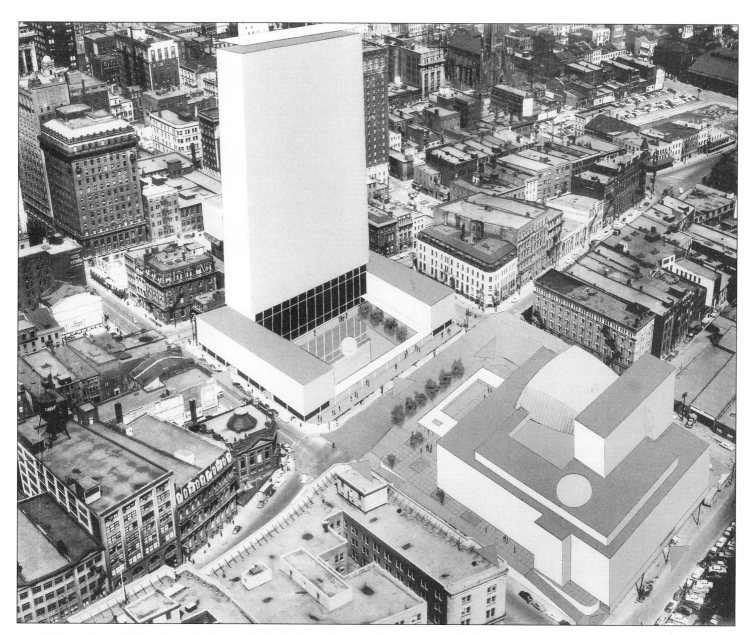

Fig. 30-2. In the 1950s, O'Keefe Breweries had plans for an office tower and plaza to rise across the street from their new performing arts centre. They were incorporated into the city's St. Lawrence Centre plans. [Panda Collection, PAN 561207-1, Canadian Architectural Archives, University of Calgary]

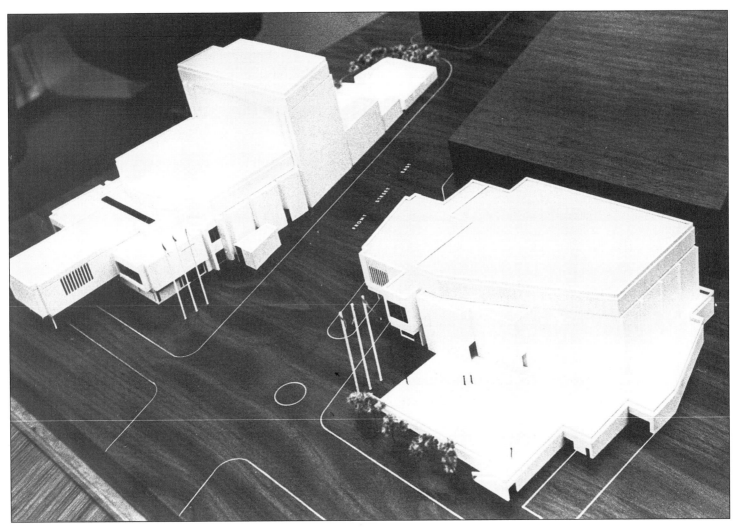

Fig. 30-3. This model shows the two-building proposal for the St. Lawrence Centre that the city took to tender at the end of 1966. Cutbacks would result in the single building that was actually built. [Clara Thomas Archives and Special Collections, York University, Toronto Telegram Photograph Collection, ASC04307]

commitment to the project, but just barely, with the motion carrying on a fourteen-to-nine majority.

By personally going out with members of the Toronto Arts Foundation to fundraise among businesses, Mayor Phil Givens helped make up for what one councillor called council's "weak, flabby, disappointing and disgraceful" support of the project. Within a month, he had reached half his personal goal of $2.3 million. But there had been further cuts to the original scheme, with the Art Gallery of Toronto and Massey Hall projects dropped. The focus was now entirely on the theatre and concert hall. Plans prepared by the architectural firm of Gordon S. Adamson and Associates at this time showed the theatre and town hall occupying the triangular parcel to the east of Scott Street, as envisaged in the original planning

board model. The entire site would be cleared of buildings, including the landmark Gooderham "flatiron" building. A 1,500-car parking structure, which could be connected underground to the theatres and the new office tower, would go on the south side of Front, beside the O'Keefe Centre. The supporting arts facilities building would be built at The Esplanade and Church.

In December of 1965, council again debated the program, this time for five hours, before finally approving a still further pared-down proposal. Gone was the arts facilities building; rehearsal space would be rented instead. Also gone was the parking garage. New plans showed the two remaining elements of the St. Lawrence Centre, the theatre and town hall, on opposite sides of Front Street (Fig. 30-3).

Fig. 30-4. The site of Toronto's centennial-project theatre as it looked only five months before 1967. It eventually became Berczy Park. [Clara Thomas Archives and Special Collections, York University, Toronto Telegram Photograph Collection, ASC04307]

The original $25-million project had been whittled down to $5,450,000 (plus $750,000 to restore St. Lawrence Hall). One Toronto Arts Foundation member quit over the cuts, and St. Lawrence Centre director Mavor Moore said he would do the same if there were any more.

With 1967 less than a year away, the project still hadn't gone out to tender. But Mayor Dennison continued to maintain that both theatres would be ready by September 1967. That dream, if it had ever been realistic to begin with, was dashed when construction bids came back in December 1966. The lowest acceptable bid came in $2,908,000 over the $5,450,000 estimate. The gap was too great. With the federal and provincial governments refusing requests for additional centennial funding, the project was stalled through 1967 (Fig. 30-4).

Again the building program was scaled back, as the theatre and town hall were combined into one facility on the south side of Front Street. The multi-block arts campus that planners had proposed at the start of the decade had been reduced to a single building, on a site that hadn't even been part of the original scheme. Even with the $2 million in savings that resulted from dropping a building, there still wasn't enough money to proceed. Finally, the promise of federal urban renewal money bridged the gap. Council approved the revised St. Lawrence Centre (again) on March 13, 1968. The building officially opened on New Year's Eve, 1969, with the mayor holding his New Year's levee in the town hall. The event was disrupted by a group called the Provocative Street Players who started to give the first (albeit unofficial) show in the new facility before being tossed out. Their intention? To protest the Spadina Expressway (see chapter 20), another troubled construction project left over from a decade on which the curtain was quickly coming down.

Chapter 31

BAY AND WELLESLEY BALLET-OPERA HOUSE

1988 / Unbuilt

ON BAY STREET, SOUTH OF Wellesley, there's a condominium development called Opera Place. An enigmatic name, given that Toronto's opera house, the Four Seasons Centre, is at University and Queen. One might assume the name commemorates some structure historically associated with the area. And it does. But not one that was ever built. In the 1980s, Bay and Wellesley was the intended site of a much-heralded and long-awaited ballet-opera house, designed by Moshe Safdie. It would have taken up an entire city block and become an instant city landmark. Instead, it became a celebrated victim of the recession of the 1990s, living on only in the name of the unremarkable condos that took its place.

When the National Ballet of Canada and the Canadian Opera Company set out to build a new ballet and opera venue on Bay Street, both companies had become internationally recognized organizations in a relatively short period. The National Ballet was founded in 1951, giving its first performances

in the auditorium at the Eaton's College Street store before moving to the Royal Alexandra Theatre in 1953. The Royal Conservatory Opera Company (precursor to the Canadian Opera Company) had been performing there since its founding in 1950. Both companies moved to the multi-purpose O'Keefe Centre after it opened in 1961, but the space was less than ideal. For one thing, at over three thousand seats, the O'Keefe was simply too big for unamplified performance. The problem was worsened by its fan-shaped auditorium. Unlike the horseshoe-shaped auditoriums of the world's great opera houses, the O'Keefe's configuration resulted in a deadened sound, with a great distance between the seats and the stage. Ironically, despite the venue's overblown size, both the orchestra pit and the backstage space were actually too small for the needs of professional opera and ballet.

In 1977 the companies looked into using the old Elgin Theatre on Yonge Street (the Loblaws warehouse at Bathurst and Front was also considered and rejected at the time). Although investigation showed that it was not suitable, the proposal did lead to the conclusion that ballet and opera would be compatible in a single theatre. Four years later, the Ballet Opera House Corporation was founded to finance and build a joint facility. The first order of business was to find a site. Six were seriously considered: the Canon Theatre (then the Imperial Six cinema), downtown North York (on Yonge Street, south of the civic centre), Harbourfront (at Maple Leaf Quay), the southeast corner of Front and Jarvis (across from the St. Lawrence Market) and the southeast corner of Bay and Wellesley. It was this last site, on surplus provincial land bounded by Bay, Wellesley, Yonge and Breadalbane, that was deemed the best in location, size and accessibility. Perhaps because of the site's proximity to Yonge Street and the University of Toronto (and in an area where there wasn't really much else going on), consultants hired to advise on a location for the new facility felt that the Bay/Wellesley location could be used to convey "an architectural image of youthfulness and vigour." No small consideration for art forms that often had to work against perceptions of playing to the old and established rather than the young and vigorous.

In December 1984 the Progressive Conservative government of Premier William Davis agreed in principle to transfer the Bay/Wellesley site to the Ballet Opera House Corporation. But when the Liberals took power in June of the following year, all bets were off. Especially with the new government's policy of developing surplus and underused provincial lands for housing wherever possible. As the Liberal government equivocated over whether to convey the land or not, the deputy minister of citizenship and culture suggested that it would be helpful if the Ballet Opera House Corporation could articulate a building plan for its proposed complex, "an architectural sketch, a little picture to give an idea of what it may look like." The ballet-opera folks did him one better. In June 1987 they sent more than 5,600 letters to members of the Royal Architectural Institute of Canada as the first phase in a limited, invitational competition.

Fifteen firms were interviewed. Three were invited to spend two weeks working through their design approach with the client before preparing plans and models: Barton Myers with Kuwabara Payne McKenna Blumberg; James Stirling, Michael Wilford and Associates; and Moshe Safdie and Associates. Safdie, who had become known across Canada for his innovative Habitat apartment complex at Expo '67, was again in the general public eye with his National Gallery of Canada in Ottawa, then nearing completion. Not everyone in the profession was happy with the concept of an invitation-only competition. In an attempt to get the directors of the Ballet Opera House Corporation to change their minds and hold an open contest, the Toronto Society of Architects held its own unofficial competition for the site, titled "Phantom of the Opera." A trip to Milan as first prize substituted for the opera house commission.

Safdie's winning design has become one of the better-remembered unbuilt projects in Toronto. It is certainly one of the more striking. The 455,000-square-foot complex would have fronted onto Bay Street. In the images shown here (Figs. 31-1 and 31-2) glass pyramids covering silver-coloured domes demarcate both the two-thousand-seat main hall and the main entrance pavilion at the corner of Bay and Wellesley. Glowing at night, they would lend an elegant and distinctive presence to the area. Windows on Bay would allow views into the great room, with its crossing grand staircases. The "Gallery of the Artists" would have stretched along Wellesley, joining the main entrance pavilion and another entrance pavilion at Yonge Street. The Yonge Street pavilion would give the complex both a presence on the city's main commercial street, as well as easy access to its principal subway line. The exterior of the building would be finished in precast panels inlaid with marble and granite.

Fig. 31-1. Moshe Safdie and Associates' Ballet-Opera House. The entrance pavilion at Bay and Wellesley is shown at left. It is connected by a block-long galleria to another pavilion at Yonge and Wellesley. The grand staircase is visible through windows behind the trees. [Safdie Fonds, John Bland Canadian Architecture Collection, McGill University Library]

Fig. 31-2. A night view of the proposed two-thousand-seat theatre. [Safdie Fonds, John Bland Canadian Architecture Collection, McGill University Library]

Finally, in July of 1988, the province agreed to donate the Bay/Wellesley site. In addition, it pledged $65 million for construction costs. In true eighties style, that money would be raised through the development of adjoining lands for 1,500 new residential units (although in keeping with the government's "housing first" policy, a third of them were for low-income occupants). The Liberals' surprise defeat to the New Democrats under Bob Rae in September 1990 placed a big question mark over the whole project again. A perfect storm was gathering. That same month, Toronto lost its bid to host the 1996 Olympics. Groups such as Bread Not Circuses had made headlines publicly questioning the morality of spending hundreds of millions of dollars on a one-off sporting event in a city with poverty and homelessness issues. Also, it had been revealed that another provincially funded leisure venue, Skydome, which had opened earlier that year, was $300 million in the red. And Ontario was deep in recession; within two weeks of being sworn in, Ontario's new treasurer, Floyd Laughren, was predicting a $2.5-billion deficit for that fiscal year. Against this backdrop, it was far from a safe bet that Ontario's newly elected NDP government would uphold the Liberals' pledge of $65 million for a ballet-opera house.

To add to the intrigue, after the provincial election, the federal Conservative government under Brian Mulroney had publicly pledged an astonishing $88 million to the project. Some observers felt that the timing of the federal announcement was calculated to force Bob Rae's government to commit to the project. If that was the plan, it didn't work. On November 9, 1990, two months before construction was set to start, Rae's cabinet announced that, although it would continue to make the land available, it was pulling its $65 million cash contribution. What was not revealed at the time was that Rae had asked the ballet-opera house board to come back with a more cost-efficient plan for the project, whose budget had climbed from $150 to $230 to $311 million. Safdie was agreeable to the idea, and had said that he could design a hall costing between $120 to $150 million. He also pointed out that in a recession, tenders could be expected to come in much lower than in a boom period. But the majority of the directors on the ballet-opera house board refused to consider a scaled-down facility. They were concerned that if the provincial grant was trimmed, cuts in the commitments from the other levels of government would follow. They didn't want to risk that, and were willing to bet that the provincial government would back down. They were wrong. The domino effect that the ballet-opera directors had feared was set in motion, but in its extreme form: once the province pulled its funding, the federal government withdrew all $88 million, and Metro Toronto withdrew the $20 million that it had pledged.

In the end, the Canadian Opera Company did end up building a no-nonsense building (with the Ballet joining in as tenant). The Four Seasons Centre for the Performing Arts opened at the corner of University and Queen in 2006. Audiences will enjoy first-rate ballet and opera performances in that facility for years to come. And for years to come, the name of the Opera Place condominiums will provide a reminder of the first-rate drama that occurred up at Bay and Wellesley in the late 1980s and early 1990s.

Chapter 32

ROYAL ONTARIO MUSEUM

2001 / Built to different plans

WHEN ARCHITECT FRANK Gehry's Guggenheim Museum opened in Bilbao, Spain in 1997, it gave rise to a new catch phrase: the "Bilbao effect," the idea that a single dramatic building could kickstart city-wide revitalization. In the first decade of the new millennium, Toronto-born Gehry returned to his hometown to design a major remodelling and addition for the Art Gallery of Ontario. A Toronto cultural institution was getting the Bilbao treatment. Only it wasn't the AGO that was getting it. Up on Bloor Street, at the same time that ground was being broken for Gehry's relatively subdued glass and wood AGO facade, contractors were finishing the steel skeleton of Daniel Libeskind's "Crystal," a controversial addition chosen through an international competition.

The ROM's original building opened in 1914. Designed by the firm of Darling and Pearson, it fronted on Philosopher's Walk, adjacent to the University of Toronto, under whose auspices the museum was operated until 1968. By that time, Chapman and Oxley had built a major addition for the museum on Queen Park's Crescent, which opened in 1933. The 1914 and 1933 buildings were joined by a central block, the entire complex taking the form of an "H," with open courtyards to the south and north. Between 1978 and 1984 those courtyards were filled in with a curatorial centre (to the south) and with the Queen Elizabeth II Terrace Galleries to the north. Moffat, Moffat and Kinoshita designed both, receiving a Governor General's Award for the latter.

By the late 1990s, the ROM's board felt that the institution's popularity was dwindling. In 2000, it retained the Zeidler Roberts Partnership to develop an architectural master plan to revitalize the museum. That same year, the ROM acquired a new director in William Thorsell. He ran with the ball, dubbing the revitalization effort "Renaissance ROM" and spearheading an international design competition that kicked off in June 2001. Fifty-two architectural firms responded to an international call for expressions of interest.

Fig. 32-1. A view of the Bloor Street entrance of Bing Thom's ROM proposal, showing the "dinosaur jar." [Bing Thom]

From that list, the ROM invited twelve to prepare designs. Interestingly, five declined, a development that Thorsell attributed to the complexity and limitations presented by working around the museum's existing historic buildings. The seven remaining firms prepared sketches that were put on display at the museum starting in November.

From those semi-finalists, a nine-member jury chose three finalists the following month. Bing Thom from Vancouver proposed an addition dominated by an undulating roof overhanging an open court on Bloor. Dinosaurs would be visible though a cylindrical glass "dinosaur jar" in front of the 1914 wing (Figs. 32-1, 32-2). Andrea Bruno from Turin also proposed a dramatic roofline, arching up from the Bloor Street entrance before descending again at the base of a twenty-storey tower. On Bloor Street, it would form a canopy for an entrance plaza. A totem pole was shown rising

Fig. 32-2. This view from the west shows the undulating roofline of the Thom design. [Bing Thom]

from the plaza, piercing through the canopy (Figs. 32-3, 32-4). And Daniel Libeskind, then based in Berlin, proposed his now-famous Crystal.

There was enormous interest in the process. Public presentations by Bruno and Thom drew six hundred people each, and Libeskind (who had gained some notoriety by displaying his initial sketches on napkins from the museum's restaurant) attracted 1600 people to his presentation. The jury declared Libeskind the winner later that month. The ROM offered practical reasons for choosing his proposal: it best met the program requirements, was deemed cheapest and fastest to build, and it didn't require the demolition of the centre block. And, for an institution looking for a revitalizing jolt, there was no denying that Libeskind's design was also seen as the most dramatic.

When the Terrace Galleries were being demolished in

Fig. 32-3. The addition proposed by Andrea Bruno of Italy featured an arching roofline punctuated at the north end by a totem pole. [Andrea Bruno]

2003 in preparation for the construction of Libeskind's Crystal, contractors found a time capsule marked "ROM 1981." It contained a twenty-two-year-old quarter, a twenty-two-year-old copy of the *Globe and Mail,* and a twenty-two-year-old letter from the ROM's curator that began "Greetings and salutations. We salute you across the years." While the builders of the Terrace Galleries presumably expected that salute to cross more than twenty-two years, they needn't have felt too bad. In

1979, when undertaking their own demolition, they had dug up a time capsule as well. It had been buried in 1959.

Fig. 32-4. A close up of the Bloor Street entrance in the Bruno submission. [Andrea Bruno]

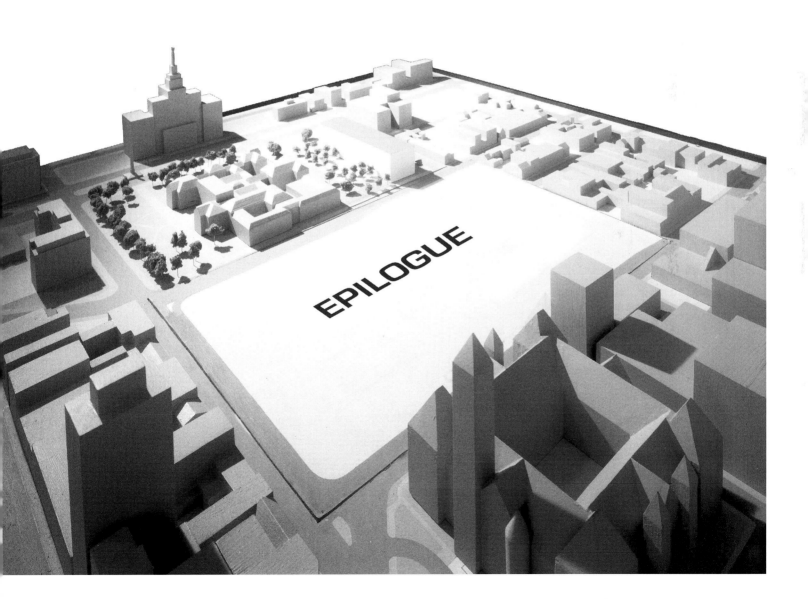

EPILOGUE

Chapter 33

THE CITY OF THE FUTURE: E.J. LENNOX'S TORONTO OF 2004

1904 / Partially built

MILES OF BEAUTIFULLY LANDSCAPED parkland lining the waterfront. More freedom for architects. Not one but two bridges to the islands. This is how one of the city's most prominent architects described the Toronto of 2004. If it doesn't sound like the Toronto you know, the architect can be forgiven: his descriptions were written over a hundred years ago.

In 1904, E.J. Lennox (Fig. 33-1, 1855–1933), designer of Old City Hall, wrote an article called "What Will the Architectural Appearance of Toronto Be in the Year 2004 A.D.?" for the first (and, it would seem, only) issue of something called *Toronto's Christmas Magazine*. While all the projects covered in this book have been someone's vision of the future, Lennox's Toronto of 2004 differs in that it is merely a speculation, not a proposal. And yet, in a history of things that never were, it seems fitting enough to end on a purely speculative note. With more than a hundred Christmases having passed since Lennox wrote his piece and the year 2004 A.D. having come and gone, we can now see how accurate his predictions were.

In 2004, millions of people will live in Toronto.
It may have seemed unfathomable, since Toronto's population in the 1901 census was only 208,040. But the era in which Lennox was writing was one of phenomenal growth: between the 1901 and 1911 census, there had been a more than 80 percent increase in Toronto's population.

"The boundary lines of Toronto will be extended many miles beyond its present limits."
Toronto had extended its boundaries through twelve separate annexations in the two decades prior to 1904. In the decade following, there would be eighteen more. And then there was the creation of the "megacity" in 1998. This prediction was undeniably correct.

Fig. 33-1. A photograph of E.J. Lennox and construction workers in front of his masterpiece, Toronto's third city hall. More than a hundred years after Lennox imagined the wonderful Toronto of 2004, few buildings have approached the splendour of his Queen Street landmark. [City of Toronto Archives, Series 958, File 106]

"All of which will have a great bearing on the architecture of the future."

Sure enough, thanks mainly to the proliferation of the automobile.

"The old city will be wiped out and a new city will be built up, laid out on a grander scheme."

Constant demolition since Lennox's time has seen the city he knew largely wiped out. But, presumably, Lennox had something different in mind. In 1904, the Guild of Civic Art was actively preparing its remake of Toronto, with the imperial European capitals as a model (see chapter 3). Not much came of that.

Boards of expert commissioners will ensure that "no building is allowed to be erected except when it is strictly of good design and one that will enhance the architectural appearance of the city."

That probably would have been a good idea.

Every building in itself will be a masterpiece of architecture.
Unfortunately, no.

People will be "so sensitive to the beautiful" that they will allow architects more freedom.

It seems unlikely we're more sensitive to the beautiful. But between Will Alsop's great tabletop for OCAD on McCaul Street and Daniel Libeskind's Crystal for the ROM (see chapter 32), architects don't have that much to complain about on the freedom front. At least those two don't, anyway.

Businesses will be strictly confined to business areas.

We take zoning for granted now. But in 1904 there wasn't any, just nuisance laws — if you were lucky — to keep out the truly noxious things like tanneries and abattoirs.

The residential areas will be divided into the "Workingman's District," "the Palatial District," and the "Boulevard District" for the classes in between.

More zoning, this time of people. Cities have always had exclusive areas. After the Second World War, strict land use laws limiting certain areas to single-family housing had the effect of separating the classes in a way the market alone never could.

Referring to the homes of the wealthy as palatial would not have been exaggeration. The previous year, Lennox had done some preliminary sketches for a new home for his client, Sir Henry Pellatt. The two had earlier toured the castles of Europe to find suitable inspiration. The result, Casa Loma, would be the largest private residence ever built in Canada.

There will be "subroadways" for the streetcar traffic.

By 1904 it was becoming clear to North Americans that the largest cities would not be able to rely on surface transit alone. It was equally clear that opposition from residents meant that new, elevated systems of the type that had been built in New York starting in the 1870s and Chicago in the 1890s were out of the question. In 1898, a one-and-a-half-mile-long streetcar subway opened in Boston. A second tunnel was added in 1904, the same year that the New York subway opened to the public. Toronto's subway — the first in Canada — followed fifty years later.

The subways will open up the streets "thereby enhancing to the mind the grandeur of the architecture of the buildings."

Well, they do open up the streets.

Buildings will be legally required to be fireproof.

In the year Lennox wrote his article, twenty acres of downtown Toronto burned to the ground in one evening (Figs. 33-2a, 33-2b). Similar fires had happened in Montreal in 1901

Figs. 33-2a (above) and 33-2b (next page). In the year that Lennox made his predictions, twenty acres of downtown Toronto burned to the ground in a single evening. The picture above shows Bay Street after the fire, with the tower of Lennox's city hall in the distance. [City of Toronto Archives, Fonds 1244, Item 2; Archives of Ontario, F 2178-1-0-22, S 5198]

and in Hull-Ottawa in 1900. Not to mention a rather famous fire in Chicago in 1871. Thanks to sprinklers and other advances in construction, you don't really hear about that kind of thing anymore.

There will be height restrictions.
Lennox called his era the "sky-scraper" age, and rightly so. After the development of steel-frame construction and passenger elevators in the late 1880s, buildings had risen to heights never before possible. In the early 1890s, Lennox had designed the seven-storey Beard Building at the southeast corner of King and Jarvis (demolished in 1935). In 1895, the ten-storey Temple Building at Queen and Bay was erected, considered Toronto's first skyscraper (see Fig. 10-1, demolished in 1970). Ten years later, the Traders Bank building at Yonge and Colborne topped off at fifteen storeys. If the laws of physics would no longer guarantee reasonable heights, the laws of city councillors would have to. Nowadays, zoning by-laws typically contain height restrictions, but Torontonians have come to embrace high-rise living.

Buildings may be of "some new style of architecture that may be developed" by 2004 or in "well-known styles of the past."
He's right on the new styles. But for commercial and institutional buildings at least, the well-known styles of the past have mostly been relegated to the past.

"Great tower buildings" will be built that straddle major intersections, serving as triumphal arches, with traffic running under them and soaring office towers on top.
Street-straddling buildings remained a futuristic favourite even decades later (appearing, for example, in the Harbour City and North York downtown plans discussed in chapters 7 and 25). None were built, however.

The railroad tracks will be elevated at Front Street from the Humber to the Don.
Something else we take for granted, but a huge issue in 1904. Imagine no grade separation in the downtown core where the tracks cross city streets. In 1909, when the government ordered a new train station built (Union Station), it was also decided that the tracks would enter the station on an elevated viaduct that would allow traffic to pass below. It would be another twenty years, however, before the new railway viaduct was finally complete.

A new road will be built at the waterfront "to accommodate the tremendous traffic that will be carried on."
Lennox was undoubtedly thinking of what would become Lake Shore Boulevard. But there's also the Gardiner. One wonders if Lennox could have imagined just how tremendous the traffic would be though: Toronto's by-laws had been updated only two years earlier to even acknowledge the existence of automobiles.

A "park drive" will be built along the waterfront, and it will connect with other park drives in the city.
Lake Shore Boulevard was planned as a park drive, but the connections that Lennox envisaged never happened.

Two bridges will be built — at the eastern and western gaps — to allow the park drive system to continue on the islands.
This idea would be proposed eight years later in the Harbour Commission's plan for the waterfront. Proposals for island bridges (and tunnels) have come up regularly since Lennox's time (see chapter 17). David Miller swept to office on the promise of defeating the last proposal in 2003. It would seem then that that idea has been put to rest. But who knows? The century is still young.

SOURCES

Chapter 1: 1788 Plan for Toronto

Arthur, Eric and Stephen A. Otto. *Toronto: No Mean City,* 3rd ed. Toronto: University of Toronto Press, 2003.

Gentilcore, R. Louis and C. Grant Head. *Ontario's History in Maps.* Toronto: University of Toronto Press, 1983.

Stelter, Gilbert A. "The Classical Ideal: Cultural and Urban Form in Eighteenth-Century Britain and America." *Journal of Urban History* 10, No. 4 (August 1984).

Chapter 2: Waterfront Walks and Gardens

Careless, J.M.S. *Toronto to 1918: An Illustrated History.* Toronto: James Lorimer & Co.; National Museum of Man; National Museums of Canada, 1984.

Doolittle, Robyn. "What happened to the city's park plan?" *The Toronto Star*, 3 August 2007.

Frith, Edith G. "Russell, Peter," in *The Dictionary of Canadian Biography*, Vol. V. Toronto: University of Toronto Press and Les Presses de l'Université Laval, 1983.

"Garrison Common History: The Western Park." *The Fife and Drum* 9, No. 4 (August 2005).

Gentilcore and Head. *Ontario's History in Maps.*

Harding, Kathryn. "Simcoe's grand idea." *The Toronto Star*, 19 May 2002.

Otto, Stephen. "The Fair Green." *Condo Voice* (St. Lawrence Condominium Ratepayers Association), No. 8 (February 1996).

———. "How the Railways Strangled Fort York." *The Fife and Drum* 11, No. 2 (July 2007).

Reeves, Wayne. *Visions for the Metropolitan Waterfront, 1: Toward Comprehensive Planning, 1852–1935.* Toronto: Centre for Urban and Community Studies, University of Toronto, 1993.

Stewart, Graeme. "History repeats itself." *Spacing* (Winter/Spring 2007).

Toronto Esplanade Act. (Statutes of Ontario, 1853, Chap. 219).

Toronto Esplanade Amendment Act. (Statutes of Ontario, 1857, Chap. 80).

(City of Toronto) Walks and Gardens Working Group. *Report on the Walks and Gardens Trust.* (31 October 2001).

Chapter 3: Plans of the Civic Improvement Committee and Advisory City Planning Commission

Advisory City Planning Commission. *Report of the Advisory City Planning Commission.* Toronto, 1929.

Carr, Angela. *Toronto Architect Edmund Burke.* Montreal and Kingston: McGill-Queen's University Press, 1995.

"The city and Dominion Square." *The Globe*, 24 April 1911.

Civic Improvement Committee. *Report of the Civic Improvement Committee.* Toronto, 1911.

"Civic Improvement in Toronto." *The Canadian Architect and Builder* 20, No. 3 (1907).

"Council to extend University Avenue." *The Toronto Daily Star*, 23 September 1930.

Dendy, William. *Lost Toronto.* Toronto: McClelland & Stewart, 1993.

"Elbow room." *The Globe*, 1 May 1911.

"Fifteen Years of Assured Steady Employment" (advertisement by the Citizens' Committee for a Greater Toronto). *The Toronto Daily Star*, 28 December 1929.

"Forces at work to delay deepening of Welland Canal." *The Toronto Daily Star*, 19 January 1912.

Gentilcore and Head. *Ontario's History in Maps*.

"A great civic centre." *The World*, 29 April 1911.

Hines, Thomas S. *Burnham of Chicago: Architect and Planner*. Chicago and London: University of Chicago Press, 1979.

Hunt, Geoffrey. *John M. Lyle: Toward a Canadian Architecture*. Kingston: Agnes Etherington Art Centre, 1982.

"The improvements." *The Toronto Daily Star*, 7 January 1930.

"Improvements for Toronto." *The Canadian Architect and Builder* 17, No. 201 (September 1904).

Lyle, John M. "Proposed Federal and Municipal Scheme for Toronto." *Construction* 4, No. 8 (July 1911).

"Plan of financing called an outrage." *The Toronto Daily Star*, 26 June 1930.

"Ratepayers reject town planning by-law in record total vote." *The Toronto Daily Star*, 1 January 1930.

Report of the Civic Department Heads Re the Advisory City Planning Commission Report for the Improvement of the City of Toronto. Toronto, 1929.

"University Ave. extension follows city plan route." *The Toronto Daily Star*, 23 April 1930.

"Vimy Circle opposed by aldermen again." *The Toronto Daily Star*, 12 April 1930.

Wilson, William H. *The City Beautiful Movement*. Baltimore and London: The Johns Hopkins University Press, 1989.

Chapter 4: Eaton Centre

Archives of Ontario. F 229-501. T. Eaton Co. Fonds. Toronto Eaton Centre Property Management Records.

Baker, Alden. "Eaton's refuses to revive $260 million development." *The Globe and Mail*, 20 May 1967.

Best, Michael. "$200 million complex in Queen-Bay area." *The Toronto Daily Star*, 15 April 1964.

"City names team to try to save Eaton centre." *The Toronto Daily Star*, 19 May 1967.

"A day that will decide the future of Toronto." *The Toronto Daily Star*, 24 June 1966.

"'Deal of century' or price too low?" *The Toronto Daily Star*, 2 December 1965.

"Decide." *The Globe and Mail*, 24 June 1966.

"Eaton's bold plan wins support of former Metro, city opponents." *The Toronto Daily Star*, 1 March 1966.

"Eaton Centre scrapped." *The Telegram*, 18 May 1967.

"The Eaton Centre issue now is public space." *The Toronto Daily Star*, 25 June 1966.

"Eaton's offer 'deal of a century' says Givens." *The Telegram*, 2 December 1965.

"Eaton plan just outline, Owen says." *The Globe and Mail*, 28 June 1966.

"Eaton's rejects new talks on scrapped centre." *The Toronto Daily Star*, 20 May 1967.

"Eaton's unveil $260 million plan for downtown area March 1." *The Toronto Daily Star*, 16 February 1966.

"$8 million for city hall." *The Toronto Daily Star*, 2 December 1965.

"Executive decision: Wreck city hall, lease land to Eaton's." *The Toronto Daily Star*, 22 June 1966.

"$500,000 'rent' hint by Eaton's." *The Telegram*, 17 June 1966.

Freedman, Adele. "1966." *Toronto Life* 30, No. 16 (November 1996).

"Futile to have anti-Eaton's forces in negotiations — Allen." *The Telegram*, 20 May 1967.

"Givens exultant, councillors OK Eaton's big plan." *The Toronto Daily Star*, 16 September 1965.

Greenberg, Ken. *Dreams of Development* [Catalogue of an Exhibition held August 18–October 28, 1984, The Market Gallery of the City of Toronto Archives]. Toronto: City of Toronto, 1984.

Haggart, Ron. "Bad deal, bad price, bad government."

The Toronto Daily Star, 27 June 1966.

———. "Why they voted to wreck the hall." *The Toronto Daily Star*, 28 June 1966.

Hanrahan, William. "Approval of Eaton Centre by Metro and City likely." *The Globe and Mail*, 2 March 1966.

———. "Unveil $260 million Eaton Centre scheme." *The Globe and Mail*, 2 March 1966.

Hunt, Paul. "Old city hall goes — Metro will lease land to Eaton's." *The Toronto Daily Star*, 25 June 1966.

Manthorpe, W.F. "The Eaton Centre scheme: how a planner sees it." *The Globe and Mail*, 16 June 1966.

Marshall, John. "Metro backs lease of old city hall site to Eaton's." *The Telegram*, 25 June 1966.

———. "Now: city of the future." *The Telegram*, 1 March 1966.

"Mayor denies his talks with Eaton's caused collapse of centre project." *The Globe and Mail*, 20 May 1967.

"Metro decides to study details before making City Hall decision." *The Globe and Mail*, 11 December 1965.

"Metro demands Eaton's guarantee project before old City Hall is sold." *The Globe and Mail*, 16 March 1966.

"Revised Eaton plan fails to win controllers." *The Toronto Daily Star*, 15 June 1966.

Smith, Kenneth. "Planning institute doubts Eaton's can fill downtown development." *The Globe and Mail*, 28 February 1966.

Snell, Richard. "3 Eaton skyscrapers in $260 million plan to rebuild downtown." *The Toronto Daily Star*, 1 March 1966.

Thompson, David. "Is this an Eaton bluff?" *The Toronto Daily Star*, 19 May 1967.

Chapter 5: Project Toronto and Project Spadina

"Aid Fuller project, Metro asks gov't." *The Telegram*, 13 August 1968.

Archives of Ontario. RG 19-6-5. Issues files of Darcy McKeough, Minister of Municipal Affairs (Buckminster Fuller Project file).

Anderson, Susan. "Fuller talks of spaceship earth's ballistics as councillors' mouths drop ever so silent." *The Globe and Mail*, 1 May 1968.

"Buckminster Fuller unveils 'livingest' city plans for Toronto." *The Toronto Daily Star*, 1 June 1968.

"Bucky's plan overwhelms city." *The Telegram*, 3 June 1968.

Cobb, David. "Gladstone in view." *The Toronto Daily Star*, 7 September 1963.

Filey, Mike. "Toronto has a history of thinking big." In *Toronto Sketches 7*. Toronto: Dundurn Press, 2003.

Fulford, Robert. "The world's most outlandish sculpture exhibition?" *The Toronto Daily Star*, 13 May 1967.

"Fuller proposes CNE at Downsview." *The Globe and Mail*, 1 June 1968.

Fuller, R. Buckminster. *The Spadina Site as an Opportunity for Urban Development; Project Spadina: A Conceptual Plan*. (undated report).

Fuller-Sadao/Geometrics. *Project Toronto: A Study and Proposals for the Future Development of the City and Region of Toronto*." Cambridge, Mass.: May 1968.

Gauther, Stanley. "Project could be the basis for jet-age progress." *The Telegram*, 1 June 1968.

Gorman, Michael John. *Buckminster Fuller: Designing for Mobility*. Milan: Skira, 2005.

Marshall, John. "Bucky's new city excites Queen's Park." *The Telegram*, 4 June 1968.

———. "Fuller proposes 'floating city' for Toronto." *The Telegram*, 1 June 1968.

———. "Gov'ts in Project Toronto study." *The Telegram*, 1 October 1968.

———. "Hellyer indicates help in Bucky's Project Toronto." *The Telegram*, 7 June 1968.

———. "Project Toronto." *The Telegram* (special section), 1 June 1968.

———. "Tantalizing hint of Bucky's Toronto." *The Telegram,* 1 May 1968.

McPherson, Jim. "TV scans Fuller's Toronto." *The Telegram*, 10 June 1968.

"R. Buckminster Fuller." *Time*, 122. (11 July 1983).

"There's hope for Toronto, says Fuller." *The Toronto Daily Star*, 3 June 1968.

Urquhart, Ian. "The big plan with a small future." *The Toronto Star*, 21 January 1972.

Chapter 6: Metro Centre

"Aid likely for Metro redevelopment." *The Globe and Mail*, 20 December 1968.

Best, Michael. "$1 billion railway Metro Centre complex to start rising in new year." *The Toronto Daily Star*, 30 December 1969.

Bragg, William. "City planners hit Metro and the TTC over centre scheme." *The Toronto Daily Star*, 15 August 1970.

———. "How Metro saved $21 million on extension of Union subway facilities." *The Toronto Daily Star*, 19 December 1970.

Calder, James. "'Niggling to blame' for Centre stall." *The Telegram*, 19 November 1970.

"Chief planner endorses $1 billion Metro Centre in downtown Toronto." *The Toronto Daily Star*, 17 October 1970.

"Citizen body out to block Metro Centre." *The Telegram*, 9 June 1971.

"City Council asks too much freedom." *The Globe and Mail*, 26 May 1971.

Coleman, Thomas. "Metro Centre a functional monstrosity cutting city off from lake conservancy head says." *The Globe and Mail*, 2 December 1971.

Community Development Consultants Limited. *Metro Centre: Development Plan and Programme*. Toronto: Community Development Consultants Limited, 1968.

Community Development Consultants Limited. *Metro Centre: Technical Report*. Toronto: Community Development Consultants Limited, 1968.

"Developer agrees to study plans of Save Union Station group." *The Globe and Mail*, 3 December 1971.

Fraser, Graham. "Council shelves Metro Centre development by rebuffing Crombie." *The Globe and Mail*, 5 November 1974.

Greenberg. *Dreams of Development*.

Hoy, Claire. "Metro Centre will start soon — or so officials say." *The Toronto Daily Star*, 19 December 1970.

Kingswell, Nicol. "'Exciting' — 200 say it with enthusiasm." *The Telegram*, 20 December 1968.

"May not build subway link to Metro Centre." *The Globe and Mail*, 19 August 1970.

"Metro approves $1 billion project for railway yards." *The Toronto Daily Star*, 16 December 1970.

"Metro Centre bogged down by red tape." *The Telegram*, 18 December 1970.

"Metro Centre boss threatens to sue over Union Station." *The Toronto Sun*, 18 July 1974.

"Metro Centre off the rails again." *The Globe and Mail*, 6 November 1974.

Moss, Tom. "Metro Centre can't make private deal with city." *The Toronto Citizen*, 8 July 1971.

"Municipal board tells Toronto to double Metro Centre parkland." *The Toronto Star*, 23 June 1972.

Purdie, James. "Cost of Metro Centre claimed to have jumped by 50% to $1.5 billion; delays in civic approval cited." *The Globe and Mail*, 8 June 1973.

Sewell, John. *The Shape of the City*. Toronto: University of Toronto Press, 1993.

———. *Up Against City Hall*. Toronto: James Lewis & Samuel, 1972.

Smith, Kenneth B. "$1 billion plan links downtown, harbour." *The Globe and Mail*, 20 December 1968.

"Talks over 9 acres of city land delay Metro Centre plan." *The Toronto Daily Star*, 23 November 1970.

Taylor, Jennifer and John Andrews. *John Andrews: Architecture a Performing Art*. Oxford: Oxford University Press, 1982.

"Union Station looms large at Metro Centre hearing." *The Toronto Star*, 26 February 1972.

Urquhart, Ian. "$1 billion Metro Centre gets 'full go-ahead' for summer start." *The Toronto Star*, 27 October 1972.

———. "City agrees to swapping station site." *The*

Telegram, 13 May 1971.

———. "Metro Centre plan: After three years the attack sharpens." *The Toronto Star*, 30 November 1971.

———. "Metro Centre start in 3 months hinges on Queen's Park." *The Toronto Star*, 15 December 1971.

———. "Metro Centre: The official plan and a critics' view." *The Toronto Star*, 10 December 1971.

Wilson, Cathy. "Metro Centre gone but not Union Station." *The Toronto Sun*, 28 May 1975.

Chapter 7: Harbour City

"Allen says Ontario 'invading' property." *The Toronto Daily Star*, 22 March 1969.

Banz, George. "Harbor City: 'Can 60,000 people be good neighbours?'" *The Toronto Daily Star*, 30 July 1970.

Bragg, William. "Forget about a Venice in Toronto." *The Toronto Star*, 21 March 1972.

Cameron, William. "City's big guns draw beads on Randall's harbor plan." *The Toronto Daily Star*, 23 May 1970.

"City hearings will discuss Harbor City." *The Toronto Daily Star*, 4 June 1970.

City of Toronto (Development Department). "Info" Sheet: *Proposed Concept by the government of Ontario for the Toronto Waterfront.* (15 February 1971).

Craig, Zeidler & Strong, Architects. *Harbour City: A Preliminary Working Report for the Planning of a New Community.* (August 1970).

———. *Habour City: Remarks.* (Press releases, Toronto Public Library Collection, 20 May 1970).

"Critics say Toronto okaying harbor plan before proper study." *The Toronto Daily Star*, 3 June 1970.

"Davis denies report Harbor City shelved." *The Toronto Daily Star*, 27 April 1971.

"500 attack proposal for harbor 'mini-city' as pollution source." *The Toronto Daily Star*, 7 May 1970.

Fraser, Graham. "Bickering stalls our waterfront development plans." *The Toronto Daily Star*, 18 April 1970.

Frayne, Trent. "This civil servant builds monuments in Montreal, Osaka and Toronto." *The Toronto Daily Star*, 6 June 1970.

"'Good' provincial harbor plan due May 18, Dennison says." *The Toronto Daily Star*, 30 April 1970.

Greenberg. *Dreams of Development.*

"Harbour City pollution 'not studied.'" *The Toronto Daily Star*, 4 December 1970.

"Harbour City: A Comment." *Canadian Architect* 15, No. 7 (July 1970).

"The Island mystery." *The Toronto Daily Star*, 5 February 1970 (editorial).

Jones, J.H. *A Conceptual Plan for the Development of the City of Toronto Waterfront.* (January 1968).

"Liberals suggest they'd end Toronto's Harbor City plan." *The Toronto Daily Star*, 25 January 1971.

Lorimer, James. "Does Harbor City fail to cater to civic needs?" *The Globe and Mail*, 25 May 1970.

Louttit, Neil. "Favourable reaction means work on Harbor City may be started in August." *The Globe and Mail*, 21 May 1970.

"Mayor denies 'secret' waterfront deal." *The Toronto Daily Star*, 19 March 1970.

Miko, Dorothy. "Town planners dazzled but puzzled by Harbor City." *The Toronto Star*, 11 July 1979.

Municipality of Metropolitan Toronto. *The Waterfront Plan for the Metropolitan Toronto Planning Area.* (December 1967).

"New law urged to keep Beaches free of jet noise." *The Toronto Star*, 21 February 1972.

Ontario Department of Trade and Development. *A New Illustrated Concept for the Harbour City Development.* Toronto, 1970.

"A new look for the lakefront." *The Telegram*, 3 March 1964.

"Ontario gets go-ahead to build islands in lake." *The Toronto Daily Star*, 8 April 1969.

Parliament, Mack. "Corporation planned to run Harbor City." *The Toronto Daily Star*, 1 May 1970.

"Projects could turn harbor into a pond, alderman says." *The Toronto Daily Star*, 12 March 1970.

"Province skips meeting on Harbor City plan." *The Toronto Daily Star*, 6 May 1971.

"Put poor on island — Randall." *The Toronto Daily Star*, 14 November 1969.

"'Sink Harbor city' campaign launched." *The Toronto Daily Star*, 25 May 1970.

"'Stalemate' reported in Harbor City talks." *The Toronto Daily Star*, 17 March 1971.

Stein, David Lewis. "Harbor City: 'An architect's artful, joyful vision.'" *The Toronto Daily Star*, 15 June 1970.

Taylor and Andrews. *John Andrews: Architecture a Performing Art.*

"True fears Harbor City will pollute." *The Toronto Daily Star*, 26 August 1970.

Vetere, Don. Personal interview. 12 March 2007.

"Waterfront city could start within a year, Randall says." *The Toronto Daily Star*, 7 October 1969.

"We're not pushing Toronto to approve harbor plan: Randall." *The Toronto Daily Star*. 5 June 1970.

Chapter 8: Ontario Legislative Buildings

Arthur, Eric. *From Front Street to Queen's Park: The Story of Ontario's Parliament Buildings.* Toronto: McClelland & Stewart, 1979.

Arthur and Otto. *Toronto: No Mean City.*

The Canadian Architect and Builder 1, No. 11 (November 1888).

The Canadian Architect and Builder 2, No. 1 (January 1889).

The Canadian Architect and Builder 3, No. 5 (May 1890).

Crossman, Kelly. *Architecture in Transition: From Art to Practice, 1885–1906.* Kingston and Montreal: McGill-Queen's University Press, 2003.

Dendy, William and William Kilbourn. *Toronto Observed.* Toronto: Oxford University Press, 1986.

Hall, Roger. *A Century to Celebrate, 1893–1993: The Ontario Legislative Building.* Toronto:

Dundurn Press, 1993.

Nasgaard, Susan. *A Critical Summary of Archival Material Relating to the History of the Parliament Buildings.* Toronto: Ministry of Government Services, 1978.

Ontario (Legislature). Sessional Papers (No. 52). 43 Victoria (1880).

Otto, Stephen A. "Tully, Kivas" in *The Dictionary of Canadian Biography*, Vol. XIII. Toronto: University of Toronto Press and Les Presses de l'Université Laval, 1983.

Stamp, Gavin. "Scott, Sir George Gilbert" in *Oxford Dictionary of National Biography*, Vol. 49, H.C.G. Matthew and Brian Harrison, eds. Oxford: Oxford University Press, 2004.

Chapter 9: St. Alban's Cathedral

An Act to incorporate the Dean and Chapter of the Cathedral of St. Alban the Martyr, Toronto. (Statutes of Ontario, 1882–83, Chap. 63).

"The Anglican Cathedral." *The World*, 2 November 1911.

Anglican Diocese of Toronto Archives. Minutes, Meeting of the Great Chapter (9 February 1906).

———. St. Alban's Cathedral Collection. Letter from Bishop Sweeny to Cram, Goodhue and Ferguson (26 November 1910); Letter from Cram, Goodhue and Ferguson to Bishop Sweeny (21 December 1910); Report of Cram, Goodhue and Ferguson (14 February 1911); Letter from Symons and Rae to G.B. Morley (5 March 1914); Letter from F.S. Baker to Bishop Sweeny (4 March 1911).

"Canadian Church Architecture." *The Canadian Architect and Builder* 2, No. 6 (June 1889).

"Cathedral of St. Alban the Martyr." *Construction* 5, No. 2 (January 1912).

Clause 9, (City of Toronto) Neighbourhoods Committee Report #8, June 17 and 18, 1991, re adoption of Intention to Designate 100 and 112 Howland Avenue.

Conservation Review Board. Decision re City of Toronto Intention to Designate 100 and 112 Howland Avenue (17 January 1992).

Cooke, William. "The Diocese of Toronto and Its Two Cathedrals" in *Journal of the Canadian Church Historical Society* 27, No. 2 (October 1985).

———, ed. *The Parish and Cathedral of St. James', Toronto, 1797–1997.* Toronto: St. James' Cathedral and University of Toronto Press, 1998.

"Laid foundation stone of south cathedral wing." *The Toronto Daily Star*, 27 August 1912.

Sweatman, Arthur. *Cathedral of St. Alban the Martyr: Its Origin, Purpose and Present Position.* Toronto: Rowsell & Hutchison, 1886.

Chapter 10: Victoria Square

"Business men favor the city hall park." *The Toronto Daily Star*, 12 April 1900.

"Civic committee re Victoria Square." *The Toronto Daily Star*, 16 April 1900.

"Create a park say citizens." *The Toronto Daily Star*, 9 April 1900.

Dendy. *Lost Toronto.*

Litvak, Marilyn M. *Edward James Lennox: "Builder of Toronto."* Toronto: Dundurn Press, 1995.

"Now for Victoria Square." *The Toronto Daily Star*, 18 April 1900.

"Park in front of City Hall." *The Toronto Daily Star*, 7 April 1900.

"People want Victoria Square." *The Toronto Daily Star*, 10 April 1900.

"Place for the Burns statue." *The Evening Star*, 17 August 1899.

"The Proposed Victorian Square." *The Canadian Architect and Builder* 10, No. 11 (November 1897).

"The Proposed Victorian Square." *The Canadian Architect and Builder* 11, No. 1 (January 1898).

"The site of the Victorian statue." *The Canadian Architect and Builder* 14, No. 8 (August 1901).

"The square Toronto didn't buy." *The Toronto Daily Star*, 20 December 1929.

"Statue of Queen Victoria by popular subscription." *The Toronto Daily Star*, 25 January 1901.

"They ask for Victoria Square." *The Toronto Daily Star*, 14 April 1900.

"Toronto cannot afford it." *The Evening Star*, 27 February 1899.

"Victoria Square." *The Evening Star*, 13 May 1899.

"Victoria Square." *The Evening Star*, 26 May 1899.

"The Victoria Square project." *The Canadian Architect and Builder* 11, No. 5 (May 1898).

"Victoria Square project." *The Toronto Daily Star*, 5 April 1900.

"A Work for the Guild of Civic Art." *The Canadian Architect and Builder* 13, No. 4 (April 1900).

Chapter 11: Toronto City Hall, 1925–1955

"'Backdoor of midway' controller says of city hall model." *The Toronto Daily Star*, 13 February 1955.

"City Hall and Civic Centre." *The Canadian Architect* 1, No. 4 (April 1956).

"City hall courthouse in new civic square advisory group urges." *The Toronto Daily Star*, 11 December 1952.

Civic Advisory Council of Toronto. *City Hall Court House Requirements in the City of Toronto.* Toronto, 1952.

"The civic square proposal." *The Toronto Daily Star*, 4 December 1946.

"Civic square, Regent Park go on new year's ballots." *The Toronto Daily Star*, 26 November 1946.

Dendy and Kilbourn. *Toronto Observed.*

"51-storey city hall unlikely." *The Telegram*, 22 June 1954.

Fulford, Robert. *Accidental City.* Toronto: Macfarlane Walter & Ross, 1995.

"Going to work at once on Regent Pk., mayor says." *The Toronto Daily Star*, 2 January 1947.

"Is that 51-storey city hall idea so 'fantastic?'" *The Telegram*, 21 June 1954.

"Metro may ask Toronto to build new city hall." *The Toronto Daily Star*, 22 October 1954.

Olins, Fabian. Letter to the Editor. *The Toronto Daily Star*, 16 December 1952.

"On straight cash basis vote for new city hall just plain horse sense." *The Toronto Daily Star*, 1 December 1956.

"Oppose 51-floor city hall." *The Toronto Daily Star*, 21 June 1954.

"Police hang up lunches or they lose them in No. 2."

The Toronto Daily Star, 9 April 1946.

Richardson, Peter. Personal interview. 28 January 2008.

"Seek 3 sets plans for new city hall." *The Toronto Daily Star*, 21 April 1956.

"'Skyscraper men serious' controllers shown plan." *The Toronto Daily Star*, 28 May 1954.

"Skyscraper City Hall has merits." *The Telegram*, 22 June 1954.

"Students call new City Hall vast funeral home." *The Toronto Daily Star*, 22 November 1955.

"U.S. money ready to build Toronto 50-storey City Hall." *The Toronto Daily Star*, 13 May 1954.

"Won't let U.S. build hall — Mayor." *The Toronto Daily Star*, 1 June 1954.

Zukowsky, John. "Prudential Building, 1952–55," in *The Sky's the Limit: A Century of Chicago Skyscrapers*, Pauline A. Saliga, ed. New York: Rizzoli, 1990.

Chapter 12: New City Hall

Arthur, Eric. *City Hall and Square Competition; Supplementary Questions and Answers.* Toronto, 1958.

Dendy and Kilbourn. *Toronto Observed.*

Fulford. *Accidental City.*

Hall, Roger. "The Toronto That Might Have Been." *Toronto Life* 34, No. 1 (January, 2000).

Kilbourn, William. *The Toronto Book.* Toronto: Macmillan, 1976.

Maloney, Mark. "The City Hall we almost had." *The Toronto Star*, 8 September 2007.

Phillips, Nathan. *Mayor of All the People.* Toronto: McClelland & Stewart, 1967.

"A Step Forward In Time: Toronto's New City Hall." Toronto Archives Virtual Exhibit. www.toronto.ca/archives.

Toronto (City Council). *Conditions of Competition, City Hall and Square, Toronto, Canada.* Toronto, 1957.

Toronto (Planning Board). *A Synopsis of the City Hall and Square Competition for Toronto, Canada.* Toronto, 1959.

West, Bruce. *Toronto.* Toronto: Doubleday, 1967.

Chapter 13: Mississauga City Hall

Arnell, Peter and Ted Bickford, eds. *Mississauga City Hall, A Canadian Competition.* New York: Rizzoli International Publications, 1984.

Baird Sampson Associates and City of Mississauga. *Mississauga City Hall, Conditions and Program: National Architectural Design Competition.* May 1982.

Banz, George. "Mississauga City Hall Competition." *The Canadian Architect* 27, No. 11 (November 1982).

City of Mississauga. News Release, 8 May 1984.

Franklin, Mark. "Subtle Symmetries." *The Canadian Architect* 32, No. 6 (June 1987).

Kalman, Harold. *A History of Canadian Architecture*, Vol. 2. Toronto: Oxford University Press, 1994.

Maxwell, Robert. "Sterling, James" in *The Encyclopedia of 20th-Century Architecture*, Vol. 3. R. Stephen Sennott, ed. New York: Fitzroy Dearborn, 2004.

The Mississauga Civic Centre Official Opening, Souvenir Program. (18 July 1987).

Platiel, Rudy. "Mississauga City Hall takes shape as centre of modern development." *The Globe and Mail*, 18 September 1985.

Zeidler, Eb. "Mississauga City Hall." *The Canadian Architect* 32, No. 6 (June 1987).

Chapter 14: Toronto and Georgian Bay Ship Canal/Newmarket Canal

Angus, James T. *A Respectable Ditch: A History of the Trent-Severn Waterway, 1833–1920.* Montreal and Kingston: McGill-Queen's University Press, 1988.

———. *A Work Unfinished: The Making of the Trent-Severn Waterway.* Orillia: Severn Publications Limited, 2000.

Cruikshank, F.D. and J. Nason. *History of Weston.* Weston: Times & Guide, 1937

Hunter, A.F. *Lake Simcoe and Its Environs.* Barrie: Barrie Examiner, 1893.

Jones, Elwood H., "Burr, Rowland" in *Dictionary of Canadian Biography*, Vol. IX. Toronto: University of Toronto Press and Les Presses de l'Université Laval, 1976.

Mason, R.B and Kivas Tully. *The Georgian Bay Canal Reports.* Chicago: Daily Press Book and Job Print, 1858.

Reports of the "Late House of Assembly" "House of Commons" and Legislative Assembly" of Ontario in Relation to the Huron and Ontario Ship Canal. Toronto: Hunter, Rose & Company, 1871.

Tully, Kivas. *Preliminary Report of the Engineer, on the Survey of the Various Routes, for the Proposed Ship Canal, to Connect the Waters of Lakes Huron & Ontario, at Toronto, to the President of the Board of Trade.* Toronto: Thompson & Co., 1857.

Chapter 15: Prince Edward Viaduct

"Ask alternative tenders." *The Toronto Daily Star*, 8 July 1914.

"Bloor Street Viaduct must follow straight line." *The World*, 25 January 1925.

"Bloor Street Viaduct will cost $1,612,000." *The Globe*, 18 November 1911.

"The Bloor Viaduct conference." *The Globe*, 17 January 1912.

"Bloor Viaduct met defeat." *The Globe*, 4 January 1912.

"Bloor Viaduct to be submitted to the people." *The World*, 18 November 1911.

Carr. *Toronto Architect: Edmund Burke.*

"City solicitor says the plan cannot be changed, but other lawyers differ." (second sub-headline). *The Toronto Daily Star*, 3 January 1912.

Civic Improvement Committee. *Report of the Civic Improvement Committee for the City of Toronto.*

"Concrete tenders lower than steel." *The Toronto Daily Star*, 14 October 1914.

"Danforth Avenue and Bloor St. Connection." *Construction* 5, No. 3 (February 1912).

"Defeat the Bloor Street Viaduct." *The Globe*, 30 December 1911.

"The expensive by-law plan, and another." *The Globe*, 28 December 1911.

Filey, Mike and Victor Russell. *From Horse Power to Horsepower Toronto: 1890–1930.* Toronto: Dundurn Press, 1993.

"A general meeting called to discuss Bloor Viaduct." *The Toronto Daily Star*, 16 January 1912.

"The municipal melting pot." *The Toronto Daily Star*, 21 February 1913.

"A new viaduct plan by Mr. J.M. Lyle." *The Globe*, 2 December 1911.

"No jiggle-joggle viaduct." *The World*, 20 November 1911.

"A plan for imposing an attractive Bloor Street Viaduct." *The Toronto Daily Star*, 19 February 1913.

"Reinforced Concrete Design For Don Section of Bloor Street Viaduct, Toronto." *The Contract Record and Engineering Review* 28, No. 43 (28 October 1914).

"Rust on the viaduct." *The Toronto Daily Star*, 17 October 1911.

"Shall Bloor St. Viaduct be of permanent concrete?" *The Toronto Daily Star* (advertisement), 31 October 1914.

"Steel forces won viaduct battle." *The Mail and Empire*, 14 December 1914.

"Steel men won, viaduct work to begin in month." *The World,* 12 December 1914.

"Suggested Design in Reinforced Concrete for Proposed Bloor Street Viaduct, Toronto." *The Contract Record and Engineering Review* 28, No. 46 (18 November 1914).

"Viaduct given big majority." *The World,* 2 January 1912

"Viaduct of steel is not determined." *The Globe*, 22 April 1913

"Viaduct problem to a committee which will select plan." *The Toronto Daily Star,* 19 January 1912.

A Visual Legacy: The City of Toronto's Use of Photography, 1856-1997. Exhibition, City of Toronto Archives (1 March–22 September 2007).

Werner, Hans. *Bridging Politics: A Political History of the Bloor Street Viaduct.* Toronto, 1989.

"Why put a crimp in the viaduct." *The World,* 28 November 1911.

Chapter 16: Hamilton Northwest Entrance

Best, John C. *Thomas Baker McQuesten: Public Works, Politics, and Imagination.* Hamilton: Corinth Press, 1991.

Filey, Mike. "Some Superhighway History" in *Toronto Sketches 3: The Way We Were.* Toronto: Dundurn Press, 1994.

Hunt. *John M. Lyle: Toward a Canadian Architecture.*

"New entrance to Hamilton cost $1,000,000." *The Evening Telegram*, 23 March 1928.

Reade, R.G. "Hamilton shows Toronto how." *The Toronto Star Weekly*, 16 November 1929.

Stamp, Robert. *QEW: Canada's First Superhighway.* Erin, Ont.: Boston Mills Press, 1987.

"Thousands view new beauty spot when new bridge opened." *The Hamilton Herald*, 18 June 1932.

Wilson, Paul. "Hamilton VIPs have no niche." *The Spectator*, 9 August 1986.

Chapter 17: Islands Tunnel

"Airport issue is held up while civic leaders argue." *The Toronto Daily Star*, 6 June 1935.

"Airport nonsensical undesirable as well Con. M'Bride asserts." *The Toronto Daily Star*, 21 December 1935.

"City must approve $425,125 expenditures." *The Toronto Daily Star*, 15 May 1935.

"City passes airport plan, island tunnel is approved." *The Toronto Daily Star,* 8 August 1935.

Filey and Russell. *From Horse Power to Horsepower.*

Filey, Mike. *I Remember Sunnyside.* Toronto: The Brownstone Press, 1981.

———. "Island Airport Bridge Up in the Air" in *Toronto Sketches 7.* Toronto: Dundurn Press, 2003.

———. "Oh, Island in the Scheme…" In *Toronto Sketches 5.* Toronto: Dundurn Press, 1997.

———. "Sunday Sports Not New." In *Toronto Sketches 7.* Toronto: Dundurn Press, 2003.

Gibson, Sally. *More Than An Island: A History of the Toronto Islands.* Toronto: Irwin Publishing, 1984.

"Liberals urge slum plan told 'tunnel or nothing.'" *The Toronto Daily Star*, 21 May 1935.

"Majority of council favour island tunnel." *The Toronto Daily Star*, 14 July 1935.

"May not drop tunnel project Ottawa states." *The Toronto Daily Star*, 30 October 1935.

"Mayor sees 45-mile drive around city." *The Toronto Daily Star*, 17 April 1935.

"M'Bride sees big savings as Ottawa halts tunnel." *The Toronto Daily Star*, 14 December 1935.

"See Toronto 'off air map' if port not started soon." *The Toronto Daily Star*, 16 May 1935.

"Sending mayor to Ottawa with tunnel protest." *The Toronto Daily Star*, 31 October 1935.

Sewell. *The Shape of the City.*

"Simpson to renew airport tunnel fight." *The Toronto Daily Star*, 16 December 1935.

Toronto Port Authority Archives. RG 3/3, Box 50, Folder 8. "Memorandum re tunnel — airport." (6 December 1935); "Memo re air harbour — western sandbar." (7 June 1935); "Report on airplane and seaplane harbour on immediate south side of western channel." (1 June 1929).

Toronto Port Authority Archives. 1930s Engineering Department Files, Islands Tunnel, 1935 (unaccessioned). Letter from J.M. Wilson, to Eugene D. Lafleur (26 January 1921); Reports of resident engineer to E.L. Cousins, General Manager, Harbour Commissioners (14 October 1935–31 January 1936).

"Tunnel, airport project of $1,656,543 is approved." *The Toronto Daily Star*, 6 August 1935.

Chapter 18: Queen Street Subway

Baker, Alden. "Construction to start after '72." *The Globe and Mail*, 15 March 1968.

Bragg, William. "A ghost subway station at Queen Street is haunting Metro Council." *The Toronto Daily Star*, 21 June 1969.

"City Council demands priority for Queen St. subway project." *The Telegram*, 11 August 1966.

City of Toronto Archives. Series 836, Subseries 2, File 17. Prince Edward Viaduct — 1970–78.

Coleman, Thomas. "Must review new subway, report says." *The Globe and Mail*, 15 February 1974.

———. "Network of express buses from suburbs is foreseen." *The Globe and Mail*, 14 January 1974.

———. "Scrap Queen subway plan for better suburban transit, study urges." *The Globe and Mail*, 28 January 1975.

"Count of passengers fails to support Queen subway needed." *The Globe and Mail*, 23 February 1967.

"8-mile Queen subway is proposed by TTC; may cost $200 million." *The Globe and Mail*, 12 June 1968.

Enright, Michael. "The Queen Street subway: a story about Toronto's ghost station." *The Globe and Mail*, 27 January 1968.

Filey, Mike. *The TTC Story: The First Seventy-Five Years.* Toronto: Dundurn Press, 1996.

"Further study of Queen subway is urged." *The Globe and Mail*, 9 December 1975.

Hunt, Paul. "E-W subway: a birth of the blues." *The Telegram*, 25 August 1965.

McKinley, Barney. "$400 million Queen subway plan gets the all-clear from TTC." *The Sun*, 10 October 1973.

Metropolitan Planning Board. *Official Plan of the Metropolitan Toronto Planning Area.* (December 1966).

"Must review new subway, report says." *The Globe and Mail*, 15 February 1974.

Parliament, Mack. "TTC ponders subway to serve 100,000 living, working south of King St." *The Toronto Daily Star*, 9 May 1969.

"Protests from Metro boroughs." *The Telegram*, 12 June 1968.

"Subway $200 million error?" *The Toronto Daily Star*, 10 March 1966.

"10-mile subway along Queen St. approved by TTC." *The Toronto Star*, 9 October 1973.

"3 boroughs ask next subway be on Eglinton." *The Toronto Daily Star*, 5 February 1968.

Toronto Transit Commission. *Queen Street Subway.* (report, 10 November 1969).

"TTC pressed by city to make decision on Queen Street subway line." *The Globe and Mail*, 27 July 1966.

"TTC spurns request to reveal route plan for Queen St. subwy." *The Globe and Mail*, 7 May 1969.

Chapter 19: A Vertically Separated City

City of Toronto, Commissioner of Development. *Pedestrian Ways — Cost Sharing Policy.* (Report to the Executive Committee, 1974).

City of Toronto Core Area Task Force. *Report and Recommendations.* 1974.

City of Toronto Department of Public Works. *On Foot Downtown.* 1970.

City of Toronto Legal Department. *Harbour Square Project — Agreement between the City, Campeau Corporation Limited and the Toronto Harbour Commissioners.* (Report to the Board of Control, 20 October 1969).

City of Toronto Official Plan. (1994)

City of Toronto Planning Board. *The Pedestrian in Downtown Toronto.* (6 October 1959).

———. *Plan for Downtown Toronto.* Toronto, 1963.

Commonwealth Holiday Inns of Canada. *Holiday Inn, Toronto Civic Square.* 1970.

Goodman, Lindy. *Streets Beneath the Towers: The Development of Toronto's Downtown Underground Pedestrian Mall System.* Toronto: Department of Geography, York University, 1984.

"Group One" (Macy Dubois, et al.) "A Plan For Central Toronto." *Canadian Architect* 7, No. 8 (August 1962).

Newton Frank Arthur Inc. and Agnew Communications Inc. *Toronto's Underground City.* 1986.

Praamsma, Wanda. "Subterranean T.O. blues." *The Toronto Star.* 16 September 2007.

Somerset, Jay. "Taking It to the Street." *Spacing* (Fall 2007).

Vattay, Sharon. "Toronto's Nathan Phillips Square: A 'Necessary waste of space.'" *Acorn: The Journal of the Architectural Conservancy of Ontario* 28, No. 2 (Summer 2003).

Chapter 20: Spadina Expressway

"Allen Expressway's name approved." *The Globe and Mail*, 28 May 1969.

"Allen extension 'speculation.'" *The Telegram*, 16 January 1970.

Cherry, Zena. "Expressway committee plans to SSSOCCC it to Toronto." *The Globe and Mail*, 17 January 1970.

"City OKs crash plan Spadina Expressway to be finished in 1975." *The Toronto Daily Star*, 30 January 1969.

Cunliffe, Alison and Mark Bonokoski. "Spadina lives: City loses court battle." *The Toronto Sun*, 22 April 1976.

"Dandy lot of trouble feared by Gardiner, Spadina plans withheld." *The Globe and Mail*, 3 October 1956.

Davis, William. *Statement by the Honourable William Davis Prime Minister of Ontario on the Future of the Spadina Expressway in the Legislature* (Press release, Toronto Public Library Collection, Thursday 3 June 1971).

Emmerson, Jim. "Davis promise of buffer strip can't stop Spadina, Tonks says." *The Toronto Star*, 5 February 1985.

"Expropriation of hundreds of homes in Forest Hill and York: anger, resignation reaction." *The Telegram*, 15 January 1964.

"Fight transit plan at rally tonight." *The Toronto Daily Star*, 5 March 1962.

Gooderham, Mary. "Land worth $28 million keeps old Spadina controversy alive." *The Globe and Mail*, 23 February 1987.

Howard, Ross. "Spadina expressway gets OK." *The Telegram*, 18 February 1971.

Hoy, Claire. "Allen Expressway highballs." *The Telegram*, 13 January 1970.

Kronby, Miles. "How a grassroots movement changed Toronto." *The Globe and Mail*, 1 June 1991.

MacFarlane, Andrew. "Confusion in planning." *The Telegram*, 15 November 1961.

MacKenzie, James. "How the 20-year political nightmare of the Spadina Expressway happened." *The Globe and Mail*, 27 January 1970.

———. "Spadina opponents plan to switch fight to Queen's Park." *The Globe and Mail*, 23

February 1970.

"Macy Dubois: Designing in Toronto, Designing in Concrete." In *Concrete Toronto: A Guidebook to Concrete Architecture from the Fifties to the Seventies*, edited by E.R.A Architects. Toronto: Coach House, 2007.

Marshall, Sean. "The Expressways of Toronto (Built and Unbuilt)." http://transit.toronto.on.ca/spare/0019.shtml.

"Metro hatches baby Spadina route." *The Telegram*, 13 December 1961.

Metropolitan Toronto Planning Board. *The Official Plan of the Metropolitan Planning Area*. Toronto, 1959.

"Must go to Bloor at least." *The Toronto Daily Star*, 26 January 1962.

Nowlan, David and Nadine Nolan. *The Bad Trip: The Untold Story of the Spadina Expressway*. Toronto: New Press, House of Anansi, 1970.

"OMB approves expressway despite protest." *The Globe and Mail*, 9 August 1963.

Oved, David. "Province given Spadina lands." *The Sun*, 2 March 1983.

"Robarts rejects pleas to step into row over Spadina Expressway." *The Toronto Daily Star*, 11 March 1970.

"2nd printing set for book on expressway." *The Globe and Mail*, 27 January 1970.

"70 groups fight Spadina plan." *The Toronto Daily Star*, 12 December 1961.

Sewell. *The Shape of the City*.

Smith, Michael. "Planners start new drive for Spadina Expressway." *The Toronto Star*, 4 May 1988.

"Spadina foes to appeal OMB vote to cabinet." *The Globe and Mail*, 24 February 1971.

"Spadina goes through, no tax rise, says Allen." *The Telegram*, 7 March 1962.

Stead, Sylvia and Geoffrey York. "Toronto gets 3-foot strip for 99 years." *The Globe and Mail*, 8 February 1985.

"Taxpayers fight 'obsolete' Spadina Expressway." *The Telegram*, 22 November 1961.

"3 aldermen defect, oppose expressway." *The Globe and Mail*, 3 February 1970.

"Tunnel or bypass asked as village expressway." *The Telegram*, 12 April 1961.

"Thruway across town out." *The Toronto Daily Star*, 13 December 1961.

"York Twp. vows to halt Spadina Expressway." *The Toronto Daily Star*, 3 November 1961.

Chapter 21: Toronto Towers/Bank of Nova Scotia Building

"Building which was proposed for King and Bay Sts." *The Evening Telegram*, 30 March 1928.

"Completed hotel plans to show new structure 29 stories in height." *The Toronto Daily Star*, 2 December 1927.

Dendy and Kilbourn. *Toronto Observed*.

"Had no hitch to date in big development." *The Toronto Daily Star*, 23 December 1927.

"Huge development in downtown Toronto." *The Contract Record and Engineering Review* 41, No. 49 (27 December 1927).

Hunt. *John M. Lyle*.

"Joke at realtor's expense." *The Toronto Daily Star*, 11 May 1928.

McHugh, Patricia. *Toronto Architecture: A City Guide*. Toronto: Mercury Books, 1985.

McKelvey, Margaret E. and Merilyn McKelvey. *Toronto: Carved in Stone*. Toronto: Fitzhenry & Whiteside, 1984.

"New Toronto syndicate behind gigantic deal in downtown realty." *The Toronto Daily Star*, 6 December 1927.

"Notes and Comments." *Construction* 23, No. 12 (December 1930).

"Property Committee approves skyscraper." *The Toronto Daily Star*, 25 November 1927.

"Say huge building scheme is ready to make a start." *The Toronto Daily Star*, 18 November 1927.

"See aldermen about plans for big work." *The Toronto Daily Star*, 24 November 1927.

"$7,000,000 head office to start in spring." *Construction* 23, No. 11 (November 1930).

"Three large buildings, costing thirty millions, planned for King Street." *The Evening Telegram*, 5 November 1927.

"Toronto Towers is to be name of new downtown street planned." *The Toronto Daily Star*, 27 January 1928.

"Toronto Towers project definitely in abeyance." *The Toronto Daily Star*, 5 April 1928.

"Wreck rear portion of Grand Opera House." *The Toronto Daily Star*, 1 June 1928.

Chapter 22: Eaton's College Street

Archives of Ontario. F 229-162-0-318. T. Eaton Co. Fonds. Building and Expansion — Ontario — Toronto — College Street Construction Committee — Minutes. (Construction Committee minutes, 1916–17).

———. F 229-162-0-319. T. Eaton Co. Fonds. Building and Expansion — Ontario — Toronto — College Street Project — Confidential. (Various memoranda from the Interior Decorating Bureau to the Board of Directors, 1931–34.)

Bird, Alf. "Firms solve challenges posed by old foundations." *The Daily Commercial News and Building Record*, 29 June 1981.

"Buchanan Street will be closed." *The Evening Telegram*, 16 July 1928.

"Carlton-College jog soon gone, mayor's lead big factor." *The Evening Telegram*, 18 October 1930.

Clark, Gregory. "Mystery's End." *The Toronto Star Weekly*, 18 October 1930.

"C.P.R. investment — $12,000,000 in new terminal." *The Evening Telegram*, 28 October 1919.

Dendy. *Lost Toronto*.

Filey, Mike. "The Legacy Continues." In *Toronto Sketches 8*. Toronto: Dundurn Press, 2004.

"Great new hotel and terminal, C.P.R. to use 'mystery block.'" *The Evening Telegram*, 27 October 1913.

Macpherson, Mary-Etta. *Shopkeepers to a Nation*. Toronto: McClelland & Stewart, 1963.

"Many buildings to be demolished in 'Mystery Block' at College and Yonge Streets." *The Evening Telegram*, 11 July 1928.

McQueen, Rod. *The Eatons*. Toronto: Stoddart, 1998.

"Mystery block deal changes complexion." *The Toronto Daily Star*, 18 May 1928.

"New Eaton block was the dream of late chief." *The Toronto Daily Star*, 16 September 1929.

"The Proposed Eaton Store Building in Toronto." *Journal of the Royal Architectural Insitute of Canada* 5, No. 12 (December 1928).

"T. Eaton Company plans vast building program over number of years." *The Toronto Daily Star*, 13 November 1928.

"T. Eaton Company Ltd., plan 7-storey building on Yonge-College site." *The Toronto Daily Star*, 12 July 1928.

"Toronto's retail trade to move toward north." *The World*, 27 March 1912.

Chapter 23: Victory Building/Bayview Ghost

"Architects will have hard task on hands." *The Toronto Daily Star*, 2 December 1927.

"The battle's on for 'the Ghost.'" *The Toronto Star*, 10 May 1980.

"Bayview Ghost loses fight for life." *The Toronto Star*, 16 May 1981.

"Bayview Ghost still haunting." *The Toronto Star*, 29 April 1980.

"Bayview Ghost story nears end." *The Toronto Star*, 27 September 1981.

"Biting the dust." *The Toronto Star*, 31 October 1981.

"Bright spots of the business week include sale of Victory Building." *The Toronto Daily Star*, 13 June 1936.

"Build armories soon military men think." *The Toronto Daily Star*, 26 August 1932.

"Cabinet sides with citizens on 'Ghost' site." *The Toronto Star*, 7 March 1981.

"Clear Victory Building." *The Toronto Daily Star*, 6 May 1932.

"Council seals fate of Ghost." *The Toronto Star*, 22 September 1981.

"Court to decide if suites legal." *The Toronto Daily Star*, 29 September 1961.

"Desire to finish Victory Building." *The Toronto Daily Star*, 29 June 1934.

"East York halts half-built apartment." *The Toronto Daily Star*, 15 August 1961.

"Full speed resumed on Victory Building." *The Toronto Daily Star*, 29 November 1929.

"Hampton Park probe demanded." *The Toronto Daily Star*, 7 September 1961.

"Have not arranged to complete building." *The Toronto Daily Star*, 14 February 1936.

"Homes ok for 'ghost of Bayview.'" *The Toronto Star*, 21 November 1980.

"Meeting called on 'Ghost.'" *The Toronto Star*, 22 July 1975.

"Metro covers up 'suite' facts — reeve." *The Toronto Daily Star*, 22 April 1961.

"Moves begin to demolish empty shell." *The Toronto Star*, 10 February 1976.

McHugh. *Toronto Architecture*.

"Must revise tenders." *The Toronto Daily Star*, 15 September 1933.

"Occupy theatre site." *The Toronto Daily Star*, 25 July 1929.

"Past East York councils made mistakes — reeve." *The Toronto Daily Star*, 10 June 1961.

"Seek to block suites after permit issued." *The Toronto Daily Star*, 20 October 1959.

"See real estate spurred by better money market." *The Toronto Daily Star*, 16 October 1931.

"'Speculators did wrong' reeve blames Gardiner." *The Toronto Daily Star*, 13 June 1961.

"Victory Building gets tenants on April 1." *The Toronto Daily Star*, 5 March 1937.

"Victory Building is sold, about 1,000,000 involved." *The Toronto Daily Star*, 12 September 1938.

"Victory Building may be completed." *The Toronto Daily Star*, 30 November 1931.

"Victory Building to be completed." *The Toronto Daily Star*, 11 September 1936.

Chapter 24: Toronto Hydro Tower

Ashworth, E.M. *Toronto Hydro Recollections*. Toronto: University of Toronto Press, 1955.

Chapman, A. H. "The New Toronto Hydro-Electric Building." *Journal, Royal Architectural Institute of Canada* 10, No. 9 (September 1933).

Chapman, Howard. *Alfred Chapman: The man and his work*. Toronto: Architectural Conservancy

of Toronto, Toronto Region Branch, 1978.

"Commerce to enlarge College-Yonge branch." *The Toronto Daily Star*, 10 October 1930.

Diamond, A.J. "Preview 1969." *Architecture Canada* 46, No. 1 (January 1969).

"An electrifying design." *The Telegram*, 11 September 1968.

Filey, Mike. "The Legacy Continues." In *Toronto Sketches 8*. Toronto: Dundurn Press, 2004.

"Head Office Project and Relief Project Announced." *Construction* 24, No. 8 (August 1931).

Kleiser, G.L. *History of 341 Church Street known as the Monetary Times Building*. Toronto: Department of Physical Resources, Ryerson Polytechnical Institute, 1988.

McHugh. *Toronto Architecture*.

"New 14-storey structure for Yonge College area." *The Toronto Daily Star*, 31 October 1930.

"New $600,000 hotel at Gerrard-Jarvis." *The Toronto Daily Star*, 11 January 1929.

"New Hydro buildings help relief program for coming winter." *The Globe*, 22 July 1931.

Sinaiticus. "Head Office Building Toronto Hydro-Electric System." *Construction* 26, No. 4 (July–August 1933).

"Yonge-Carlton area expected to expand." *The Toronto Daily Star*, 12 June 1931.

Chapter 25: Willowdale Telecommunications Tower

"Bid to submerge part of Yonge St." *The Telegram*, 20 October 1967.

"Board approves 59-storey North York global tower." *The Telegram*, 5 February 1970.

"Board approves erecting tower in North York." *The Globe and Mail*, 12 March 1966.

"Council shown pan for $80 million civic centre." *The Willowdale Mirror*, 3 July 1974.

"Developer threatens to kill civic centre." *The Toronto Daily Star*, 10 March 1971.

Duff, Morris. "N. York's downtown dream — can Service pull it off?" *The Toronto Daily Star*, 20 February 1966.

Enright, Michael. "$164,000 for civic study." *The*

Globe and Mail, 11 August 1966.

———. "North York about to buy key parcel along Yonge." *The Globe and Mail*, 19 August 1966.

"Is it a glamorous 'downtown' or just 'cemetery square?'" *The Toronto Daily Star*, 9 May 1967.

"Library, school boards in centre?" *The Willowdale Mirror*, 14 May 1973.

MacKenzie, James. "North York plan faces city opposition." *The Globe and Mail*, 28 February 1968.

———. "The problems of giving a borough a new heart." *The Globe and Mail*, 31 August 1968.

"Municipal building expansion?" *The Telegram*, 4 June 1970.

Murray V. Jones and Associates Limited, John B. Parkins Associates. *Yonge Redevelopment Study*. Toronto: February 1968.

"N. York wants cemetery land." *The Toronto Daily Star*, 19 August 1966.

"North York '65: image of a city." *The Globe and Mail*, 31 December 1965.

"North York buys cemetery land." *The Toronto Daily Star*, 14 September 1966.

"N.Y. considers $102 million civic centre." *The Willowdale Mirror*, 3 March 1965.

"North York Council again discusses proposal for a municipal centre." *The Globe and Mail*, 28 January 1974.

"North York faces $65 million cost for civic centre." *The Toronto Star*, 29 January 1974.

"North York grows 'like Topsy.'" *The Telegram*, 20 October 1966.

"North York hopes to get 1,000-foot tower for its civic square." *The Toronto Daily Star*, 2 July 1968.

"North York seeks own heart." *The Globe and Mail*, 16 May 1967.

"North York told development could cost public 'millions.'" *The Telegram*, 7 March 1969.

"North York tower plan choice due Monday." *The Toronto Daily Star*, 25 January 1969.

"Plans for $65 million North York civic centre." *The Toronto Sun*, 28 June 1974.

"Service's vision sees North York a city." *The Globe and Mail*, 2 November 1966.

"Service wants North York to be city with new name." *The Toronto Daily Star*, 1 November 1966.

"$600 million North York plan." *The Telegram*, 27 February 1966.

"$6,000,000 tower plan for North York." *The Toronto Daily Star*, 27 February 1968.

"Tall TV tower wins backing in North York." *The Globe and Mail*, 5 November 1968.

"Tower at Willowdale would rise 740 feet." *The Globe and Mail*, 5 February 1970.

"TV tower delay called 'sabotage.'" *The Toronto Daily Star*, 28 January 1969.

"TV tower may add shop plaza apartments." *The Toronto Daily Star*, 18 August 1970.

"$25 million complex set for North York." *The Globe and Mail*, 23 May 1973.

Chapter 26: Bay-Adelaide Centre

Barber, John. "Toronto beneficiary despite unfinished business." *The Globe and Mail*, 20 August 1993.

Blanchaer, Carl. Personal interview. 16 January 2008.

Cowan, James. "No objections as city approves two towers." *National Post*, 10 May 2006.

Demb, Alan. "Bay-Adelaide Centre: super-dealing on a super-block development." *Business Journal* 78, No. 6 (July/August 1988).

Fulford, Robert. "Artificial Sweeteners." *Toronto Life* 27, No. 6 (April 1993).

Hemson Consulting Ltd. *A Review of the Bay-Adelaide Centre*. May 1989.

Heinzl, Mark. "Markborough delays project completion: Bay Adelaide put off to 1994." *The Globe and Mail*, 30 May 1991.

Kerr, Tom. "Bay-Adelaide deal ripe for review, Layton says." *The Toronto Star*, 16 November 1988.

Markborough Properties Limited and Trizec Equities Limited. *The Bay-Adelaide Centre.* (undated pamphlet).

Monserbraaten, Laurie. "Reformers 'never dreamed of sweep.'" *The Toronto Star*, 16 November 1988.

Stein, David Lewis. "Approval of highrise rekindles opposition." *The Toronto Star*, 5 November 1988.

Watson, Albert. "Downtowns Are Back!" *Building* 48, No. 1 (March/April 1998).

"'We want change' is voters' message." *The Toronto Star*, 15 November 1988.

Won, Shirley. "End nears for Toronto's Bay-Adelaide 'stump.'" *The Globe and Mail*, 19 July 2006.

Wong, Tony. "Office tower a sign of new 'cycle.'" *The Toronto Star*, 20 July 2006.

Chapter 27: University of King's College

Arthur. *From Front Street to Queen's Park*.

Dendy. *Lost Toronto*.

Freidland, Martin L. *The University of Toronto: A History*. Toronto: University of Toronto Press, 2002.

Otto, Stephen and Pleasance Crawford. "André Parmentier's 'Two or Three Places in Upper Canada." *Journal of the New England Garden History Society*, 5 (Fall 1997).

Richardson, Douglas. *A Not Unsightly Building: University College and its History*. Toronto: Mosaic Press for University College, 1990.

Chapter 28: CNE Fifty-Year Plan/1971 CNE Master Plan

Archives of Ontario. Alfred H. Chapman Fonds. Accession 48506. *Canadian National Exhibition: Report of Plans Committee* (undated report).

"At Last an Electrical Building at the Canadian National." *The Electrical News* 32, No. 2 (15 January 1923).

"British Building for the Exhibition." *The Mail and Empire*, 15 August 1924.

Canadian National Exhibition Archives, Corporate Secretary Fonds, Minutes of the Canadian National Exhibition Association (16 February 1928; 21 February 1928).

Canadian National Exhibition Archives exhibit text, "One Brick at a Time, Architecture at the Ex, Past, Present and Imagined," 2006.

G.G. "The Great Exhibition Bursts Its Bounds

Eastward." *The Toronto Star Weekly*, 18 August 1923.

Hunt. *John M. Lyle.*

Lorimer, James. *The Ex: A Picture History of the Canadian National Exhibition.* Toronto: James Lewis & Samuel, 1973.

Metropolitan Parks Department and Staff of the Metropolitan Planning Board. *Proposals for the Rehabilitation of Exhibition Park.* April 1971.

"New Electrical and Engineering Building for C.N.E." *The Toronto Daily Star*, 8 March 1928.

"1928 Exhibition time capsule is opened." *The Toronto Star*, 26 May 1972.

Policy Steering Committee on Exhibition Place Development, Technical Committee. *Exhibition Place Development Concept Plan and 1982 Study Program.* 1982.

"Progress Made Visible: American World's Fairs and Expositions." Online exhibit of the University of Delaware Library (curator Iris R. Snyder). www.lib.udel.edu./ud/spec/exhbits/fairs

"A Souvenir of the Pan-American Exposition." Online exhibit. www.buffalohistoryworks.com.

"Step toward Empire Court taken by C.N.E. directors in laying corner stone." *The Globe*, 2 June 1926.

Chapter 29: St. Michael's College

"Campaign for $3,000,000 for new buildings." *The Evening Telegram*, 11 May 1929.

The Catholic College of the University: St. Michael's College in the University of Toronto. Toronto: University of Toronto Press, 1929.

McCorkell, E.J. *Memoirs of Rev. E.J. McCorkell, C.S.B.* Toronto: Basilian Press, 1975.

———. "The New St. Michael's." *The Basilian* 1, No. 3 (May 1935).

Oliver, M.J. "The New Buildings." *St. Michael's College Yearbook*, 1929.

"Property transfers precede campaign of united colleges." *The Globe*, 14 May 1929.

"St. Basil's Novitiate, St. Clair Avenue." *The Catholic Weekly Review* 6, No. 12 (30 April 1892).

"St. Michael's College plans expansion." *University of Toronto Monthly* 29, No. 6 (March 1929).

St. Michael's College v. Toronto (City). [1926] S.C.R. 318 (decision of the Supreme Court of Canada, 13 March 1926).

"St. Michael's enhances grace and grandeur of ensemble." *The Evening Telegram*, 5 April 1929.

Thomas, Christopher A. "A Thoroughly Traditional Architect: A.W. Holmes and the Catholic Archdiocese of Toronto, 1890–1940." *Bulletin, Society for the Study of Architecture in Canada* 10, No. 1 (March 1989).

———. "A High Sense of Calling: Joseph Connolly, A.W. Holmes, and their Buildings for the Roman Catholic Archdiocese of Toronto, 1885-1935." *Canadian Art Review* 13, No. 2 (1986).

University of St. Michael's College Archives. Presidents' Files. Pr10.5, E. J. McCorkell, Building and Endowment Fund 1929, Campaign News.

———. *Property and Building Dates: St Michael's College.* Undated pamphlet.

Chapter 30: St. Lawrence Centre

"Arts centre tender date moved up." *The Toronto Daily Star*, 8 October 1966.

Best, Michael. "These are the contestants … this is the prize … in the CBC sweepstakes." *The Toronto Daily Star*, 3 February 1964.

"City Council debates 5 hours then OKs art centre saw-off." *The Toronto Daily Star*, 18 December 1965.

"City council 21-1 for the arts centre." *The Toronto Daily Star*, 19 February 1964.

"City rules $1,250,000 too high for museum." *The Toronto Daily Star*, 25 February 1965.

Cohen, Nathan. "A go-go campaign." *The Toronto Daily Star*, 28 August 1965.

———. "No need for tears." *The Toronto Daily Star*, 21 June 1965.

"Council OKs arts centre — finally." *The Toronto Daily Star*, 14 March 1965.

"Dennison gives MPs civic plan." *The Toronto Daily Star*, 5 October 1967.

Ferry, Anthony. "Well, are we going to get a centre or not? Now we'll know." *The Toronto Daily Star*, 17 December 1965.

"Festival Hall and Arts Building, Toronto." *Canadian Architect* 10, No. 8 (August 1965).

"Firm offers to save St. Lawrence Centre." *The Toronto Daily Star*, 18 June 1965.

"42 per cent are willing to help on centennial." *The Toronto Daily Star*, 22 June 1965.

"Fund raiser: too late to revive centre." *The Toronto Daily Star*, 22 June 1965.

Haggart, Ron. "How gut politics saved the arts centre." *The Toronto Daily Star*, 11 May 1965.

Hicklin, Ralph. "Mayor points to Charlottetown." *The Globe and Mail*, 5 September 1965.

"Mayor halfway there in Arts Centre Drive." *The Toronto Daily Star*, 15 July 1965.

"Piccininni switches, Centennial centre squeaks through." *The Toronto Daily Star*, 11 May 1965.

"Queen's Park won't provide extra cash for arts centre." *The Toronto Daily Star*, 22 June 1967.

"St. Lawrence Centre for the Arts, Toronto." *Canadian Architect* 15, No. 5 (May 1970).

"Tomorrow may decide Ottawa aid to centre." *The Toronto Daily Star*, 24 October 1967.

"Too many fingers in centennial pie." *The Toronto Daily Star*, 21 October 1963.

"The Toronto Arts Foundation, Ontario." *Canadian Architect.* (Yearbook, 1966).

Toronto (Ont.) Planning Board. *The City's Centennial Project.* Toronto, 1965.

———. *The St. Lawrence Centre for the Arts and Entertainment in Toronto: A Proposal.* Toronto, 1962.

"Unveil plans for city's $16 million arts centre." *The Toronto Daily Star*, 18 February 1964.

Whittaker, Herbert. "St. Lawrence Hall: a cultural dichotomy." *The Globe and Mail*, 21 August 1965.

———. "Theatre of the Future — Designer's Note Book." *Canadian Interiors* 3, No. 6 (June 1966).

Chapter 31: Bay and Wellesley Ballet-Opera House

Arcop Associates. *A Home for the Canadian Opera Company and the National Ballet of Canada.* February 6 1983.

"Ballet-opera house the sequel: priced to sell?" *The Globe and Mail*, 24 March 1992.

Brent, Bob and Peter Cheney. "Cost of ballet-opera house can be cut, architect says." *The Toronto Star*, 16 November 1990.

Drainie, Bronwyn. "We don't want to look a gift house in the mouth but ..." *The Globe and Mail*, 6 October 1990.

Du Toit, Roger. "Toronto Ballet Opera House: 1 — Selection Process." *The Canadian Architect* 33, No. 8 (August 1988).

Franklin, Mark. "Toronto Ballet Opera House: 2 — Design Critique." *The Canadian Architect* 33, No. 8 (August 1988).

Gooderham, Mary. "Toronto opera centre finds home; plan includes downtown housing." *The Globe and Mail*, 28 July 1988.

———— and Paul Taylor. "Ontario gives downtown land for housing, opera-ballet theatre." *The Globe and Mail*, 29 July 1988.

Hume, Christopher. "Ballet Opera House that wouldn't die." *The Toronto Star*, 30 March 1990.

————. "Opera house 'protest' designs set high standard." *The Toronto Star*, 23 February 1988.

Jones, Edward. "Closing Doors Across Canada." *The Canadian Architect* 33, No. 6 (June 1988).

Knelman, Martin. "Fans pine for old opera house plans." *The Toronto Star*, 7 June 2006.

————. "How the curtain came down on Toronto's opera house dream." *The Toronto Star*, 27 August 2000.

Mackie, Richard. "Ontario forecast $2.5 billion deficit." *The Globe and Mail*, 12 October 1990.

Maychak, Matt. "Opera house may be dead as province backs out." *The Saturday Star*, 10 November 1990.

McGill University Library, John Bland Canadian Architecture Collection, Safdie Fonds. Undated pamphlets: "Ballet Opera House" and "Canada's Ballet Opera House."

Monsebraaten, Laurie. "Housing to surround new opera house." *The Toronto Star*, 29 July 1988.

Moshe Safdie and Associates. "Toronto Ballet Opera House: 3 — Winning Submission." *The Canadian Architect* 33, No. 8 (August 1988).

O'Malley, Sean. "Ballet-opera plans still alive." *The Globe and Mail*, 4 March 1991.

"Ontario cabinet to meet on financing opera house." *The Globe and Mail*, 6 October 1990.

Polanyi, Margaret. "Ottawa comes up with funds for opera 'World-class facility' to get $88 million." *The Globe and Mail*, 27 September 1990.

Rochon, Lisa. "Ten years later, Ballet Opera House is still just a dream." *The Globe and Mail*, 13 June 1987.

Taylor, Kate. "Arts cutbacks: private financing makes the difference." *The Globe and Mail*, 9 March 1991.

————. "House dream dies: Upgraded O'Keefe offered instead." *The Globe and Mail*, 5 November 1992.

Theatre Projects Consultants. *Toronto Opera Ballet Theatre.* March 1985.

Chapter 32: Royal Ontario Museum

Browne, Kelvin. *Bold Visions: The Architecture of the Royal Ontario Museum.* Toronto: Royal Ontario Museum, 2008.

Immen, Wallace. "ROM opens time capsule — from 1981." *The Globe and Mail*, 27 May 2003.

Mays, John Bentley. "Public Building." *Canadian Architect* 47, No. 5 (May 2002).

Rochon, Lisa. "Crystallizing an Image." *Canadian Architect* 47, No. 5 (May 2002).

Chapter 33: The City of the Future

Armstrong, Frederick H. *A City in the Making.* Toronto: Dundurn Press, 1988.

Benn, Carl. *The History of Toronto: An 11,000-Year Journey.* Culture Toronto, on-line publication (www.toronto.ca/culture/history/index).

Careless. *Toronto to 1918.*

Dendy. *Lost Toronto.*

Filey and Russell. *From Horse Power to Horsepower.*

Fogelson, Robert M. *Downtown: Its Rise and Fall, 1880–1950.* New Haven: Yale University Press, 2001.

Lennox, E.J. "What Will the Architectural Appearance of Toronto be in the Year 2004 A.D.?" in *Toronto's Christmas Magazine* 1, No. 1 (December 1904).

Litvak. *Edward James Lennox: Builder of Toronto.*

INDEX

OF RELATED INTEREST

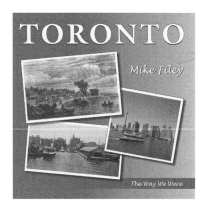

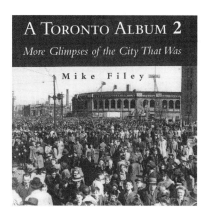

Toronto: The Way We Were
by Mike Filey
978-1-55002-842-3 $45.00

A Toronto Album 2: More Glimpses of the City That Was
by Mike Filey
978-1-55002-393-0 $24.99

For decades Toronto historian Mike Filey has regaled readers with stories of Toronto's past. Now, in one lavishly illustrated volume, he serves up the best of his meditations on the city's people and places.

A companion edition to Mike Filey's immensely popular *A Toronto Album*, *A Toronto Album 2* is a photographic journey through the bustling metropolis from the late 1930s to the early 1970s.

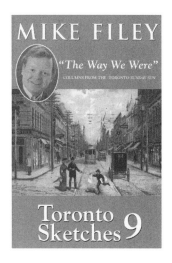

Toronto Sketches 9: "The Way We Were" Columns
from the Toronto Sunday Sun
by Mike Filey
978-1-55002-613-9 $19.99

A lively and fascinating collection of Mike Filey's "The Way We Were" columns, which have enjoyed an uninterrupted stretch as one of the *Sunday Sun*'s most popular features.

Available at your favourite bookseller.
Tell us your story! What did you think of this book? Join the conversation at www.definingcanada.ca/tell-us-your-story by telling us what you think.

DUNDURN
www.dundurn.com